CLOUI COMPUTING

Master the Concepts, Architecture and Applications with Real-world examples and Case studies

by

Kamal Kant Hiran

Ruchi Doshi

Dr. Temitayo Fagbola

Mehul Mahrishi

Distributors:

BPB PUBLICATIONS
20, Ansari Road, Darya Ganj
New Delhi-110002
Ph: 23254990/23254991

DECCAN AGENCIES
4-3-329, Bank Street,
Hyderabad-500195
Ph: 24756967/24756400

MICRO MEDIA
Shop No. 5, Mahendra Chambers,
150 DN Rd. Next to Capital Cinema,
V.T. (C.S.T.) Station, MUMBAI-400 001
Ph: 22078296/22078297

BPB BOOK CENTRE
376 Old Lajpat Rai Market,
Delhi-110006
Ph: 23861747

Published by Manish Jain for BPB Publications, 20 Ansari Road, Darya Ganj, New Delhi-110002 and Printed by him at Repro India Ltd, Mumbai

About the Author

Kamal Kant Hiran works as an Associate Professor and Head, Academics at the BlueCrest University College, Liberia, West Africa as well as a Research Fellow at the Aalborg University, Copenhagen, Denmark. He has a rich experience of 14+ years as an academician and researcher in Asia, Africa and Europe. He has several awards to his credit such as International travel grant for Germany from ITS Europe, Gold Medal Award in M. Tech (ICT), IEEE Ghana Section Award, IEEE Senior Member Recognition, IEEE Student Branch Award, Elsevier Reviewer Recognition Award and the Best Research Paper Award from the University of Gondar, Ethiopia. He has published 35 research papers in peer-reviewed international journals and conferences. He has authored the book, "The Proliferation of Smart Devices on Mobile Cloud Computing" and was published by Lambert Academic Publishing, Germany in 2014. He is a reviewer and editorial board member of various reputed International Journals in Elsevier, Springer, IEEE, Bentham Science, IGI Global, IJSET, IJTEE, IJSTR and IJERT. He is an active member and helps organize many international seminars, workshops and conferences in India, Ghana, Liberia, Denmark, Jordan, and Ethiopia.

His Website: *http://www.kamalhiran.in/*
His Linkedin Profile: *https://www.linkedin.com/in/kamal-kant-hiran-4553b643/*

Ruchi Doshi has more than 10 years of academic, research and software development experience in Asia and Africa. She works as a Registrar at the BlueCrest University College, Liberia, West Africa and also worked with the BlueCrest University College, Ghana; Amity University, India, and Trimax IT Infrastructure and Services as a software engineer. She has received the ITS European award for presentation of her research paper at the University of Passau, Germany in the year 2017. She is a reviewer, advisor, ambassador, Keynote Speaker, and editorial board member of various reputed International Journals and Conferences such as MIR Labs, USA, IEEE W4S, IJCS, IGI Global, IJSET, IJTEE, IJSTR and IJERT. She is an active member and helps organize many international events in India, Ghana, and Liberia.

Her Linkedin Profile: *https://www.linkedin.com/in/ruchi-doshi-96bb63b4/*

Dr. Temitayo Fagbola is currently a Post-Doctoral Fellow (PDF) at the Durban University of Technology, South Africa and an Assistant Professor at the Department of Computer Science, Federal University, Oye-Ekiti, Nigeria with over 10 years of proven teaching and research experience. He has Ph.D., M.Sc, and B.Tech degrees in Computer Science with strong research interests in cloud computing ecosystem, deep learning, computational intelligence, social media big data analytics, information security, decision support system and video processing. Dr Fagbola is a member of the **South African Institute of Computer Scientists and Information Technologists (SAICSIT)**, **Asian Council of Science Editors (ACSE)**, **Machine Intelligence Institute of Africa (MIIA)**, **Computer Professionals (Registration Council) of Nigeria (CPN)**, the **International Association of Engineers (IAENG)** and DataHack4FI in Africa. He has published over 50 peer-reviewed papers in reputed international journals and conferences and currently works as a reviewer for over 15 reputable international journals. He is also a recipient of the ACM FAT's grant in November 2018.

His Linkedin Profile: *https://www.linkedin.com/in/temitayo-fagbola-5941a2169/*

Mehul Mahrishi currently works as an Associate Professor at the Department of Computer Science & Engineering, Swami Keshvanand Institute of Technology, Management and Gramothan, Jaipur, India. He is a life member of International Association of Engineers and has published several research articles in National/International Journals, Conferences, including Global Journals, ICCCTAM-Dubai, ICMLC-Singapore, IACC and chapters in books. He is also an active technical reviewer of Journal of Parallel and Distributed Computing (SCI & Scopus-Elsevier). His research activities are currently twofold: while the first research activity is set to explore the developmental enhancements, video processing and analysis, the second major research theme is focused on the emerging capabilities of cloud computing. Mr. Mahrishi has won many awards in various domains, including recognition as an active reviewer by Journal of Parallel and Distributed Computing (JPDC, Elsevier, SCI & Scopus Indexed) and IEEE Continuing Education Certification for *Cloud Computing Enable Technologies and Recognition for outstanding performance in Campus Connect Program* by Infosys, India.

His Linkedin Profile: *https://in.linkedin.com/in/mehul-mahrishi-30979026*

Preface

In today's world, cloud computing is moving in its seventh heaven and is affecting the way through which businesses are done and will be done in the future. IT enabled services are now our bread and butter with Internet providing an extra topping to the dish. The concept of 24*7*365 availability and on-demand access to resources gives the basic definition of cloud computing as 'a style of computing where massively scalable and elastic IT capabilities are provided *as a service* to external customers using Internet technology.' This is a paradigm of computing which tells us about both the applications providing the services and the scalable hardware and the software resources that provide the services.

In this book, relevant frameworks and applications of cloud computing in the modern era are presented. It also provides a practical start-to-finish guide to some important implementations of the cloud, including migration steps from traditional (local) servers to the cloud, disaster recovery, risk management, cloud performance monitoring and management. The content is written in simple language and suitable for undergraduates, degree and postgraduate students who would like to improve their understanding of cloud computing. Furthermore, this book can help the readers to understand how cloud computing evolves, how it is accepted worldwide and how it becomes an integral part of several organizations. A key objective of this book is to provide a systematic source of reference for all aspects of cloud computing. This book comprises of nine chapters with close co-operation and contributions from four different authors spanning four countries and providing a global, broad perspective on major cloud computing topics.

Chapter 1, *Foundation of Cloud Computing*, takes on a proactive and practical approach to discuss the foundation, background concepts, characteristics as well as the pros and cons of the cloud computing paradigm. The evolution from the old traditional computing practice to the most recent cloud computing technology, provisioning sophisticated systems and infrastructures as utilities for retail access and use over the internet is also discussed. This chapter concludes by discussing the approaches of migration and economics of potential business impacts as well as prospects for the future of the cloud ecosystem.

Chapter 2, *Cloud Services and Deployment Models*, addresses key enterprise cloud infrastructures' deployment and service models. It generally exposes you to deployment and service models of the cloud computing infrastructure and concepts adopted by cloud service providers for deploying hardware, software, networks and storage components as services to their subscribers. The economic cost, performance expectations and service benefits of the varying deployment models are discussed in this chapter. The concluding part of this chapter presents a narrative of sustainable solutions that are currently being used for the management of cloud computing infrastructures in practice.

Chapter 3, *Cloud Computing Architecture*, discusses the fundamental elements which make up cloud computing services. Notably, cloud computing requires the synchronization of various technologies and service providers who collectively make this new computing concept a success. It also fosters the understanding of the roles and responsibilities of each provider and the predominant technologies utilized in the cloud computing. The benefits and limitations of these technologies are also explored.

Chapter 4, *Virtualization Technology*, discusses the scalability and agility characteristics of cloud computing resources are product of virtualization. In this chapter, a detailed fundamental concept of virtualization as it affects the cloud computing ecosystem is presented. This Chapter explains different type of virtualization techniques and software tools used to implement virtualization at different levels.

Chapter 5, *Service Oriented Architecture (SOA)*, This chapter focuses on elementary introduction of Service Oriented Architecture. The architecture, protocol stack and SOA services that are discussed in this chapter are the founding concept behind successful adoption of cloud computing paradigm.

Chapter 6, *Cloud Security and Privacy*, discusses the key fundamental concepts of cloud security and privacy. It identifies basic cloud threats and presents corresponding mitigation approaches and emphasizes on the CIA security model. It provides an explicit narrative of a prototype cloud computing security architecture with its composite layered structure. Furthermore, it presents and discusses some performance monitoring and management solutions for cloud systems. Legal issues relating to cloud computing, risk management, business continuity and disaster recovery, threats in the cloud, cloud vendors, step by step procedures and requirements to successfully migrate a local server to the cloud are also extensively discussed. Issues of quality of cloud services, cloud service level agreements and trust management in the cloud are also discussed and form the concluding part of this chapter.

Chapter 7, *Cloud Computing Applications*, lays emphasis on cloud computing, complemented by numerous applications and platforms that deliver cloud services. As technology makes noteworthy developments throughout the modern world, the most essential driving force is unquestionably a greater computing capacity with cloud computing serving as a significant element to this hi-tech progression. Additionally, prevailing companies along with their cloud computing products, cloud storage, and virtualization technologies are briefly explored.

Chapter 8, *Cloud Computing Technologies, Platform and Services*, discusses the base layer and concepts behind development and application of such tools. The cloud paradigm presents new opportunities for software vendors, developers and programming communities by using cloud-based IDE for their development process. Development tools like Amazon Toolkit for Eclipse, Cloud9 IDE with integrated support for Microsoft Azure and Cloud Foundry supports the ability to collaborate during development. It covers the study of Apache Hadoop with MapReduce models, Open Stack Cloud Platform and OpenNebula Cloud Platform which are open source frameworks for sensing a cloud environment.

Chapter 9, *Adoption of Cloud Computing,* lays emphasis on the issues affecting and strategies for the adoption of cloud computing. Additionally, existing applications in key socio-economic areas along with case studies are briefly explored. It also covers the various cloud computing international recognized certifications from Google, IBM and Amazon Web Services (AWS).

This book is a peer-reviewed, highly recommended and an excellent instructional guide for cloud computing newbies, university students at both undergraduate and postgraduate levels, developers, cloud stakeholders, educators, engineers, and researchers. Each chapter interestingly ends with a key summary and exercise questions. As already mentioned, cloud computing is an emerging discipline; as such, new concepts, methodologies and applications are constantly emerging, making this a challenging and rewarding area of research. All suggestions and corrections are welcome to research further in this area to build the ever increasing knowledge base of cloud computing.

All the best in the latest cloud computing technology world!

Acknowledgements

It is very important to acknowledge the tireless support and endless contributions received from many people in completing this work. Furthermore, this book would not have been a reality without the support of the BPB Publication family, mentors, colleagues and friends. Their unique contributions, advice, time, energy and expertise have improved the quality of this book immensely.

Firstly, we would like to thank Manish Jain, Nrip Jain, and BPB Publishing house for giving this wonderful opportunity and the staff members, especially Sourabh, Amrita and Sneha for their relentless effort to make this book a reality.

Kamal Kant Hiran: I would like to thank Prof. Anders Henten, Prof. Kund Erik Skouby, Prof. Reza Tadayoni, Anette Bysøe, Aalborg University, CMI, Copenhagen, Denmark for providing in-depth scientific knowledge in cloud computing and support during work. Most importantly, I would like to thank my Parents, wife and my daughter Cherry for their sacrifice during the past years.

Ruchi Doshi: I would like to extend my sincerest thanks to Dr. Anurag Mehta, Pacific University, Udaipur, India for their valuable scientific guidance and support during work. My deepest thanks go to my family, especially my beautiful daughter Bhuvi Jain, and my parents, Dr. M. K. Doshi and Pushpa Doshi, for the love, understanding, and support they have shown in my partial absence during my work. Specially, I would also like to thank the BlueCrest University College, Liberia, West Africa for providing a healthy academic environment during my consistent work.

Dr. Fagbola Temitayo: I would like to thank my wife, Funmilola, for her love, prayers, encouragement and support. I also commend Kamal for his doggedness to see the successful completion of the writing, reviewing, editing and publication of this book. This book was his idea all along. Special thanks to Prof. Stephen Olabiyisi, Prof. Justice Emuoyibofarhe, Prof. Elijah Omidiora, and Prof. Cecilia Akintayo for being great role models and excellent mentors over the years. I am also grateful to all those with whom I had the pleasure to work with during this and other related projects.

Mehul Mahrishi: I would like to thank my wife, Ratika, for always believing that I can complete this project and also my parents and family for the continuous support and motivation. I would like to dedicate this book to my son Rihaan. Special thanks to Prof. Kamal for his idea and implementation.

Finally, the authors would like to appreciate the reviewers Dr. Dharm Singh, Professor, Namibia University of Science and Technology and Dr. Vijandra Singh, Associate Professor, Amity University, Rajasthan for their time, dedication, expertise and immeasurable contributions to make this book a great success. They have kept us technically accurate as well as helped us with readability.

Errata

We take immense pride in our work at BPB Publications and follow best practices to ensure the accuracy of our content to provide with an indulging reading experience to our subscribers. Our readers are our mirrors, and we use their inputs to reflect and improve upon human errors if any, occurred during the publishing processes involved. To let us maintain the quality and help us reach out to any readers who might be having difficulties due to any unforeseen errors, please write to us at :

errata@bpbonline.com

Your support, suggestions and feedbacks are highly appreciated by the BPB Publications' Family.

Foreword

Mastering Cloud computing is a must in this day and age of digital era. This book will elegantly guide you through everything which is worth knowing on this subject.

Dr. Maria-Alexandra Paun, Chair of IEEE Switzerland

The authors provide an easy and comprehensive perspective of cloud computing concepts. The explanation is clear and concise with appropriate diagrams and real-world examples that demystify this important technology.

Deepak Modi, Senior Software Engineer, Microsoft Radmond Woods, USA

Cloud computing is the dawn of new era in the world of computing that provides a new way to share resources, software and data over web in a highly capable, scalable and secure environment. I recommend this book to anyone who wants to understand the basics of cloud computing and how it works in real world scenarios.

Sushil Choudhary, SAP Consultant, USA

This is a very useful and valuable book. It is, on the one hand, a primer on the various aspects of what cloud computing is in terms of concepts and technologies and, on the other hand, a discussion on critical issues regarding cloud computing with respect to for instance security and privacy and adoption of cloud solutions. It is therefore a book which addresses readers who are new to the field as well as experienced readers who wish to acquire an overview of central issues concerning cloud computing.

Dr. Anders Henten, Professor, Aalborg University, Denmark

The two most important technological shifts in the 21st century are the adoption and prevalence of mobile and cloud computing in our day to day lives. It's essential for every business to adopt these technologies, and more importantly for our educational systems to teach and train the next generation of learners on cloud technologies. This book provides a concise, clear and lucid understanding of the fundamentals of cloud computing technologies and concepts.

Siddharth Ajith, IITK, Oxford University Alumni, Education Sector Strategist

It's a very useful book, especially for a beginner in cloud learning. The authors used step-by-step approach, which makes it ideal for a beginner. The diagrams are self-explanatory, and the language is easy but evident.

Trilok Nuwal, Software Architect, McAfee, India

A genuine book for beginners who wants to understand and implement cloud computing concepts.

Dr. Do Manh Thai, Executive, Govt. of Vietnam

Cloud computing is everywhere in our digital age. Masterminding the ideas and tools behind the many uses of cloud computing is a must. This book will help you grasp and deepen your understanding helped by its clear and concise teaching.

Dr. Silvia Elaluf-Calderwood, Telecommunications Expert
Research Fellow, Florida International University, USA

Cloud comping is an interesting and important topic of research in current days. It covers from water to cloud, home to office, or village to city. The IoT, ubiquitous, or pervasive are the subdomains of cloud computing. This book covers the fundamentals, models, architecture, its applications. It really helps the reader in enhancing their knowledge and provide a conceptual understanding in this domain. The book also moves from academic to research aspects. So, it is very helpful for any researcher and academician, from beginning to advance level.

Prof. Hari Prabhat Gupta, Dept. of CSE, IIT BHU, India

Cloud computing is a very important tool that keeps whole business handy. You don't have to carry anything still you have everything. In short, for present and coming era cloud computing is a must for any business and for cloud computing the book by Prof. Kamal and other distinguished authors is a must. He has explained difficult theories so beautifully that it becomes just a cake walk afterward. Case studies are relevant and very useful to understand the whole concept. I really appreciate his hard work and wish him luck with his new book.

Dr. Anil Sharma, Amity University Dubai, Dubai, UAE

The book is truly comprehensive and can be associated with any university's curriculum. The best part of the book is that it discusses the case studies of major cloud service providers like Google, Amazon, Microsoft and even Eucalyptus and OpenStack.

Dr. Anil Chaudhary, Professor & Head (Department of IT, SKIT, Rajasthan, India)

In the era of digitization, cloud computing is truly a game changer. The market share of cloud computing is increasing exponentially to an unforeseen level. Cloud computing platforms and applications are gaining wide popularity across enterprises today. Therefore, it has become imperative for IT professionals to acquire knowledge of cloud computing and its applications. This book covers almost all the aspects of cloud computing starting from fundamental to enterprise-level strategies. It incorporates case studies and several advanced topics that may help learners to build strong concepts in the area of cloud computing.

Prof. Anurag Jagetiya, MLVTE College, Rajasthan, India

Table of Contents

CHAPTER 1

Foundation of Cloud Computing

"Cloud computing is a spectrum of things complementing one another and building on a foundation of sharing."

~ Chris Howard, Research Vice President at Gartner

Objectives

- To learn about the basic concepts of new evolving/emerging technologies in cloud computing
- To learn about the fundamentals of the cloud computing ecosystem and its characteristics
- To learn about the advantages and disadvantages of cloud computing
- To evaluate the cloud's business impact and economics
- To identify the difference between cluster, grid and cloud computing
- To identify the drivers of cloud computing adoption and discuss **future of cloud (FoC)**

Cloud computing is the delivery of on-demand computing services from applications to storage and processing power over the internet and on a pay-as-you-go basis. Organizations have moved to cloud platforms for better scalability, mobility, and security.

One benefit of using cloud computing services is that organizations can avoid the upfront cost and complexity of owning and maintaining their own IT infrastructure, and instead simply pay for what they use, when they use it.

This chapter takes on a proactive and practical approach to discuss the foundation, background concepts, characteristics as well as the pros and cons of the cloud computing paradigm. We will discuss the evolution from the old traditional computing practice to the most recent cloud computing technology, provisioning sophisticated systems, and infrastructures as utilities for retail access and use over the internet. This chapter concludes by discussing the approaches of migration and economics of potential business impacts as well as prospects for the future of the cloud ecosystem.

In this chapter, we will discuss the following topics:

- Introduction to cloud computing
- History of cloud computing
- Fundamentals of the cloud computing ecosystem
- Characteristics of cloud computing
- Advantages and disadvantages of cloud computing
- Comparison of traditional and cloud computing paradigms
- Evaluating the cloud's business impact and economics
- Business drivers of cloud computing adoption
- Future of cloud (FoC)

Introduction to cloud computing

Cloud computing is a service that integrates the characteristics and functionalities of *cloud* and *computing* as a technological revolutionized approach or system. Cloud can be defined as a wide-area network community that houses data centers and their associated software/hardware applications, other **Information Technology (IT)** resources and infrastructures that can be accessed using internet connectivity. It was further conceptualized as *a unique IT environment principally designed to remotely provision regular and scalable IT resources*.

On the other hand, according to Technopedia, computing is defined as the process of adopting computer technology to solve a given goal-oriented problem. It can further symbolize the process of gathering, processing and organizing information using some computer software and/or hardware as well as a computer system for a myriad of purposes.

By unifying the concept of *cloud* and *computing*, cloud computing has enjoyed a broad and diverse perspective to its definitions. At present, there is no standard and generally acceptable definition for cloud computing. Nevertheless, let us take a look at some definitions of cloud computing:

- A dynamically scalable system that provides internet-based services often virtually.

- A model for enabling ubiquitous, convenient, on-demand network access to a shared pool of configurable computing resources (for example, networks, servers, storage, applications and services) that can be rapidly provisioned and released with minimal management effort or service provider interaction (the National Institute for Standards and Technology of the United States).

- A type of parallel and distributed computing system consisting of a collection of inter-connected and virtualized computers that are dynamically provisioned and presented as one or more unified computing resources based on **Service Level Agreements (SLAs)** established through negotiation between the service providers and consumers.

- The delivery of IT infrastructure and applications as a service on-demand to individuals and organizations via internet platforms.

- Forrester Research provided its own definition of cloud computing as: *"...a standardized IT capability (services, software, or infrastructure) delivered via Internet technologies in pay-per-use, self-service way."*

- Forrester defines cloud computing as *"A pool of abstracted, highly scalable, and managed compute infrastructure capable of hosting end-customer applications and billed by consumption."*

The following figure shows the basic operating mode of cloud computing. The resources are provisioned and released with less effort from the management and the interaction of a service. Thus, an organization or individuals can use the resources whenever it is required from anywhere and at any time:

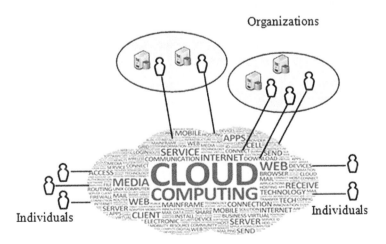

Figure 1.1: Basic operating mode of a cloud

Cloud computing offers virtualized pay-per-use platforms which are dynamic, scalable and self-service flexible for resource sharing. It is a distributed computing paradigm embodying the delivery, development and application platforms for utility-based services. It can be seen as a delivery platform when it deploys an application via on-demand services.

An example of cloud computing is the Amazon Elastic Cloud. It acts as a development platform when it provides a general-purpose development environment for programming via the internet. Examples also include Google Sites and Coghead. It allows you to design, build and deploy end-users' applications as an application platform. It also includes Google docs, NetSuite and Cisco-WebEx.

History of cloud computing

Cloud computing has its roots from technologies, including the mainframe computing, grid computing, cluster computing, the internet, multi-core systems, parallel and distributed systems and virtualization. However, cloud computing can easily be distinguished from these baselines via characteristics like resource pooling, on-demand self-services, measured service, broad network access and rapid elasticity.

The gradual evolution dated back to the 1950s with mainframe computing. Intergalactic computer network, proposed in 1969 by J.C.R. Licklider who co-developed the **Advanced Research Projects Agency Network (ARPANET)**, now known as the internet, was envisioned to allow people in the universe to be interconnected together via computers and equally-capable electronic devices for the purpose of information access and sharing from anywhere. This now serves as the gateway to access the cloud. Virtualized services came to the limelight in the 1970s with the evolution of virtual machines that mimic real computers together with their associated fully-functional operating programs. The internet allows private networks to be accessible virtually offering these infrastructures as rentable services via a concept known as **virtualization**. By early 1990s, more virtual computers were in use which led to the modern cloud computing systems. The economic intrigues of cloud computing became a little evident in the late 1990s. For example, Salesforce pioneered the delivery of software applications to their end users using the internet. However, later in the 1990s, virtualized private network connections were being offered as a service by telecommunications companies.

By the early 2000s, Amazon leveraged on the cloud computing infrastructure model to efficiently utilize the capacity of their systems with the **Amazon Web Services (AWS)** launched in 2006 to offer streamlined online services to their clients. For example, **Amazon Mechanical Turk (MTurk)** and **Amazon Elastic Compute Cloud (Amazon EC2)**. Similarly, Google Docs services were launched in 2006. With this application suite, word processing, including editing and saving of documents were made possible and offered as services via the internet. In 2008, IBM developed and introduced the IBM SmartCloud framework while Apple launched the ICloud system. By 2012, Oracle Cloud was launched by Oracle Corporation to offer **Software-as-a-Service (SaaS)**, **Platform-as-a-Service (PaaS)** and **Infrastructure-as-a-Service (IaaS)**. In 2014, Cloud has fully grown to maturity and most researches primarily focused on enhancing its security features. Currently, there has been enormous widespread of cloud computing systems specifically designed to meet the targeted organizational performance needs.

The emerging evolutionary trends of cloud computing is listed below:

- **Mainframe systems**: These are high-performance systems used for critical-mission applications and large processing tasks.

- **Grid computing**: This introduces the concept of parallel computing to solve large problems.

- **Utility computing**: This offers a metered service to access and use computing resources.

- **SaaS**: This offers remote use of applications via network-based subscriptions.

- **Cloud computing**: This dynamically provides ubiquitous, real-time access to IT resources, including applications and IaaS.

Fundamentals of the cloud computing ecosystem

The **Cloud Computing Ecosystem (CCE)** is a dynamic and complex community of the cloud computing system components and the stakeholders. The interdependent components of the CCE include cloud consultants, cloud service providers, cloud end-users (customers), cloud product manufacturers, cloud engineers, cloud partners, high speed network, the cloud management environment as well as the cloud computing infrastructures and IT resources that are provisioned as services.

Cloud stakeholders

The three primary stakeholders of the cloud include the end users, the cloud users and the cloud providers:

- **Cloud service providers**: They provide and render on-demand, pay-as-you-go utility computing services to cloud users. For example, telecommunication companies, systems integrators, large organization process outsourcers and internet service providers offer services accessible over the internet to cloud users, service brokers, consumers and resellers.

- **The cloud users**: The provisioned services are used by the cloud users to develop personalized products and web services (for example, software applications and websites) for the end users' consumption based on prior formal requirements specifications:

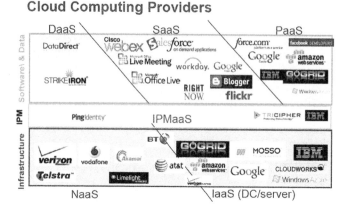

Figure 1.2: Cloud computing providers

- **The end users**: These are the direct consumers of the products developed by the cloud users.

The other stakeholders of the cloud ecosystem include:

- **Cloud service brokers**: These are influencers, professional service organizations, technology consultants, registered brokers and agents that assist cloud users to choose appropriate cloud computing solutions that best suit their organizational needs. Service brokers manage and negotiate on the terms of agreement and relationship between the cloud users and the providers to make other extra services available.

- **Cloud resellers**: These make expansion of cloud service provisioning business globally a reality in the cloud market. For each particular region, cloud providers may choose and establish contractual agreements with local IT resellers of their existing cloud products to resell their cloud products.

- **Cloud consumers**: These are the main stakeholders of the cloud ecosystem. End users, customers of cloud resellers, providers or brokers are the major cloud consumers. The cloud consumer could be a person, a group of people or an organization that subscribes to and uses cloud service(s). Service level agreements are established between a cloud consumer and a service provider on the technical performance requirements that are expected to be met by the cloud service provider.

- **Cloud brokers**: Cloud brokers are entities that facilitate efficient and effective use of cloud services while ensuring peak performance and seamless delivery of such services. They normally establish relationships between cloud consumers and cloud providers. They offer service intermediation, aggregation and arbitrage.

- **Service intermediation**: A cloud broker enhances a given service by improving some specific capabilities of a cloud service like access management, performance reporting, and identity management and providing rewards or value-added services to the cloud consumers.

- **Service aggregation**: A cloud broker consolidates a number of fixed cloud services into one or new services.

- **Service arbitrage**: This is similar to service aggregation except that the services being aggregated are not fixed.

- **Cloud carrier**: This is the intermediate communication medium between the cloud provider and the consumer. It makes cloud services accessible to cloud consumers through network connectivity and network access devices like mobile phones, laptops and other internet-enabled digital devices.

Cloud computing characteristics

Cloud computing characteristics are typically distinctive features and qualities that differentiate such systems from other seemingly-related systems. These characteristics can be categorized as either technical or basic.

Technical characteristics of cloud computing

The five technical characteristics of cloud computing is as follows:

- **Large-scale computing resources**: Cloud computing systems are often implemented in large scale to reduce cost and providers can benefit from significant economies of scale.

- **Shared resource pooling**: Resource pooling forms the foundation for cloud scalability. Pooling of virtual and physical resources into the cloud provides an abstraction of resource location independence phenomenon, which in turn shields cloud consumers from being aware of the real location of share resources in use.

- **Dynamic resource scheduling**: Via software automation, cloud resources are provisioned dynamically based on the current demand requirements and ensures that the cloud service capability is being expanded or contracted based on demand. However, great considerations should be given to high levels of reliability and security during this process.

- **High scalability**: Cloud computing architecture allows you to add new nodes and servers with no reconfiguration and remodification requirements to cloud software and infrastructure.

- **Rapid elasticity**: Computing resources can be rapidly and elastically provisioned and released based on the demand of the consumer. Consumers view these resources as if they are infinite and can be purchased in any quantity at any time. Capabilities provided to each user can be scaled rapidly and automatically in line with changes in demand.

Basic characteristics of cloud computing

- **On-demand self-service**: Cloud services are automatically made available without human interference when required by a potential consumer. These services include, but are not limited to processing power, web applications, server time, storage and networks.

- **Broad network access**: Real-time access and use of cloud services via the internet using any platform (laptops, mobile phones and so on) is made possible anytime regardless of the geographical location.

- **Measured service**: A pay-per-use metering model is being used by the cloud service provider to monitor, control and effectively manage cloud services and resources. This service sends an appropriate pricing bill to the user based on the type of services requested and extent of usage.

- **Multitenancy**: Multiple users can access the same cloud services at the same time. Although, sharing of cloud resources among multiple users is possible at the host, network and application levels; however, each user operates as an instance of a customized virtual application.

- **Reliability**: The use of multiple redundant sites is an approach being adopted to attain reliability. The higher the reliability the lower the cloud service usage risks. It also increases the confidence of potential cloud consumers and users to adopt cloud for business-critical tasks and disaster recovery.

- **Cost effectiveness**: Cloud adoption relieves the users of heavy investments in high performance complex and expensive computing systems and the technical expertise involved. Sophisticated infrastructures and resources that perfectly match business requirements are being leased out as a service. This helps to lower the operational cost of IT organizations and individuals.

- **Customization**: Cloud provides a highly flexible and reconfigurable environment that allows you to customize a set of cloud services, infrastructures and applications to meet users' specifications.

- **Efficient resource utilization**: The cloud architecture ensures that resources that are delivered are efficiently utilized and made available only for the period needed.

- **Maintainability**: Use of cloud ensures that the burden of technical know-how and the cost of maintaining software and hardware are taken away from the users.

- **Collaboration**: Collaborative interaction among disparate users of cloud PaaS is possible.

- **Virtualization**: Physical resources are provisioned virtually, thus allowing users' work accessible from anywhere and at any time. Cloud computing provides IT solutions as a service rather than as conventional physical products.

- **Green technology**: Cloud computing is an energy-efficient technology that does not require huge power consumption.

- **High performance**: Cloud computing has very large storage and high computing specifications that characterize high-performance computing environments.

- **Shared infrastructure**: Cloud allows you to share of resources (storage, physical services and networking capabilities) using a virtualized software model.

- **Network Access**: Cloud allows resources and services to be accessed using any internet-ready devices like the portable digital assistants, laptops, personal computers and so on using protocols like the **Hyper Text Transfer Protocol (HTTP)**, internet and transmission control technologies.

Advantages and disadvantages of cloud computing

A number of motivational factors make cloud computing adoption the best decision for most organizations. These factors form the basic benefits of using cloud.

The following are the advantages of cloud computing:

- **Economical**: Cloud computing offers cost-effective use of cloud applications and resources that would ideally require huge upfront investments, thereby reducing the expenses of the organization.

- **Almost unlimited storage**: Cloud provides access to very large storage space based on users' requirements.

- **Backup and recovery**: Cloud offers backup and recovery services for the most traditional physical computing infrastructures. It is relatively much easier and safer to backup and restore important data than to store data on tertiary devices.

- **Automatic software integration**: Cloud ensures real-time and seamless integration of its applications to the users' environment and system. Users do not need to reinvent the wheel of such capability.

- **Easy access to information**: The user has unprecedented and unrivalled access to data from anywhere and at any time.

- **Quick deployment**: The cloud is ready for use once the relevant cloud functionalities and parameter settings are completed.

The other advantages of cloud computing are as follows:

- Users need not worry about upgrading the technology stack and software. This is done by the provider and the latest releases and services are always available.

- Users need not worry about compatibility of the infrastructure and the development environment. The provider needs to ensure this.

- Cloud provides flexible switching between multiple staging environments.

The disadvantages of cloud computing are as follows:

- **Technical issues**: These issues occur if there is a bad internet connection or dysfunctional systems.

- **Prone to attack**: Cloud is more potentially prone to security threats and external hack attacks as there is a large amount of sensitive information on the cloud. The fact that it is in the cloud does not mean it is safe from external interference and attacks.

- **Security and privacy**: Cloud computing still suffers from some security and privacy challenges. The major concerns are data protection and confidentiality, disaster and data breach as well as user authentication. Data protection is often managed using data encryption with defined roles and privileges on data encryption keys management. Analysis of audit trails and data access logs is a major operational procedure to be practiced by companies to ensure integrity of user authentication. A single centralized cloud repository is at a higher risk due to natural disasters and data breaches. Availability and integrity of data is critical to manage mission-critical operations relying on the data. Companies should take measures to mitigate against the damages this potential occurrence may pose.

- **Lack of standards**: Most documented interfaces of cloud have no associated standards which might later pose interoperability issues. This challenge is currently being pursued by the open grid forum.

- **Continuously evolving**: Cloud is continuously evolving and so are the user requirements and the requirements for storage, interfaces and networking.

- **Compliance concerns**: The policy and compliance concerns are significant challenges as data usage and protection laws differ from one country to another.

- **Service migration**: User lock-in to a particular provider is a problem after service migration to the cloud. This is due to non-existence of a standardized external interface in cloud computing.

Comparison of traditional and cloud computing paradigms

Cloud computing is an evolving composite computing system that builds on the characteristics and technologies of such traditional computing platforms and technologies like **Service-oriented Architecture (SOA)**, cluster computing, grid computing and virtualization technology. We have referred to the evolutionary trends of computing before the emergence of cloud computing as traditional. In this chapter, we will use traditional computing to refer to both the cluster and the grid computing systems. The traditional computing paradigms are the clusters and grid computing.

Cluster computing

A cluster is an embodied set of stand-alone systems inter-connected via a local area network or a group of linked computers, working together as a single integrated system for scaling workloads. The main motivation for cluster computing is performance improvement, fault tolerance, scalability, huge cost-savings, throughput, redundancy, high memory, enormous speed, load balancing and high availability. It is a local network that is often characterized by high speed interconnections and centralized job management and scheduling system commonly used to execute modern high-performance computing tasks.

The following diagram depicts a cluster computing network. Cluster networks eliminate a single point of failure by ensuring that if a node fails in a network; a standby node takes over:

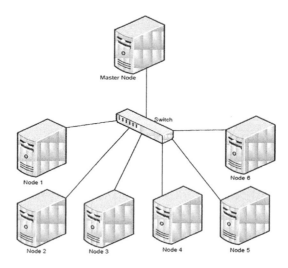

Figure 1.3: Cluster computing

Here is a list of advantages and disadvantages of cluster computing:

Advantages	Disadvantages
It is cost-effective.	There are a lot of issues associated with programming the network.
High manageability	It is very difficult to trace and locate faults.
It provides a single system image.	It requires deep technical know-how.

Table 1.1

Grid computing

Grid computing is the amalgamation of several computing resources from several supervisory domains into one or more logical entity, coordinated with a high-performance distributed grid and applied to solving large batch processing problems. Such problems require a computing infrastructure with a great deal of processing cycles to run to completion. It can be described as a form of distributed and parallel system that fosters seamless and dynamic runtime sharing, accumulating, hosting and providing services globally.

The following diagram represents a grid computing structure. Grid computing is also referred to as a *super virtual computer*. In grid computing, computing resources are located on loosely-coupled but geographically dispersed, distributed and heterogeneous networks unlike in cluster computing. However, it shares some similar characteristics such as resource pooling, scalability, network access and resiliency with cloud computing. Resource sharing, virtualization, service workflow coordination, security and scalability are the basic characteristics of a grid infrastructure.

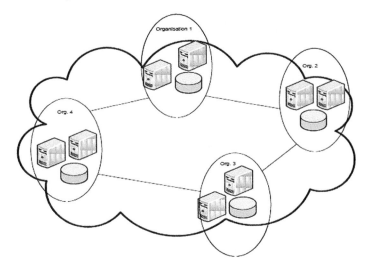

Figure 1.4: Grid computing

The advantages of grid computing are as follows:

- It ensures easy scaling of applications.
- It utilizes underused resources more adequately.
- It allows the consolidation of the power and capabilities of several low configuration systems into one.
- It adopts the use of open source, trust, transparency, and technology.
- It increases the computing reliability power.
- It allows seamless sharing and distribution of computing resources across networks.
- It supports parallel processing of programs and data.
- It guarantees optimal resource balancing.

The disadvantages of cloud computing are as follows:

- It suffers from proprietary approach.
- It is very complex.
- If a node on the grid is down, a single point of failure occurs.

Cloud computing

Cloud computing paradigms have been discussed in the previous section of this chapter. However, the following diagram presents a structure of the cloud computing system. Furthermore, the tables represent the characteristics of cluster, grid and cloud computing systems and the difference between the three computing paradigms:

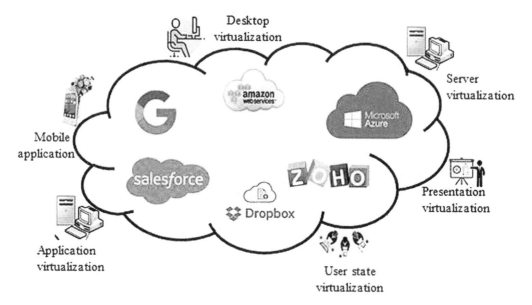

Figure 1.5: Cloud computing

The characteristics of cluster, grid and cloud computing are as follows:

Cluster computing	Grid computing	Cloud computing
• Tightly-coupled architecture. • Single system image. • Job management and scheduling is centralized.	• Loosely-coupled architecture (de-centralization). • Dynamism and diversity. • Job management and scheduling is distributed.	• Dynamic computing architecture. • Information technology service-centric approach. • Usage model is based on self-service. • Minimally or self-managed platform. • Consumption-based billing.

Cluster computing	Grid computing	Cloud computing
• Identical systems are directly connected together locally in the same physical location with very high speed connections to function as a single computer.	• The systems need not be in the same physical location and can work independently. Each node on the grid is a distinct system.	• The systems could be at any physical location.
• All systems share the same hardware and operating system.	• Different hardware and operating systems are possible.	• All cloud computing resources are managed by the operating system of the physical cloud units.
• All nodes comprising the cluster behave like a single system. Resources are centrally managed by the resource manager.	• Autonomous nodes with each node behaving independently and executing its own resource manager.	• Each node is an independent entity.
• The systems forming a cluster are kept together in a single location.	• Grids are essentially distributed over a local area network, metropolitan or wide area network.	• Cloud distribution covers a metropolitan area network.
• Application areas of cluster computing. • Medical research. • Educational resources provisioning. • Industrial promotion in commercial sectors.	• Application areas of grid computing. • Visualization. • Energy resources exploration. • Predictive modeling and simulations. • Engineering design and automation. • Medical, military and basic research.	• Application areas of cloud computing. • Space exploration. • Weather forecasting. • Banking. • Insurance.

Table 1.2

The difference between cluster computing, grid computing and cloud computing are shown in the following table:

Characteristics	Clusters	Grids	Clouds
Ownership	Single ownership	Multiple ownership	Single ownership
Service pricing	Limited	Private or public assigned	Utility /large user discount
Virtualization	Half	Half	Yes
Resource management	Centralized resource	Distributed resource	Both
Scalable size	100s	1000s	100 to 1000s
Standardized	Yes	Yes	No
Interoperability	Yes	Yes	Not full
Speed/ Interconnected network	Dedicated high end with low latency and high bandwidth	Mostly internet with high latency and low bandwidth	Dedicated high end with low latency and high bandwidth
Self-service	No	Yes	Yes
Single system image	Yes	No	Yes/optional included
Multi-tenancy	No	Yes	Yes
Service negotiation	Limited	Yes, SLA-based	Yes, SLA-based
Membership discovery	Membership service discovery	Decentralized information services and centralized indexing	Membership service discovery
Operating system	Windows/Linux	Any standard but dominated by Unix	Uses a hypervisor
Application drivers	Business, data centres, enterprise computing	Collaborative scientific and high-throughput applications	Web App. content delivery, dynamic provisioning
Standards/ interoperability	**Virtual Interface Architecture (VIA)**	Some open grid forum	Web services (SOAP and REST)
Scalable	No	Half	Yes

Characteristics	Clusters	Grids	Clouds
Failure management	Limited (often failed task/ application and restarted	Limited (often failed task/application restarted	Failover, content replication, virtual machine migration from one node to another supported
Capacity	Stable and guaranteed capacity	Varies, but high capacity	Provisioned on-demand capacity
Security	Traditional login/ password-based	Public/private pair -based authentication and mapping of a user to an account	Each user and/ or application is provided with a virtual machine
Privacy	Medium level of privacy depends on user privileges	Limited support for privacy	High security/ privacy is guaranteed. There is support for file **Access Control List (ACL)** settings.
Population	Commodity computers	High-end computing systems (including clusters and servers)	Commodity PCs, high-end servers' network, attached storage
End-user presentation	Presented as a dynamic and diversified system	Presented as a single system image	Presented as a self-services-based usage model

Table 1.3

Evaluating the cloud's business impact and economics

Cloud solutions offer a range of economic benefits to their users and to the economy as a whole. In particular, it has the potential to help growing businesses and organizations from having to spend more capital on their information technology requirements. Forrester research has predicted a global economic diffusion of cloud computing with the market growing in 2018 from $117 billion to $162 billion in 2020, as shown in the following diagram, depicting that the cloud market is growing in size:

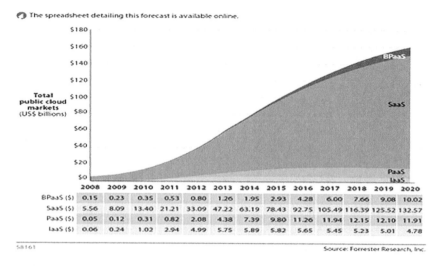

The spreadsheet detailing this forecast is available online.

	2008	2009	2010	2011	2012	2013	2014	2015	2016	2017	2018	2019	2020
BPaaS ($)	0.15	0.23	0.35	0.53	0.80	1.26	1.95	2.93	4.28	6.00	7.66	9.08	10.02
SaaS ($)	5.56	8.09	13.40	21.21	33.09	47.22	63.19	78.43	92.75	105.49	116.39	125.52	132.57
PaaS ($)	0.05	0.12	0.31	0.82	2.08	4.38	7.39	9.80	11.26	11.94	12.15	12.10	11.91
IaaS ($)	0.06	0.24	1.02	2.94	4.99	5.75	5.89	5.82	5.65	5.45	5.23	5.01	4.78

Source: Forrester Research, Inc.

Figure 1.6: Global public cloud market size from 2008 to 2020

Business drivers of cloud computing adoption

Cloud computing is a cost-reducing technology that allows small and medium-scale enterprises to contribute to the economic growth by strengthening their pro-activeness and productivity. Among the several economic advantages of cloud computing, the on-demand and pay-per-use pricing models help convert fixed cost into marginal cost. The cost savings realized can be used to start a new business which in turn could facilitate more job opportunities, innovations and macroeconomic growth.

Some key business drivers of cloud computing adoption include:

- **Help to pursue new business opportunities**: This drives improved customer relationship by providing a platform to locate and interact with potential customers over the internet.

- **Upfront costs reduction**: This reduces capital expenditure costs that include the cost of computer systems, physical data center and technical staff. The organization only pays for the computing resources actually used and makes a few reasonable operational expenditures.

- **Potential improvement in business continuity**: With guaranteed available and efficient network connectivity, cloud ensures seamless availability of computing infrastructure with its increased capacity for improved disaster recovery.

- **Potential reduction in carbon footprint**: Inevitable provisioning of electricity and air conditioning is greatly eliminated due to the efficient use of computer resources with limited demand for electricity and air conditioning.

Business users expect the cloud to assist them in the following ways:

- Meet customer cloud performance requirements for more and improved services.

- Innovate via mobility and ubiquity of cloud-based resources and great technologies.

- Lower business operational costs through operational excellence.

- Improve financial performance and its basis for competitive advantages.

- Focus more on core competencies by redistributing the non-tangible activities and saving more capital.

A number of costs primarily associated with the use of cloud computing is as follows:

- **Server costs**: A server has the capability to support a number of workloads. However, support costs grow as the disparate workloads of the server grows.

- **Storage costs**: Costs associated with the requirements of the storage hardware can contribute to a rise in storage costs. The storage costs vary based on the types of applications, including email and complex analytics.

- **Network costs**: These costs include costs of incurring additional bandwidth requirement if an internally-hosted web app needs to be moved into the cloud.

- **Backup and archive costs**: The backup and archiving strategy, the personnel responsible for the backup, the amount of cloud-based backup required, and cost of making contingency plans are all direct influencers of backup and archive costs.

- **Disaster recovery costs**: This is an extra cost from the cloud service provider towards disaster recovery responsibilities.

- **Software maintenance costs**: The potential cloud user must be aware of this cost and plan as required.

- **Platform costs**: This is basically a component of the overall annual cost of maintaining the platform and operating systems. Examples of platforms and systems include Windows, Linux, HP-UX, IBM z/OS, AIX.

- **Support personnel costs**: This cost includes the cost of the staff support for everyday operations.

Future of the cloud (FoC)

The **FoC** is the one envisioned to encapsulate both on-premise compute and cloud-based software products as a single entity with greater scalability and flexibility balance between cloud, private data center control and security.

FoC is further described as a standard architecture that leverages on technologies for seamless on-demand availability of software infrastructure, network segmentation, data management, authentication, encryption and data integrity over several public clouds.

A multi-cloud operational mode has a promising future ahead which will have the capacity to avoid lock-in to a single provider.

Future clouds are expected to make ubiquitous computing a reality and experience proliferation of consolidated applications communicating together and with the environment.

Tech Funnel envisages an expanded growth in cloud services solutions, increased storage capacity and enhanced internet quality. It is also believed that future cloud will leverage on serverless computing technologies to provide more resilient architectural patterns.

The factors driving the future of cloud computing are as follows:

- **Defining and comparing services**: A consolidated definition language explicitly exhibiting the functional and non-functional cloud service characteristics, including the standardized service benchmarks to help customers in the decision making process on which provider to choose.

- **Enabling the next generation data centers**: The cloud-enabled infrastructure for the next generation FoC is expected to be adaptive, configurable, open and flexible.

- **Managing a hybrid world**: Hybrid integration of on- and -off premise services of the cloud is part of the expectation of FoC. It is expected to offer agility and greater choice to the customers. Increasingly agile cloud computing services is expected to seamlessly grow new capabilities that can help achieve organizational objectives. Hybrid cloud environments address complex management challenges to gain and maintain control over cloud resources that are external to their resource limitation.

- **Everything as a service**: Future cloud tends to offer everything as a service. Influx of open source composable solutions and services, which can be integrated with an application, to solve a computational problem, will become trending in the near future.

Summary

NIST defines cloud computing as a model for enabling ubiquitous, convenient, on-demand network access to a shared pool of configurable computing resources that can be rapidly provisioned and released with minimal management effort or service provider interaction.

The CCE is a dynamic and complex community of the cloud computing system components and the stakeholders. The three primary stakeholders of the cloud include the end users, the cloud users and the cloud providers.

Cloud computing characteristics are typically the distinctive features and qualities that differentiate such systems from other seemingly-related systems.

There are basically five technical characteristics of cloud computing:

- Large-scale computing resources
- Shared resource pooling
- Dynamic resource scheduling
- High scalability
- Rapid elasticity

Advantages of cloud computing:

- Economical
- Unlimited storage
- Backup and recovery
- Automatic software integration
- Easy access to information and quick deployment.

Disadvantages of cloud computing:

- Technical issues
- Prone to attack
- Security and privacy
- Compliance concerns
- Service migration

Cloud computing is an evolving composite computing system that builds on the characteristics and technologies of such traditional computing platforms and technologies like SOA, cluster computing, grid computing and virtualization technology.

The main motivation for cluster computing is performance improvement, fault tolerance, scalability, huge cost-savings, throughput, redundancy, high memory, enormous speed, load balancing, and high availability.

Grid computing is the amalgamation of several computing resources from several supervisory domains into one or more logical entity, working together as a high-performance distributed grid and applied to solving large batch processing problems.

Cloud computing is a cost-reducing technology that allows small and medium-scale enterprises to contribute to economic growth by strengthening their pro-activeness and productivity.

The FoC is described as a standard architecture that leverages on technologies for seamless on-demand availability of software infrastructure, network segmentation, data management, authentication, encryption and data integrity over several public clouds.

Exercise

Tick the correct option

1. Which of these is NOT a technical characteristic of the cloud?

    a. High scalability

    b. Resource pooling

    c. Resource scheduling

    d. Multi-tenancy

2. Which of the following is associated with cluster computing?

    a. Loose coupling

    b. Tight coupling

    c. Distributed job management

    d. Diversity

3. Which of these is a key business driver of cloud computing?

    a. Costs reduction

    b. Scalability

    c. Sharing

    d. Mobility

4. In which year was Oracle Cloud launched?

    a. 2014

    b. 2012

    c. Late 1990s

    d. Early 2000s

5. Who proposed Intergalactic computer network?

    a. IBM

    b. Oracle

    c. J.C.R. Licklider

    d. Salesforce

6. Remote use of applications via network-based subscriptions is known as

    a. Cloud service

    b. Infrastructure-as-a-Service

    c. On-demand service

    d. Software-as-a-Service

7. Metered service to access and use computing resources is tagged

    a. Pay service

    b. Utility computing

    c. Metered access

    d. Pay-as-you-go

8. Energy efficiency in cloud computing is termed

    a. Energy-aware computing

    b. Energy virtualization

    c. Green computing

    d. High performance computing

9. Difficulty in locating faults is common to?

    a. Mainframe systems

    b. Cloud computing

    c. Grid computing

    d. Cluster computing

10. Which of the following costs is associated with the server costs?

    a. Network cost

    b. Storage cost

    c. Support cost

    d. Recovery cost

Answers:

1. d. Multi-tenancy
2. a. Loose coupling
3. a. Costs reduction
4. b. 2012
5. c. J.C.R. Licklider
6. d. Software-as-a-Service
7. b. Utility computing
8. c. Green computing
9. d. Cluster computing
10. c. Support cost

Fill in the blanks:

1. Data protection is often managed using _____ with defined roles and privileges on data encryption keys management.

2. The main stakeholders of the cloud ecosystem are the _____.

3. The consolidation of fixed cloud services into one or new services is known as_____.

4. _____ are entities that facilitate efficient and effective use of cloud services while ensuring peak performance and seamless delivery of such services.

5. _____makes an expansion of cloud service provisioning business globally a reality in the cloud market.

Answers:

1. data encryption
2. cloud consumers
3. service aggregation
4. Cloud brokers
5. Cloud resellers

Descriptive questions

1. Why cloud computing is essential for organizations?
2. Explain the basic operating mode of a cloud.
3. What are the essential technical characteristics of cloud computing?
4. What are the advantages of cloud computing?
5. What are the disadvantages of cloud computing?
6. Explain the primary stakeholders of the cloud computing ecosystem.
7. Differentiate between clusters, grid and cloud computing.
8. What are the drivers of cloud computing adoption?
9. Explain in brief about the Future of cloud (FoC).
10. Explain about the traditional and cloud computing paradigms.

CHAPTER 2

Cloud Services and Deployment Models

"If someone asks me what cloud computing is, I try not to get bogged down with definitions. I tell them that, simply put, cloud computing is a better way to run your business."

~ Marc Benioff, Founder, CEO and Chairman of Salesforce

Objectives

- To be able to learn about the concepts and different types of cloud deployment models
- To be able to learn and analyze the various cloud service models with examples
- To be able to learn about cloud infrastructure mechanisms
- To be able to learn about cloud service management

This chapter addresses key enterprise cloud infrastructures' deployment and service models. It generally exposes the reader to deployment and service models of the cloud computing infrastructure and specifically to concepts adopted by cloud service providers for deploying hardware, software, networks and storage components as services to their subscribers. The economic cost, performance expectations and service benefits of the varying deployment models are discussed in this chapter. The concluding part of this chapter presents a narrative of sustainable solutions that are currently being used for the management of cloud computing infrastructures in practice.

In this chapter, we will cover the following topics:

- Cloud deployment models: Public, private, hybrid and community clouds

- Cloud service models: **Infrastructure-as-a-Service (IaaS)**, **Platform-as-a-Service (PaaS)** and **Software-as-a-Service (SaaS)**

- Cloud infrastructure mechanisms

- Cloud service management

Cloud deployment models

A cloud deployment model can be described as a distinct parameterized configuration of the cloud computing environment. These parameters include storage size, ownership and accessibility. There are four main cloud deployment models: public, private, hybrid, and community. Web-based organization systems like the *inter-cloud* and *virtual private* are also two other emerging deployment models but yet to gain widespread popularity. Choosing the right cloud deployment model depends on the business, storage, networking and computing requirements of an organization.

Public (external) cloud

A public cloud also known as an external cloud is a cloud environment.

- **Ownership**: Possession of a third-party cloud service provider

  Public cloud platforms are fully owned and maintained by a third-party cloud service provider, creating **virtual machines (VMs)** for use.

- **Accessibility**: Publicly accessible (open access)

  Public cloud models in which cloud computing services are provided and accessed over a public network (with permission) such as the internet.

- **Storage size**: Huge storage size

  Public cloud storage enables individuals and organizations to store, edit and manage huge storage amount of data. This type of storage exists on a remote cloud service provider server and is accessible over the internet. A cloud service provider hosts, manages and sources the storage infrastructure publicly to many different users.

The data and application in the public cloud are created and retained on third-party servers for general public access and use. Provisioning of resources is done dynamically by the off-site third-party cloud service provider and offers access to these resources via a web application or a web service or over the internet as shown in *Figure 2.1*.

The other responsibilities include the administration and maintenance of the pool resources and the entire cloud infrastructure is done by the cloud service provider. This way, public cloud consumers are relieved of the cost of application, bandwidth and hardware acquisition and maintenance requirements in their daily business operations. However, the public cloud subscriber (consumer) is offered a *pay-as-you-go* fine-grained utility pricing model that ensures that the billing is made only for services used and for the period of the usage. In other words, the utility pricing model ensures that the consumer pays only for the amount of shared resources used within a stipulated amount of time. This makes the public cloud very economical and easy to use. Examples of public cloud include Rackspace, **Amazon Elastic Compute Cloud** (**Amazon EC2**), Sun Cloud, IBM's Blue Cloud, Windows Azure Services Platform, and so on.

The characteristics care as follows:

- Resources are homogenous
- Operates a common administrative control and privacy policies
- Multitenancy and shared resources
- Leased or rented cloud resources
- Economies of scale

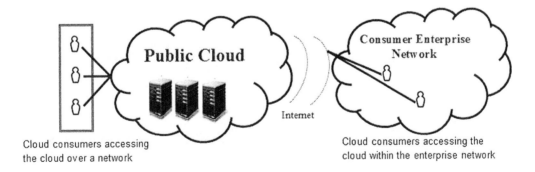

Cloud consumers accessing the cloud over a network

Cloud consumers accessing the cloud within the enterprise network

Figure 2.1: Structure of a public cloud

The advantages and drawbacks of a public cloud are summarized as follows:

Advantages	Disadvantages
Easy setup and use	Data privacy and security
Easy data accessibility	Compromised reliability
Flexibility to add and reduce required capacity	The lack of administrative power
Scalability	Third-party data access
Continuous operation time	
24/7 upkeep	
Cost effectiveness	
Saves cost of procuring software and updates	

Table 2.1

Private/Internal/Corporate cloud

The private cloud can also be described as an internal cloud. Some also refer to it as a corporate cloud. The private cloud is a cloud environment.

The advantages of using a private cloud model are:

- **Ownership**: A private cloud model provides the total ownership that is equal to total control. This is the strength of the private cloud. This type of a cloud is managed by a single (specific) organization and cloud service provider.

- **Accessibility**: A private cloud model has controlled/limited access (only for clearly defined set of persons). A private cloud model is a cloud model in which cloud computing services are provided and accessible over a private network (with permission) such as the internet.

- **Storage size**: Limited storage; in a private cloud model, computing resources are dedicated to serving a single organization. This means the software, hardware, and VMs are all exclusively at the disposal of a single organization.

A private cloud only permits limited access because its highly-virtualized data center architectures are housed by the organization's firewall, making it less risky. In the same vein, it also allows consumers to define and set their preferred customized privacy policies and security requirements. These features make it far more secured than the public cloud. However, unlike the economical public cloud, a private cloud is capital intensive as it requires some capital to buy, build and manage. Some examples of a private cloud include **Simple Storage Service** (**S3**), Red Hat, SaM CloudBOX and Amazon EC2.

A private cloud has many advantages and certain limitations which are summarized in the following table:

Advantages of a Private Cloud	Disadvantages of a Private Cloud
Computational resources and network access is made available to users	Not economical: Incurs considerable cost of hardware, software and staff training
Customizable network and storage and components	Not financially feasible to adopt by small and medium organizations
Greater control over the corporate cloud information	
High privacy, security and reliability: That is, it can safeguard mission-critical operational data/sensitive data	
Maximum level of scalability	

Table 2.2

Hosting of a private cloud server is done on-premise or externally:

- **On-premise private cloud**: On-premise private cloud also referred to as internal cloud is hosted within an organization' own data center as shown in *Figure 2.2*. It provides a more standardized process and security but is often limited in scalability and size. Operational and capital costs for the organization's physical resources are incurred by the organization. The internal cloud is best used for applications that require complete control and configurability of the infrastructure and security:

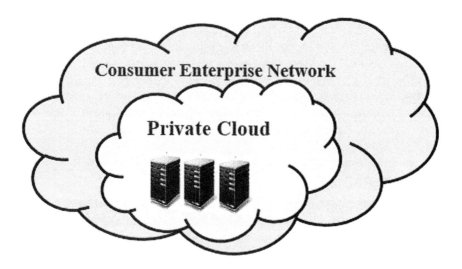

Figure 2.2: On-premise private cloud

- **Externally-hosted private cloud**: The private cloud server is hosted externally and with an exclusive privacy and data security guarantee facilitated by a cloud provider as presented in *Figure 2.3*. It shields the organization from undue risks associated with the sharing of physical resources as seen in the public cloud. Technically, the external cloud, including the pool of resources and infrastructure, is made exclusively for the subscriber by partitioning and separating the private solution from the entire resources of the cloud service provider:

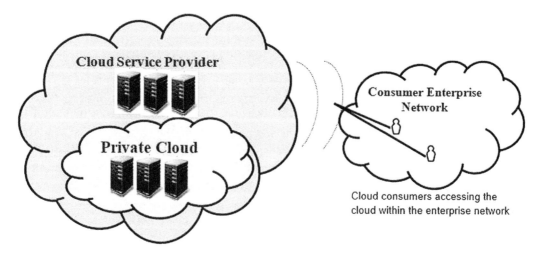

Figure 2.3: Out-sourced private cloud

The general characteristics of a private cloud are as follows:

- Self-service resource provisioning and compute capability
- Automated and well-managed virtualized environments
- Optimized computing resources and servers' utilization
- Support specific workloads
- Heterogeneous and dedicated infrastructure
- Customized policies and end-to-end control

Hybrid cloud

A hybrid cloud environment integrates the operational characteristics of two or more public and private clouds such that some part of the organization's resources are partially hosted within the organization and the rest are hosted externally in a public cloud. A typical structure of a hybrid cloud is presented in *Figure 2.4*. The integration follows a standardized technology that ensures application and data portability. However, with this deployment model, a private cloud could be used to process sensitive (critical) cloud services while other auxiliary cloud service tasks are outsourced to the public cloud. It is often used for backup purpose and to keep records due to its high scalability and cost-effectiveness. The other advantages and challenges of a hybrid cloud are summarized in Table 3:

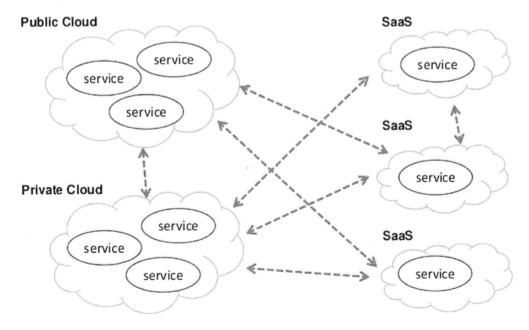

Figure 2.4: The Structure of a typical hybrid cloud

The advantages and disadvantages of a hybrid cloud are as follows:

Advantages of a hybrid cloud	Disadvantages of a hybrid cloud
Enhanced privacy and security	Complex maintenance of two or more deployment architectures
Greater flexibility and scalability	Disparity in cloud environments
Reasonable price	Split responsibilities between the private cloud provider organization and the public cloud provider

Table 2.3

Community cloud

This cloud environment is similar to a private cloud except for the ownership of the cloud resources and infrastructure. Using a community cloud, several organizations with very similar technical and business-specific requirements and objectives can jointly share the cloud resources and infrastructure. It can be described as a close private cloud for some specific set of mutual users. A community cloud is characterized by centralized multi-tenant data center architecture, facilitating easy and efficient project initiation, development, management and implementation. However, it offers high cost savings because it is shared among all the cooperating users in the community cloud. Some examples of community clouds include Google Government Cloud, IGT Cloud, Optum Health Care Cloud, and so on. Similar to a private cloud, a community cloud can also be hosted internally or externally.

Outsourced community cloud

In this arrangement, the server is outsourced to a cloud service provider. However, the infrastructure of an outsourced community cloud exists off-premise and is configured to serve a number of companies that request and use cloud services. A structure of an outsourced community cloud is represented in the following figure:

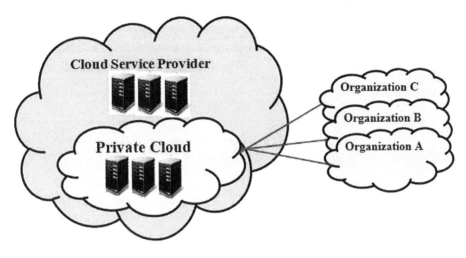

Figure 2.5: Out-sourced community cloud

On-site community cloud

The cloud infrastructure is accessed and used by several companies in the same cloud community having similar and closely-related shared concerns, including privacy and security requirements, compliance considerations and policies. In the following figure, a structure of an on-site community cloud is shown. However, the advantages and disadvantages of the community cloud are summarized in *Table 2.4*. In *Table2.5*, a summary of a comparative analysis of the cloud deployment models is presented:

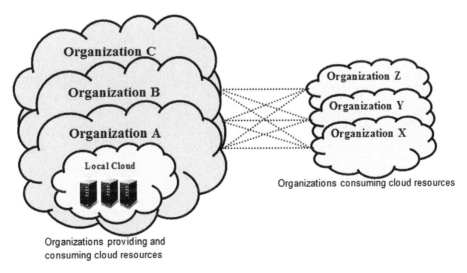

Figure 2.6: On-site community cloud

The advantages and disadvantages of a community cloud are as follows:

Advantages of a Community Cloud	Disadvantages of a Community Cloud
Cost reduction	Higher cost than that of a public one
Improved security, privacy and reliability	Sharing of fixed storage and bandwidth capacity
Ease of data sharing and collaboration	Broad adoption is slow

Table 2.4

The comparative analysis of cloud deployment models is given in the following table:

Attribute	Public	Private	Community	Hybrid
Ease of setup and use	Easy	Requires proficiency in IT	Requires proficiency in IT	Requires proficiency in IT
Data privacy and security	Low	High	Relatively high	High
Data control	Little to none	High	Relatively high	Relatively high
Reliability	Vulnerable	High	Relatively high	High
Scalability and flexibility	High	High	Fixed capacity	High
Cost-effectiveness	The most cost-effective	Cost-intensive, the most expensive one	Cost is shared among the community members	Cheaper than a private model but more expensive than a public model
Need for in-house hardware	No	Depends	Depends	Depends
Upfront costs	Low	High	Medium	Medium

Attribute	Public	Private	Community	Hybrid
Ongoing costs	High	Low	Medium	Medium
Security	Low	High	Medium	Medium
Compliance	Low	High	Medium	Medium
Quality of service	Low	High	Medium	Medium
Integration	Low	High	Medium	Medium
Configurability	Low	Medium	Medium	Medium

Table 2.5

The following figure summarizes all the concepts explained:

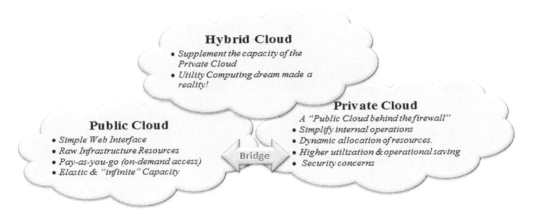

Figure 2.7: Cloud deployment models

Cloud Service Models

There are basically three service models for a cloud computing system, namely, Infrastructure-as-a-Service, Platform-as-a-Service and Software-as-a-Service. The service models can be viewed as mapped layers as represented in Figure 2.8:

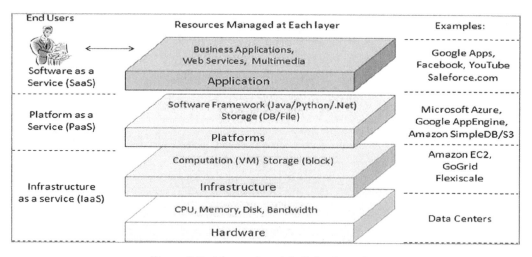

Figure 2.8: A layered model of cloud services

Infrastructure-as-a-Service (IaaS)

Infrastructure-as-a-Service (IaaS) is a service-oriented and secure enterprise-level computing infrastructure that includes the computing resources and the storage, which can be efficiently scaled and managed to assist organizations in meeting their different business objectives. Technically, it follows the concept of the virtual private server. The computing resources (include the CPU hours, bandwidth, storage space, and so on) and infrastructure (data transfers, virtual servers, storage, computing, content distribution networks, and so on) are metered based on a pay-as-you-go utility pricing model. For example, IaaS cloud storage offers consumers scalable online storage access. Virtual server instances having unique internet protocol addresses and storage blocks are also similarly offered on demand. The unique flexibility of IaaS allows subscribers to use **application program interface (API)** of service providers to initiate, stop, access, adjust and set up storage and virtual servers as required. Some examples of IaaS cloud include Eucalyptus, Nimbus, Amazon EC2, S3 and Rackspace. It is important to note that IaaS can be public, private and hybrid.

The advantages of IaaS are reliability, almost limitless computing power and storage, cost reduction, business agility, scalability, and privacy.

Public, private and hybrid IaaS

In a public IaaS, shared resources are accessed by the consumers via a simple sign-up mechanism and managed by a service provider.

In a private IaaS, a secure and on-demand access to resources of an organization is provided by the service provider to the consumer(s).

Hybrid IaaS combines the functionalities and characteristics of both the public and the private IaaS. Both internal and external service providers are responsible for maintaining the cloud computing resource and infrastructure as the case may be.

The characteristics of IaaS are as follows:

- Resources are provisioned as a service
- Availability is based on a utility-based pricing model
- Scaling of resources is dynamic and on-demand
- Supports multiple users to concurrently access a single piece of hardware

Platform-as-a-Service (PaaS)

PaaS is a product development-oriented cloud service model which provides subscribers (developers) with a virtualized set of partial or full integrated development environment and tools to create, develop, execute, test, and deploy new applications directly in the cloud with a particular programming language via the internet as a service. It has associated tools and services to facilitate efficient coding and deployment of completed applications. The developed applications using PaaS are provisioned as SaaS to the end-users via the internet. Using this model, absolute control and maintenance of the key cloud infrastructure, especially the operating systems, storage and the server, resides with the service provider and not the consumer. Using PaaS, collaborative projects can be jointly developed by several members of a project team irrespective of their wide geographical proximity. Some examples of PaaS are Apache Stratos, Microsoft Azure, IBM Bluemix, Force. com and Google Apps. PaaS is characterized by failover and security capabilities, high server speed, load balancing, availability, uniform authentication, robust scalability, automated backups creation, and high storage capabilities.

The advantages of PaaS are as follows:

- **Implements standardization**: PaaS seamlessly allows the developers and the technical operations professionals to access the same services on the same platform.

- **Provides ease of service provisioning**: PaaS offers easy distribution of development tools and repository services, thereby eliminating interoperability challenges that may be associated with non-standard environments. Consequently, reduced errors, high consistency and improved efficiency often characterize the development life cycle management processes. PaaS also offers easy provisioning of scaling applications and runtime services.

Some other advantages are as follows:

- Offers an abstracted interface and platform to optimize the development life cycle of an application
- Relieves organizations of installation and operational burden
- Provides a unified environment to develop, build, distribute, host, and maintain applications
- Provides web-based interface development tools for designing appealing graphical user interfaces
- Offers a multi-tenant architecture that supports remote collaborative team work and concurrent usage

Software-as-a-Service (SaaS)

SaaS is typically the functional layer of the cloud service model. Via a multi-tenant architecture, SaaS grants multiple users remote and exclusive access to a single application through a web browser. To the consumer, the SaaS model is more or less a web-based application platform with an interface to present and deliver hosted software applications and services on the internet which are accessible via a web browser. Using SaaS, consumers are relieved of capital investment in servers, software licensing, upgrading or maintaining software applications on their local systems. However, running and maintenance of the computing resources, the operating system and the application software are the responsibilities of the cloud service provider. Characteristics of SaaS include configurability, scalability, high efficiency, and multi-tenant architecture among others. Multi-tenant architecture enables a single software application to be delivered through a web browser to numerous users. Some examples of SaaS hosted applications include Microsoft Office 365, Google Docs, Salesforce, NetSuite, Hotmail, Gmail, WebEx and Microsoft LiveMeeting which can be accessed by a client using devices such as smartphones, iPads and laptops. In particular, Google Docs provide users with interfaces to create, edit, delete, and share their documents, presentations or spreadsheets with anyone while Google retains the responsibility to ensure that the software and hardware that support the applications are routinely maintained. SaaS applications are offered as a service on demand at no charge via a subscription or billed as per the *pay-as-you-go* utility pricing model.

The characteristics of SaaS are as follows:

- Commercial software gets centralized web-based access

- Provides flexibilities that makes the entire business process to shift to the cloud

- No burden of software patches and upgrades of some sorts

- Integration with different applications is possible via application programming interfaces

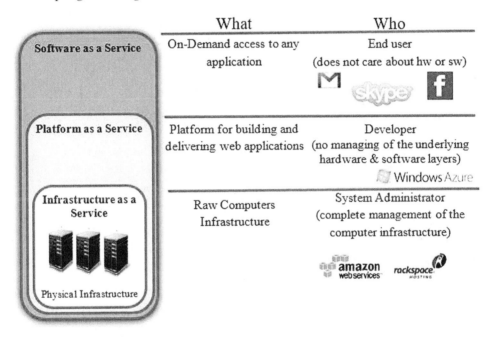

Figure 2.9: Cloud service models

A summary of personnel responsibilities in cloud service models is given in Table 2.6:

	Application Software	**Operating System**	**Hardware and Virtual Resources**
SaaS	Cloud service provider	Cloud service provider	Cloud service provider
PaaS	Customer	Cloud service provider	Cloud service provider
IaaS	Customer	Customer	Cloud service provider

Table 2.6

Cloud infrastructure mechanisms

The cloud infrastructure mechanisms are the basic foundational building blocks of the cloud computing environments. They create the principal underlying structural elements that make up the fundamental cloud technology architecture. They formally represent the major system elements that are common to all cloud platforms. These mechanisms include the logical network perimeter, virtual server, cloud usage monitor, cloud storage device, resource replication and ready-made environments.

Logical network perimeter (LNP)

The **logical network perimeter** (**LNP**) is defined as the creation of a logical boundary to partition a segment of a network environment from the entire communication network. With LNP, a virtual or implicit network partition can be established which in turn is capable of enclosing and separating a group of related cloud-based computing resources and infrastructure that may be physically distributed. Network devices can be used to establish a logical network perimeter. These network devices are those that provide and manage the connectivity of data centers. However, LNP are typically deployed as virtualized environments comprising of a virtual firewall and a virtual network:

- **Virtual firewall**: Given an isolated network, a virtual firewall is a technology-based security and access control resource that actively filters the network traffic to and from the isolated network while managing its interactions and communications with the internet.

- **Virtual network**: This technology-based resource, usually acquired via virtual local area networks, is being used to isolate the network environment within the data center infrastructure. However, the LNP mechanism can be applied to:

- Isolate and shield computing resources and cloud infrastructure from non-authorized users

- Isolate and shield computing resources and cloud infrastructure from non-users

- Isolate and computing resources and cloud infrastructure from cloud consumers

- Adjust the bandwidth that is available to isolated computing resources and cloud infrastructure

Virtual server

A virtual server is an abstraction of a physical (dedicated) server that runs via a virtualization process. It is actually a high configuration virtual computer with a considerable number of virtual server programs typically used by cloud providers to share software and hardware resources as well as the physical server with several cloud subscribers such that each subscriber has a virtual server instance running. Virtual servers offer the possibilities for subscribers to access and manage their file directories, statistics, logs and passwords without the intervention of the internet service provider. Each virtual server has its own operating system, independent reboot provisioning and software. It uses a unique combination of the host name, IP address and port number to be identified. Virtual servers are cost-effective and provide efficient resource control. However, resource hogging may set in if multiple virtual servers are concurrently running on a physical machine.

Cloud storage devices (CSD)

This mechanism represents storage devices that are primarily designed and tailored for cloud-based distribution and provisioning. These devices can be accessed as virtual instances through cloud storage services, following a similar mirroring process of how dedicated servers mimic images of virtual servers. CSD's flexibility allows fixed-increment capacity allocation complementing the metered pay-per-use utility pricing model. However, the paramount concerns of cloud storage include regulatory and legal implications of data relocation, integrity, security and confidentiality of data. This is because data is susceptible to compromise should a third-party or an external cloud provider gain access to it. CSD mechanisms provide standard logical classes of data storage known as cloud storage levels.

The cloud storage levels include files, blocks, datasets and objects:

- **Files**: This is a collection of information or data with a unique name which is typically located in folders. The different types of files can be data, text, and directory or program files, etc.

- **Blocks**: This is the smallest unit of data and the lowest level of storage, the closest to the hardware, and which can be accessed individually.

- **Datasets**: This is an aggregation of related sets of data organized as byte streams logically into a table-based, delimited, block or record format which may be accessed in combination or individually.

- **Objects**: This is the composite data together with its associated metadata which are grouped as web-based resources.

Cloud usage monitor

The **cloud usage monitor** mechanism is an autonomous and lightweight software application that is responsible for harvesting and processing the usage data of computing IT resources. The cloud usage monitor is technically composed of a monitoring agent and a resource agent:

- Monitoring agent: A monitoring agent is a mediating, event-driven program that functions as a service agent and occupies existing communication paths to ensure a clear and apparent monitoring and analysis of dataflows. Monitoring agents are mostly used to estimate message metrics and the network traffic. When a cloud service user makes a request to use a cloud service, the request is intercepted by the monitoring agent to enable it to extract pertinent usage data. Before releasing the intercepted message to access the cloud service, the monitoring agent will store the usage data collected in a log database. However, the cloud service will reply with a response message that is sent back to the cloud service user without any interference by the monitoring agent.

- Resource agent: A resource agent is a processing program (module) that harvests usage data via event-driven communications with esoteric resource software. A resource agent program is typically used to track usage metrics by following some pre-defined, perceptible events at the resource software level such as vertical scaling, initiating, resuming, and suspending.

Resource replication

Generally, the goal of a replication process is to allow an open access to resources if a system failure occurs. However, a resource replication in cloud can be regarded as the initiation of manifold instances of cloud-based resources which is implemented via virtualization technology. This procedure is typically performed when the need to optimize the performance and availability of a cloud resource arises.

Ready-made environment

The **ready-made environment** mechanism is a fundamental and typical component of the PaaS delivery model that depicts a pre-defined, cloud-based environment that is composed of a number of pre-installed cloud-based resources, ready to be accessed and personalized by a cloud user. Cloud users may use ready-made environments to design, implement, test and deploy their own self-tailored applications and services within a cloud. This environment is equipped with a complete **software development kit** (**SDK**) that offers programmatic direct access to the underlying pre-installed technologies that comprise the programming stacks preference of the cloud users. Some examples of ready-made environments with pre-installed cloud resources are middleware, databases, governance, and development tools.

Cloud service management

Cloud service management refers to all activities that are performed by a cloud service provisioning organization to monitor, maintain and manage cloud computing products and services to ensure a 24/7 availability and exclusive access by subscribers. A standard cloud service management reference architecture must be in place and adopted by cloud service providers to guide effective planning, analysis, provisioning, and optimization of their services.

The functional requirements and purpose of cloud service management are as follows:

- To demonstrate appropriate techniques for easy and automated management cloud-oriented services

- To incorporate cloud service management practices in the current support and development methodologies

- To maximize cloud service supply chains and reduce costs by integrating cloud services and products

- To enable constant and uninterrupted provisioning of new cloud service capabilities effectively and efficiently as a way of improving quality of service

- To effectively mitigate new threats from multiple interconnected infrastructure and computing resources and manage change in a sustainable manner

- To harness practices for rapid detection of problems and speedy restoration of service

Here are the ten cloud service management tips for cloud service providers and architects:

1. Cloud service providers can harness the power of cloud service monitoring and management tools to ensure peak performance, availability and efficiency of cloud services in on-demand virtualized platforms.

2. Cloud service providers should be aware of the constant changing capacity demands of a high-elastic cloud computing environment for effective cloud service administration and management at par with best practices.

3. Cloud service providers should provide the visibility, automation and control required for seamless and efficient cloud service provisioning.

4. Cloud service providers should simplify the interactions of cloud users with cloud IT resources.

5. Cloud service providers should maintain an up-to-date cloud service catalogue.

6. Cloud service providers should ensure that cloud services provisioned are self-service and user friendly.

7. Cloud service providers and architects should implement a policy of economies of scale for cloud service distribution.

8. Cloud service providers and architects should automate resource allocation and de-allocation processes for efficiency.

9. Cloud architects should maintain an index of cloud resources to gain greater scalability.

10. Pre-defined alarms should be provided by cloud architects to inform cloud users regarding the service threshold reached.

Dimensions to cloud service management

Cloud service management can be described from three basic dimensions namely—the business support, the provisioning/configuration and the portability/ interoperability as shown in *Figure 2.10*.

Business support

This implies the actual set of business-related services that affect the cloud subscribers and their supporting processes. This may include the elements that drive business operations that are cloud subscriber-facing. These elements can be identified as a customer, contract, inventory, accounting and billing, reporting and auditing as well as pricing and rating:

- **Customer management**: Keep customer accounts up to date, open/ close/terminate accounts, ensure effective management of users' profiles, imbibe know-your-customer initiative to largely maintain customers' relationship and the endeavor to seamlessly resolve customer problems and complaints.

- **Contract management**: Manage all service contracts; set up/negotiate/ close/terminate contract as required.

- **Inventory management**: Set up and manage all inventory logs and service catalogs.

- **Billing and accounting**: Manage the customers' billing and account details, promptly send billing statements and process all payments and invoices.

- **Auditing and reporting**: Audit all financial reporting of business transactions from time to time, monitor user operations and generate appropriate reports.

- **Rating and pricing**: Evaluate provisioned cloud services and determine appropriate pricing, address pricing policies based on each user's subscription type.

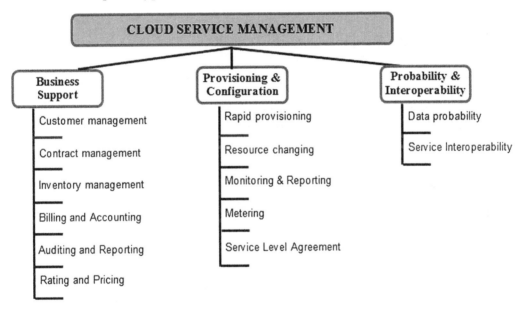

Figure 2.10: Cloud service management dimensions

Provisioning and configuration

Provisioning and configuration include rapid provisioning, resource changing, monitoring and reporting, metering and service level agreement management:

- **Rapid provisioning**: Deploy cloud services automatically with respect to the requested resource(s), service(s) and configuration capabilities.

- **Resource changing**: Fine-tune resource/configuration request for overhaul, upgrades and connection of new nodes to the cloud.

- **Monitoring and reporting**: Discover and monitor virtual resources, cloud services and events generating relevant performance reports.

- **Metering**: Ensure that a metering model at some level of abstraction commensurable with the type of cloud service (for example, processing, storage, bandwidth and so on) is provided.

- **Service Level Agreement (SLA) management**: Interpret and implement the SLA contract requirements definition (basic schema with the QoS parameters), SLA monitoring and SLA enforcement according to standard defined policies.

Portability and interoperability

Cloud computing adoption lies solely on how users' concerns about cloud security, portability and interoperability issues are addressed.

Requirements for portability and interoperability are as follows:

- In the case of portability, prospective subscribers are keen to know the possibility of moving their data and/or applications across multiple cloud environments at minimal interference and low cost.

- From an interoperability dimension, the extent of interoperability support to communicating between or among multiple clouds.

Cloud providers are expected to provide methods and systems offering greater support for data portability, system portability and service interoperability:

- Data portability allows the cloud users to copy stored data objects into or out of a cloud for bulk data migration using an external storage disk

- System portability is the ability to seamlessly migrate to a machine image or a fully-stopped virtual machine instance from one service provider to another service provider, or migrate to services, applications and their associated contents from one service provider to another.

- Service interoperability involves the ability of cloud users to access their unique set of data and provisioned services from multiple cloud providers via a unified management interface.

However, it should be noted that these requirements vary from one cloud service model to another.

Summary

- A public cloud is also known as an external cloud. The data and application in the public cloud are created and retained on third-party servers for general public access and use.

- A private cloud can also be described as an internal cloud or corporate cloud. A private cloud is a computing model where IT services are provisioned over the private IT infrastructure for the dedicated use of a single organization.

- A hybrid cloud is a type of cloud computing which uses a mix of one or more private and public clouds to perform distinct functions.

- A community cloud is a type of cloud computing which is shared by one or more organizations forming a group with common computing concerns.

- A community cloud is categorized in the outsourced community cloud and on-site community cloud.

- There are basically three service models for a cloud computing system, namely, Infrastructure-as-a-Service, Platform-as-a-Service and Software-as-a-Service.

- Infrastructure-as-a-service (IaaS) is a service-oriented and secure enterprise-level computing infrastructure. IaaS provides hardware, storage, servers and data center space or network components. It may also include software.

- Some examples of IaaS cloud include Eucalyptus, Nimbus, Amazon EC2, S3 and Rackspace. IaaS is also known as hardware-as-a-service (HaaS).

- PaaS provides a platform and environment to allow developers to build applications and services over the internet.

- Some examples of PaaS are Apache Stratos, Microsoft Azure, IBM Bluemix, Force.com and Google Apps.

- Software-as-a-Service (SaaS) allows data and applications to be accessed from any device with internet connection and a web browser. SaaS applications are sometimes called web-based software, on-demand software, or hosted software.

- Some examples of SaaS hosted applications include Microsoft Office 365, Google Docs, Salesforce, NetSuite, Hotmail, Gmail, WebEx and Microsoft LiveMeeting.

- Cloud infrastructure mechanisms are the basic foundational building blocks of the cloud computing environments.

- Cloud infrastructure mechanisms include the logical network perimeter, virtual server, cloud usage monitor, cloud storage device, resource replication and ready-made environment.

- The cloud usage monitor mechanism is an autonomous and lightweight software application that is responsible for harvesting and processing the usage data of computing IT resources.

- Cloud service management refers to all activities that are performed by a cloud service provisioning organization to monitor, maintain and manage cloud computing products and services to ensure a 24/7 availability and exclusive access by subscribers.

Exercise

Tick the correct option

1. A public cloud is defined by?

    a. Portability

    b. Ownership

    c. Storage size

    d. Accessibility

2. One of the following is not a characteristic of the public cloud.

    a. Homogenous resources

    b. Multi-tenancy

    c. Economies of scale

    d. Heterogeneous resources

3. One of the following is not true about the on-premise private cloud.

    a. Highly standardized process

    b. Also referred to as the internal cloud

    c. High scalability

    d. High level of security

4. IGT Cloud is an example of

    a. Public cloud

    b. Private cloud

   c. Hybrid cloud

   d. Community cloud

5. The composite data together with its associated metadata which are grouped as web-based resources is called

   a. File

   b. Object

   c. Block

   d. Dataset

6. Cloud storage device mechanisms provide standard logical classes of data storage known as

   a. Cloud storage stages

   b. Cloud storage blocks

   c. Cloud Storage levels

   d. Cloud storage steps

7. Eucalyptus is an example of

   a. PaaS cloud

   b. Private cloud

   c. IaaS cloud

   d. SaaS cloud

8. Identify the odd out of the following:

   a. Cloud storage driver

   b. Resource replication

   c. Resource aggregation

   d. Cloud usage monitor

9. A ready-made environment is a peculiar component of

   a. On-premise IaaS

   b. PaaS

   c. SaaS

   d. Out-sourced IaaS

10. Examples of a ready-made environment pre-installed cloud resources are all of the following except
    a. Middleware
    b. Databases
    c. Development tools
    d. Resource agents

11. The smallest unit of data and the lowest level of storage is called
    a. Objects
    b. Dataset
    c. Block
    d. Files

12. A virtual server uses a combination of all of the following for identification except
    a. Host name
    b. Password
    c. IP address
    d. Port number

Answers:
1. a. Portability
2. a. Heterogeneous resources
3. c. High scalability
4. d. Community cloud
5. b. Object
6. c. Cloud storage levels
7. c. IaaS Cloud
8. c. Resource aggregation
9. b. PaaS
10. d. Resource agents
11. c. Block
12. b. Password

Fill in the blanks

1. _____ are the basic foundational building blocks of the cloud computing environments.

2. Network devices can be used to establish _____.

3. _____ is being used to isolate the network environment within the data center infrastructure.

4. Service interoperability involves the ability of cloud users to access their unique set of data and provisioned services from multiple cloud providers via a _____.

5. Cloud users may use _____ to design, implement, test and deploy their own self-tailored applications and services within a cloud.

6. A _____ is a processing program (module) that harvests usage data via event-driven communications with esoteric resource software.

7. A monitoring agent is a mediating, event-driven program that functions as a service agent and occupies existing communication paths to ensure a clear and apparent monitoring and analysis of _____.

8. _____ are mostly used to estimate message metrics and the network traffic.

9. The _____ mechanism is an autonomous and lightweight software application that is responsible for harvesting and processing the usage data of compute IT resource.

10. _____ may set in if multiple virtual servers are concurrently running on a physical machine.

Answers:

1. Cloud infrastructure mechanisms
2. logical network perimeter
3. Virtual network
4. unified management interface
5. ready-made environments
6. resource agent
7. dataflows
8. Monitoring agents
9. cloud usage monitor
10. Resource hogging

Descriptive questions:

1. Differentiate between private and public clouds.

2. Draw a diagram to explain in brief a hybrid cloud computing infrastructure.

3. Explain a outsourced community cloud and on-site community cloud with diagrams.

4. Give a detailed analysis of cloud deployment models.

5. What is the difference between IaaS, PaaS and SaaS?

6. Is Gmail SaaS or PaaS? Explain in detail.

7. What is an example of PaaS?

8. Explain cloud infrastructure mechanisms in detail.

9. What are the three basic dimensions cloud service management? Describe them with diagrams.

10. What is the purpose of cloud service management? List any five functional requirements of cloud service management.

CHAPTER 3

Cloud Computing Architecture

"Architecture is a visual art and the buildings speak for themselves."

~ Julia Morgan, American architect

Objectives

- To discuss the cloud computing architecture design principles
- To discuss the cloud computing life cycle (CCLC) phases in detail
- To learn about the cloud computing reference architecture
- To learn about the concepts of load balancing approach
- To learn about the mobile cloud computing (MCC)
- To discuss the Oracle cloud management as a case study

In this chapter, we will discuss the fundamental elements which make up cloud computing services. Cloud computing requires the synchronization of various technologies and service providers who collectively make this new computing concept a success. We will understand the roles and responsibilities of each provider and the predominant technologies utilized in cloud computing. We will also explore the benefits and limitations of these technologies.

In this chapter, we will discuss the following points:

- Cloud computing architecture design principles
- Cloud computing life cycle (CCLC)

- Cloud computing reference architecture
- Load balancing approach
- Mobile cloud computing (MCC)
- Case study – Oracle cloud management

Cloud computing architecture design principles

Cloud computing is one of the boons of technology, making storage and access of data easier and more efficient. An acceptable cloud system design should take advantage of some of the essential characteristics of cloud computing such as on-demand availability, ability to automate infrastructure management, scalability, elasticity, and so on.

There are certain principles of architecture that one needs to follow in order to take advantage of the incredible abilities of the cloud. The following seven design principles you must consider for cloud architecture are as follows:

- **Adaptive and elastic**: Cloud architecture should foster growth of users, traffic, or data size with no drop in operational performance. It should also make provision for adjustments whenever additional computing resources are added.

- **Implement loose coupling**: Cloud architecture should ideally be designed in such a way that software and hardware components are made separate and distinct so as to reduce inter-dependencies. This design is meant to prevent changes or failure in one or more components from adversely affecting others.

- **Managed database services**: Cloud architecture should help remove constraints that arise with licensing costs and the ability to support diverse database engines that were an inherent part of the traditional IT infrastructure. You need to keep in mind that limitless access to the information stockpiled on these databases is the primary objective of cloud computing.

- **Be sure to remove single points of failure**: A cloud computing system is consistently accessible if it can endure the failure of a single component or multiple ones (for example, hard disks, servers, network links, operating systems, and so on). Through virtualization, automatic recovery can reduce system disruption at each layer of the cloud architecture.

- **Optimize for cost**: Cloud architecture should be designed to optimize costs, considering that costs can be reduced by selecting the configurations and data storage arrangements to suit users' needs by taking advantage of a variety of Instance Purchasing choices.

- **Caching**: Data caching should be applied to multiple layers of the cloud architecture for optimum application performance and efficiency of costs.

- **Security**: Both organizations and individual users expect their private information to not only be safe but also secure. Therefore, cloud architecture should be designed notwithstanding legal obligations for providers to adhere to high data security standards.

Cloud user interfaces and formats must be in line with appropriate industry standards. The cloud computing system must represent only the interface relevant for the user to perform individual functions. Cloud service providers' claims of dependability, accessibility, security, and performance must be certified by some IT authority. The cloud architecture should observe every aspect of computing resources being used as well as the responsibilities and tasks performed by both the Cloud provider and consumer.

The following are the benefits of the designing aspects of the cloud computing architecture:

- **Transparent architecture and control**: Cloud service consumers should have access to the design and operation of the cloud system.

- **Improved productivity**: Cloud systems should provide significant improvements in the levels of efficiency and productivity than those in traditional IT settings.

- **Assured data protection**: Cloud service consumers should be confident that data privacy standards and regulations are being followed by the provider.

- **Automate operations**: Cloud service consumers' platform services runtime should have manual operations in marginal amounts.

- Accessibility should not be hindered by expected hardware failures.

- **Robust identity domain separation**: Cloud service consumers should not be subjected to any impairment caused by other users.

Cloud computing life cycle (CCLC)

A cloud life cycle developed by a group of organizations using an open-innovation approach encompasses nine steps that can be followed for both the migration to cloud computing and perpetual management of public cloud-based services. Each step in this life cycle is described in terms of the primary difficulties faced, and the prescribed activities, with ensuing outputs required to resolve these problems.

Cloud computing has the potential of noteworthy benefits, including but not limited to reduced costs, better service delivery, and a move to a pay-per-use model. The objective of the cloud lifecycle is to negotiate the ever-changing nature of the cloud environment, expedite service speed, increase flexibility, and promptly satisfy the needs of individuals and organizations.

The principal benefits of a cloud lifecycle management solution should include:

- Expediting the delivery of cloud services in response to users' needs and requirements

- Automating services and other work processes from initiation to completion for efficiency

- Facilitating users with flexible and customizable cloud services for their specific uses

- Supporting the use of public cloud infrastructures to supplement internal computing resources

- Maximizing computing resource deployment by ensuring idle cloud services are retrieved

There are four stages/phases within the cloud life cycle which can be further segmented into nine steps as illustrated in *Figure 3.1*. Each step serves as a precursor for the subsequent step. Accordingly, the series must be followed in succession to achieve favorable results.

In sequential order, the four phases of the cloud computing life cycle are as follows:

1. **Architect**: This phase begins with the analysis and preparation of the cloud scheme. Usually, an organization will only commit a nominal amount of resources in order to decide if they should go forward with comprehensive development.

2. **Engage**: This phase involves choosing a cloud service provider that can provide the necessary services. A lot of organizations decide to stop at this stage whenever the suitable cloud services are not offered, or because they do not have the assurance that any cloud provider can deliver the required services.

3. **Operate**: This phase comprises the execution of and regular management of the cloud service.

4. **Refresh**: This phase includes the continued appraisal of cloud services provided.

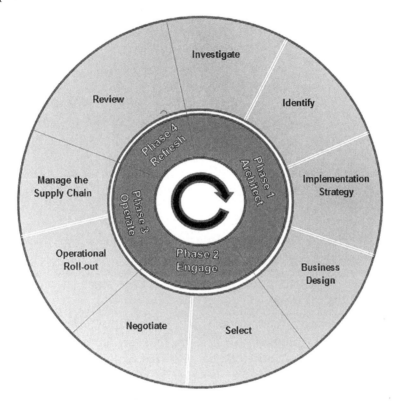

Figure 3.1: Cloud computing life cycle

Phase 1 – Architect

The following steps are as follows:

- **Step 1**: Examine prospects—provide an understanding of what firms want to achieve by moving to the cloud, and how they expect to accomplish specific objectives and overall goals. This will be based on an analysis of the relevant industry sector with insights from experts and experiences from industry experts.

- **Step 2**: Classify facilities—impartially evaluate the components of the business that are suitable to outsource to the cloud and the effect it will have on the firm's current delivery model. This cataloging will require a thorough understanding of the business's present state of affairs so that it can be compared to the desired future. Factors to consider during classification include customer interaction and IT infrastructure.

- **Step 3**: Define services—outline a strategy of how the outsourced cloud services will be implemented. During this step, key decisions on employment, communication, project execution, organizational policies, and risk assessment strategies should be well-defined.

- **Step 4**: Design model—create a detailed service model of the proposed outsourced cloud service package. This comprehensive plan will expound the new service, its operation management, how it fits into the existing business systems, and how results will be reported.

Phase 2 – Engage

- **Step 5**: Select supplier—choose the best cloud provider based on interface, quality, cost, and continuity.

- **Step 6**: Negotiate service terms—finalize discussions based on design criteria and sign service contracts.

Phase 3 – Operate

- **Step 7**: Implement plan—assemble a team that will manage the migration to the new cloud platform. Make sure that communication is disseminated to all stakeholders via email, letters, faxes, bulletins, and so on regarding the transition of the new services provided.

- **Step 8**: Manage the supply chain—manage the new cloud service efficiently and effectively. The company staff will need to familiarize themselves with the new cloud interface, particularly at the IT management level. Instead of directly managing internal resources, monitoring and controlling the cloud provider should be the focus.

Phase 4 – Refresh

- **Step 9**: Review—periodically review the cloud service requirements based on the service itself, other changes within the business, changes within the supplier organization, or the need to change the supplier. Note that changing the supplier can create some difficulties, so carefully consider **Step 5**.

The importance of using life cycle stages are illustrated as follows:

Architect	**Step 1: Investigate**
	1. Determine the organization's IT objectives and its alignment with the business.
	2. Determine what role cloud computing will play within the IT strategy.
	3. Gather intelligence on cloud service offerings.
	4. Validate results with cloud subject matter experts and peer organizations.
	Step 2 (a): Identify
	1. Determine what services will be outsourced to the cloud and consider impacts on the service, people, cost, infrastructure, and stakeholders.
	2. Decide what type of cloud outsourcing model will be used and why it is suitable.
	3. Document the current and future states of the IT infrastructure.
	Step 2(b): Implementation Strategy
	1. Determine the roll out approach and how the program will be managed.
	2. Detail how the program will be staffed and reported.
	3. Decide how cloud suppliers will be engaged, selected and managed.
	4. Determine how risk will be assessed and managed, including security, data recovering and in-sourcing.
	Step 3. Business Design
	1. Detail the service offering for tender.
	2. Define negotiable/non- negotiable issues around: contracts, service-level agreements (SLA), and pricing model.

	Step 4. Selection
Engage	1. Define the tender/bid process.
	2. Select and staff an evaluation team.
	3. Invite bids/tenders.
	4. Evaluate suppliers against the defined criteria.
	5. Short list the suppliers.
	6. Carry out due diligence.
	Step 5: Negotiate and sign-off
	1. Define the negotiation strategy.
	2. Select and staff the negotiation team.
	3. Carry out negotiations.
	4. Select the preferred cloud supplier.
	5. Get internal approvals and sign the contract.
	Step 6: Operational roll-out
	1. Finalize and publish transition plans.
	2. Select and staff the transition team.
	3. Agree and publish acceptance criteria.
	4. Carry out the transition.
	5. Communicate progress.
Operate	6. Carry out knowledge transfer.
	7. Manage staff (directly and indirectly) impacted.
	Step 7: Management
	1. Manage and report on cloud service operations.
	2. Capture and manage issues, variations and disputes.
	3. Manage the supplier relationship.
	4. Change management.
	5. Continuous improvement.
	6. Assess and validate how the cloud service is performing.

Step 8: Review
1. Gather intelligence in your relevant market segment for cloud service technology trends and supplier offerings.
2. Audit cloud supplier performance and compare to alternatives.
3. Understand and assess how other changes in the organization impact on the existing cloud service arrangement.
4. Make and present a business case for any significant change to the current cloud service arrangement to get approval to start a new cycle.

Table 3.1

The cloud life cycle proves to be a marvelous instrument for an organization's management structure to plan and oversee not only the migration to the cloud environment but also its continuous management. Each of the nine steps presented previously clearly exhibits the importance of using a cloud life cycle to control and manage the migration to the cloud.

Cloud computing reference architecture

The cloud computing reference architecture is a practical plan for a system with a distinct range of operations. It fulfills specific system requirements through carefully crafted architectural schemes to ensure quality and consistency over the course of system development and delivery projects.

The conceptual reference model

Figure 3.2 illustrates the **National Institute of Standards and Technology (NIST)** cloud computing reference architecture. It shows the five main participants in the cloud computing environment and the roles they play. The diagram depicts a generic high-level architecture and is intended to simplify the comprehension of the requirements, usages, features and principles of cloud computing:

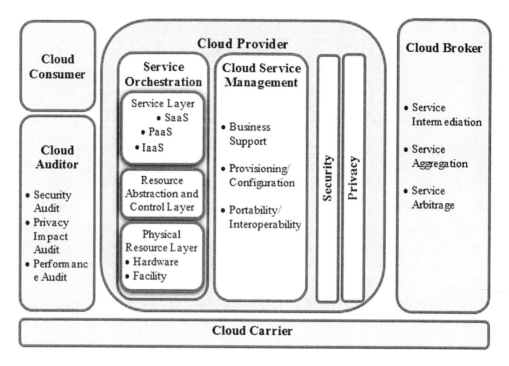

Figure 3.2: NIST cloud computing reference architecture

As shown in *Figure 3.2*, the NIST cloud computing reference architecture defines five major actors:

- Cloud consumer
- Cloud provider
- Cloud carrier
- Cloud auditor
- Cloud broker

Each participant is either an individual or an entity that participates in a transaction or process and/or performs various tasks within the cloud system. *Table 2* briefly lists the functions of each participant depicted in the NIST cloud computing reference architecture.

Figure 3.3 shows the interactions between the actors. As implied, cloud consumers may request services directly from providers or through brokers while auditors may collect relevant information from any of the three aforementioned parties in efforts to conduct independent audits:

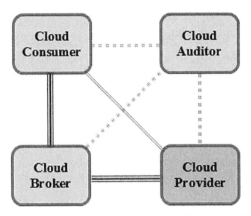

═The communication path between a Cloud Provider and a Cloud Consumer
░░ The communication path for a Cloud Auditor to cloud auditing information
≡The communication paths for a Cloud Broker to provide service to a Cloud Consumer

Figure 3.3: Interactions between the actors in cloud computing

The actors in cloud computing are presented in the following table:

Actor	Definition
Cloud Consumer	A person or organization that maintains a business relationship with and uses service from cloud providers.
Cloud Provider	A person, organization, or entity responsible for making a service available to interested parties.
Cloud Auditor	A party that can conduct independent assessment of cloud services, information system operations, performance and security of the cloud implementation.
Cloud Broker	An entity that manages the use, performance and delivery of cloud services, and negotiates relationships between **Cloud Providers** and **Cloud Consumers.**
Cloud Carrier	An intermediary that provides connectivity and transport of cloud services from **Cloud Providers** to **Cloud Consumers.**

Table 3.2

Let us understand each actor in detail:

- **Cloud Consumer**: A cloud consumer is the primary stakeholder for the cloud computing service. A cloud consumer may be an individual or an organization. After browsing the cloud service catalogs from a cloud provider, requests the service applicable to their business processes, sign **service-level agreements (SLAs)** or contracts with the provider, and use the service(s) for which they are billed on a pay-per-use basis. Cloud SLAs stipulate the technical performance commitments between the provider and the client/customer and cover particular aspects of the service concerning issues such as the availability and quality of service, security measures, client obligations, and remedies for performance letdowns. Normally, a cloud provider's pricing policy and SLAs are non-negotiable, unless the customer anticipates heavy data usage and might not be in a position to negotiate for better contracts.

- **Cloud Provider**: A cloud provider is the entity in charge of rendering cloud services to interested clients. A cloud provider procures and controls the computing infrastructure necessary for providing the services. Cloud providers manage the cloud hardware and software components through network access.

  As shown in *Figure 3.4*, a **Cloud Provider's** activities can be described in five major areas:

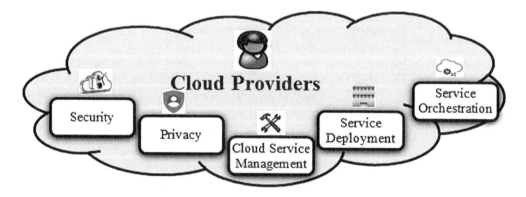

Figure 3.4: Cloud provider activities

- **Cloud Auditor**: A cloud auditor is the entity that can perform objective examinations of cloud services in conformity with IT standards. Cloud auditors assess the services delivered by a cloud provider regarding the adherence to security and privacy protocols, quality service performance, and so on.

- **Cloud Broker**: Cloud Brokers are companies that foster relationships between a cloud provider and the client. They facilitate the use, performance and delivery of cloud services. Usually, when clients are not sure which cloud providers or services to acquire, they hire brokers to make recommendations.

In general, a cloud broker provides the following three types of services:

1. **Service intermediation**: A cloud broker improves services by refining some specific characteristics and providing value-added features to cloud consumers. These features include the managing of client access to cloud services, identity management, performance reporting, enhanced security, and so on.

2. **Service aggregation**: A cloud broker merges numerous facilities into one or more new service by providing data integration and ensuring secure data migration between the cloud consumer and the cloud provider.

3. **Service arbitrage**: Service arbitrage is analogous to service aggregation, but with service arbitrage, the cloud broker has the flexibility to integrate services from multiple cloud providers.

- **Cloud Carrier**: A cloud carrier acts as a go-between that provides network access and transference of cloud services between cloud consumers and cloud providers through network and telecommunication devices such as personal computers, cellphones, tablets, and so on.

Load balancing approach

Load balancing is a virtualization process in which the workload is spread out across multiple nodes, cluster of computers, or other computing resources to accomplish peak resource utilization, maximize throughput, minimize job response time, and avoid system overload. Load balancing ensures that workloads are evenly distributed across nodes so that some are not left idle or underutilized in their capacity.

If computing resources are efficiently utilized, the system's overall performance in speed will automatically improve, resulting in better quality, reduction in energy consumption and carbon emission, and ultimately lower costs.

The objectives of the load balancing are to:

- Improve the overall system performance
- Construct a fault-tolerant system
- Increase computing resource availability
- Maintain system consistency and stability

- Increase user satisfaction

- Improve the computing resource utilization proportion

The cloud is an amalgamation of seemingly unrelated computer hardware and software resources. Therefore, in order to take full advantage of these resources in an ideal way so that resources are not overloaded, left idle or underutilized, efficient load balancing algorithms are required. These algorithms can be allocated differently depending on the cloud environment:

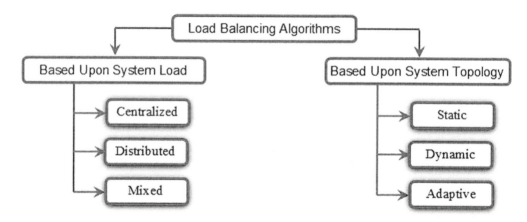

Figure 3.5: Load balancing classification

Load balancing classification

The **Load Balancing Algorithm** arrangement is displayed in *Figure 3.5* stemming from its two major classifications:

- **The system load**: How the workload is evenly distributed among computing resources.

- **The system topology**: How the data/information is utilized for effecting load balancing.

Mobile cloud computing (MCC)

The fundamental technology underlying cloud computing is centralizing computing facilities, and specific applications provided as a utility to end users. MCC is the incorporation of cloud computing into mobile device applications. As the wireless network technology rapidly grows with the proliferation of mobile gadgets, smartphones are considered the flagship of these electronic devices. Ubiquity and mobility are two of the foremost features in the next generation of IT, offering a range of personalized computing services over a seemingly infinite network, that is, the internet.

Much like its precursor, mobile cloud computing systems are virtualized, and resource capacity is distributed over a network of interconnected computers rather than in traditional local computers or servers. The only difference is that the cloud services are provided to mobile devices such as smartphones, tablets, laptops, and so on, (see *Figure 3.6*). Moreover, applications based on mobile cloud computing have been created and provided to users on Android, Apple, and Microsoft platforms encompassing mobile emails, navigation systems, social media apps, games, knowledge content, and productivity tools.

Figure 3.6: Mobile cloud computing

Mobile computing is comprised of three key concepts—hardware, software, and communication. Hardware can be grouped into several categories of portable devices and their mobile components. Software consists of mobile applications installed on these devices such as the mobile browser, anti-virus software, diagnostics, games, and so on. Communication includes the infrastructure of mobile networks, access point protocols, and data packet delivery.

Mobile computing features

The features of mobile computing are as follows:

- **Mobility**: Each node within the mobile computing network can establish connection with others. Even fixed nodes in wired networks can connect through a **Mobile Support Station (MSS)**.

- **Diversity of network conditions**: Usually, the networks utilized by mobile nodes can be a wired network with high bandwidth, or a **Wireless Wide Area Network (WWAN)** with low bandwidth.

- **Frequent disconnection and consistency**: Mobile nodes do not always maintain their connection. They disconnect from the wireless networks passively or actively based on bad network conditions, limited battery power, and so on.

- **Dis-symmetrical network communication**: Servers, access points, and other MSS permit strong send/receive signals. However, such ability in mobile nodes is comparatively weak. Consequently, the communication bandwidth and overhead between downlink and uplink are incongruent.

- **Low reliability**: Mobile data signals are more vulnerable to interference.

Challenges

Due to the wireless environment and numerous mobile nodes, mobile computing networks may face various complications than a conventional wired network. These constraints include signal disturbance from landforms, weather, and buildings, security, handoff delay, limited power, low computing ability, and so on.

Although mobile computing has some constraints, it also has some advantages. They include:

- **Improving data storage capacity and processing power**: MCC is developed to enable mobile users to store/access cloud data.

- **Improving reliability**: Storing data on multiple computers in the cloud improves reliability. On-demand provisioning of resources and scalability allows applications to be accessed without reserving computing resources or paying for additional services.

- **Multi-tenancy**: Service providers can pool resources to support an assortment of applications with a multiplicity of users.

- **Ease of integration**: Services from diverse service providers can be assimilated through the cloud.

The advantages are represented in *Figure 3.7* as follows:

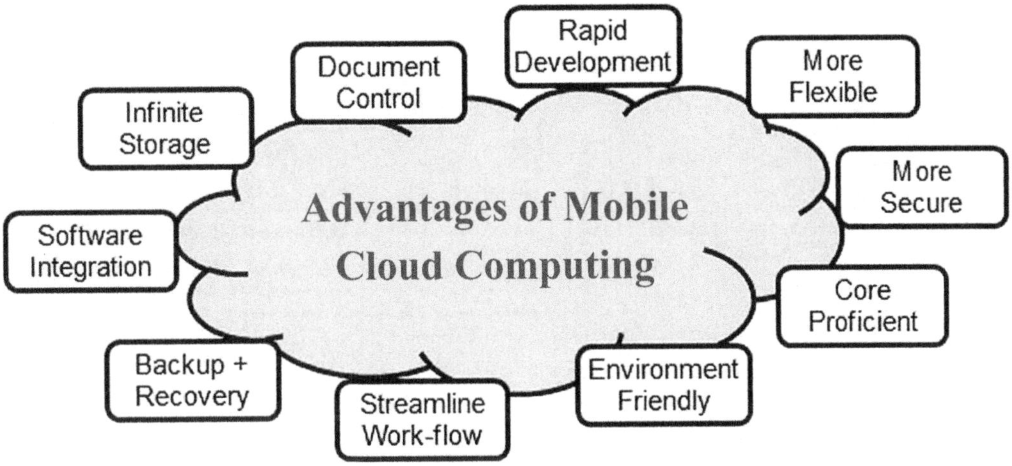

Rapid Development
Document Control
More Flexible
Infinite Storage
More Secure
Advantages of Mobile Cloud Computing
Software Integration
Core Proficient
Backup + Recovery
Environment Friendly
Streamline Work-flow

Figure 3.7: Mobile cloud computing advantages

Mobile cloud computing architecture

This architecture offers a model that links the benefits of both mobile technology and cloud computing. Different mobile devices connected to the networks via the **Base Transceiver Station** (**BTS**) or satellite allows mobile users to access servers that offer mobile services. Then, the users' requests are distributed to the cloud via an internet connection, and the cloud controllers provide the users the requested cloud services. The following is represented in *Figure 3.8* as follows:

Cloud Service
Cloud Platform
Web Service API
Cloud Infrastructure
Cloud Storage
Base Transceiver Station
Users
Mobile Device

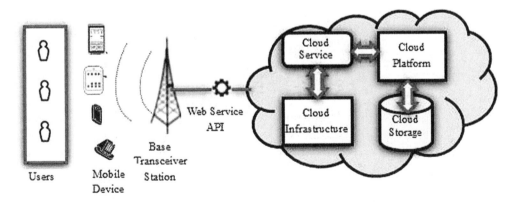

Figure 3.8: Mobile cloud computing architecture

As shown in *Figure 3.9*, mobile cloud computing can be separated into cloud computing and mobile computing. Mobile devices connect to a hotspot or base stations by 3G, WIFI, or GPRS:

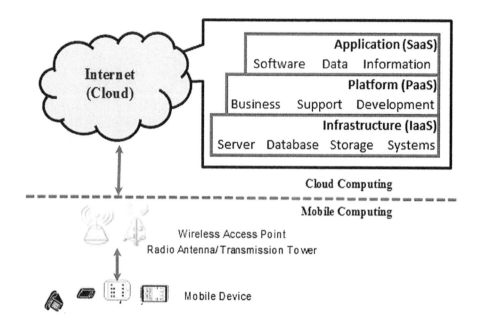

Figure 3.9. (Mobile + Cloud) Computing

Case study – Oracle cloud management

Oracle management cloud is a suite of management services that eradicate the human effort associated with conventional solutions for monitoring, managing and safeguarding applications and infrastructure:

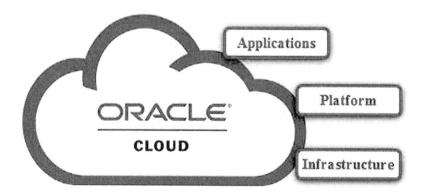

Figure 3.10: Oracle cloud

Conceptual view

The conceptual view of the Oracle cloud architecture, shown in *Figure 3.11*, brings together three key cloud perspectives—the **Cloud Provider**, **Cloud Consumer**, and **Cloud Broker**:

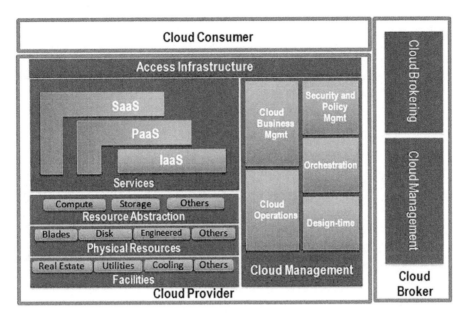

Figure 3.11: Cloud computing conceptual view

The role of the cloud provider is the most significant and most difficult of all. A cloud provider can spread the costs of computing resources across clients to achieve economies of scale. The expenses of facilities may include the cost of real estate, physical equipment, utilities, and so on.

The physical infrastructure may include server blades, network components, engineered systems, and storage disks. These resources must be pooled and provisioned through grid technologies in order to support the elasticity and scalability demands of the cloud infrastructure.

These physical resources must be logically segregated in order to support multi-tenancy. Conventional deployment models require interruption for scaling and maintenance, but the cloud infrastructure does not. The methodology is to create and deploy new instances on the fly to grow, shrink, or repair the existing deployments. The resource abstraction layer provides the abilities to logically virtualize the physical infrastructure.

Many computing resources are offered as services, but three general layers of services are listed as follows:

- **Infrastructure-as-a-Service (IaaS)**

- **Platform-as-a-Service (PaaS)**

- **Software-as-a-Service (SaaS)**

There is no particular dependency between these three layers. For example, PaaS and SaaS may exist autonomously without the overhead of an IaaS layer. In this case, a dedicated infrastructure for running the PaaS and SaaS may be utilized. Alternatively, they may use any of the underlying layers. For example, SaaS may leverage a PaaS service that is built on an IaaS service platform.

The access infrastructure controls access to the services and provides the appropriate interfaces to the consumers to access the services.

Logical view

Figure 3.12 shows the logical layers and crucial logical components of the cloud infrastructure.

The access layer splits into two important sets of functionality—interfaces and network components. The cloud needs a variety of user interfaces to permit access to the underlying services as well as its management capabilities. In addition to the end-user facing interfaces present in the access layer, there will be several operator-specific capabilities present:

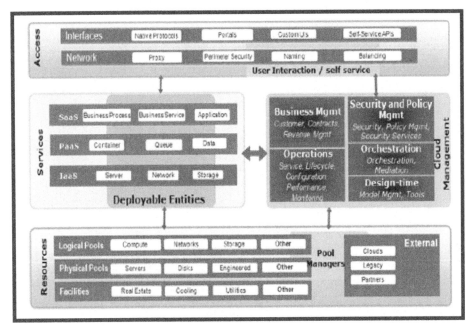

Figure 3.12: Cloud computing logical view

A shared cloud management layer provides the capabilities required for all kinds of services. A unified management framework provides a general view of the infrastructure and end-to-end visibility. The management layer provides support for both build-time and run-time activities.

Logical and physical pools of computing resources include virtualized or physical resources controlled by the pool manager. These resources may be simple in nature as the single virtualized server or complex such as clustered computers.

External resources may include third-party cloud services, legacy systems, and partner services.

The services layer illustrates the concept of deployable entities that are self-contained and logically grouped so as to automate and speed up the provisioning of services.

Oracle cloud mapping to the logical view

Currently, Oracle powers the cloud and is the foundation for many of the world's public and private clouds. It provides one of the most comprehensive and integrated cloud software and hardware products to facilitate public, private and hybrid clouds, thereby enabling clients to choose the right approach for their business models.

For private PaaS clouds, Oracle offers an extensive collection of industry applications that run on standards-based, shared services platforms. Engineered systems such as Oracle Exadata Database Machine, and Oracle Exalogic Elastic Cloud, provide high-performance platforms for building platform services. For private IaaS clouds, Oracle offers leading computing hardware resources. Customers can also choose to run new generation Oracle applications through third-party public clouds using on-premise or off-premise private models.

Figure 3.13 shows the mapping of Oracle products to the cloud logical view:

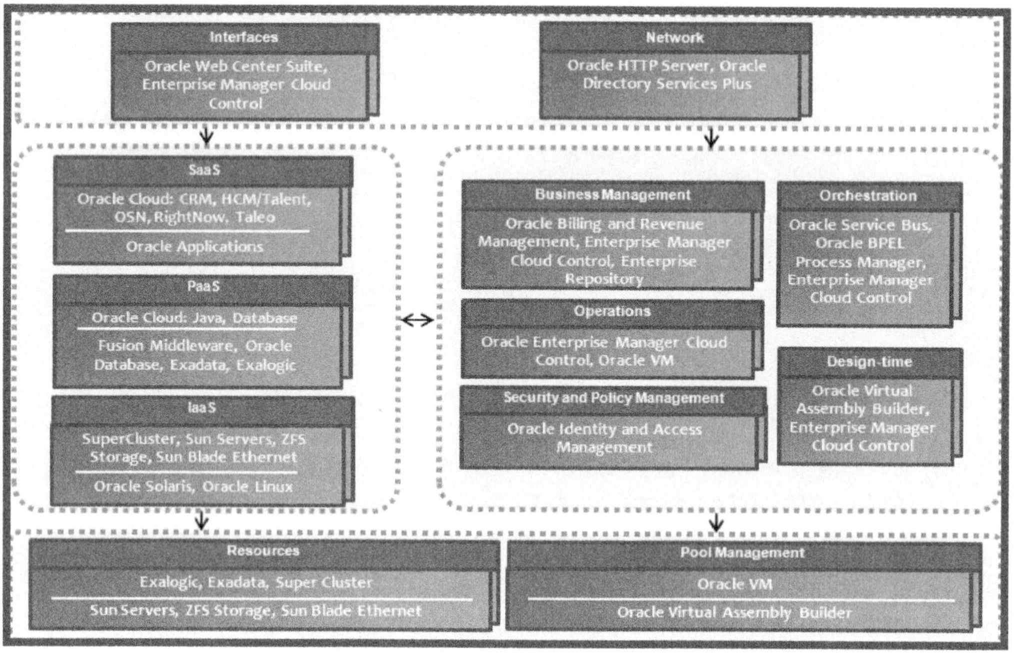

Figure 3.13: Oracle cloud mapping to the logical view

Summary

- Cloud computing is one of the boons of technology, making storage and access of data easier and more efficient. An acceptable cloud system design should take advantage of some of the essential characteristics of cloud computing.

- Seven cloud architecture design principles are adaptive and elastic, implement loose coupling, manage database services. Make sure you remove single points of failure, optimize for cost, caching and security.

- The objective of the CCLC is to negotiate the ever-changing nature of the cloud environment, expedite service speed, increase flexibility, and promptly satisfy the needs of individuals and organizations.

- There are four stages/phases within the cloud life cycle—architect, engage, operate and refresh.

- The NIST cloud computing reference architecture defines five major actors—Cloud Consumer, Cloud Provider, Cloud Carrier, Cloud Auditor and Cloud Broker.

- Load balancing is a virtualization process in which the workload is spread out across multiple nodes, cluster of computers, or other computing resources to accomplish peak resource utilization, maximize throughput, minimize job response time, and avoid system overload.

- The load balancing algorithm can be classified into two major categories— system load and system topology.

- MCC is the incorporation of cloud computing into mobile device applications.

- Mobile computing is comprised of three key concepts—hardware, software, and communication.

- Mobile cloud computing architecture offers a model that links the benefits of both mobile technology and cloud computing.

- Oracle management cloud is a suite of management services that eradicate the human effort associated with conventional solutions for monitoring, managing and safeguarding applications and infrastructure.

- Cloud consumer/client: An individual or organization that retains a professional relationship with and uses service from cloud service providers.

- Cloud Provider: An entity responsible for making cloud services available to clients.

- Cloud Carrier: The intermediary that provides connectivity and transference of cloud services between cloud providers and cloud consumers.

- Cloud Broker: An entity that manages the use, performance and delivery of cloud services, and negotiates relationships between cloud providers and cloud consumers.

- Cloud Auditor: A neutral party that can conduct objective, independent assessments of cloud services, information system operations, performance, and security of the cloud implementation.

Exercise

Tick the correct option

1. Which of these techniques is vital for creating cloud computing centers?

   a. Virtualization

   b. Transubstantiation

   c. Cannibalization

   d. Insubordination

2. Which of the following cloud concept is related to pooling and sharing of resources?

   a. Polymorphism

   b. Abstraction

   c. Virtualization

   d. None of the mentioned

3. Which of the architectural layer is used as front end in cloud computing?

   a. Cloud

   b. Soft

   c. Client

   d. All of the mentioned

4. Tick the correct statement

   a. Cloud architecture can couple software running on virtualized hardware in multiple locations to provide an on-demand service.

   b. Cloud computing relies on a set of protocols needed to manage inter process communications.

   c. Platforms are used to create more complex software.

   d. All of the above.

5. What are the two traits of a cloud computing architecture? (Choose two)

   a. Single tiered

   b. Not scalable

   c. On-demand access to resources

    d. Internet/intranet accessible server

    e. Client and server run in the same physical environment

6. What is a common design element often found in cloud architectures?

    a. Single tiered

    b. Terminal emulators

    c. Synchronous web services

    d. Asynchronous web services

7. What is a common trait of cloud architectures?

    a. It dictates monolithic application designs.

    b. It must use publicly accessible computing resources.

    c. A fixed set of computing resources is pre-allocated to each application.

    d. While in operation the application automatically scales up or down based on resource needs.

Answers:

1. a. Virtualization

2. c. Virtualization

3. c. Client

4. d. All of the above

5. c. On-demand access to resources, D Internet/intranet accessible server

6. d. Asynchronous web services

7. d. While in operation the application automatically scales up or down based on resource needs.

Fill in the blanks

1. Four phases within the Cloud Computing Life Cycle (CCLC) are Architect, Engage, _____ and Refresh.

2. The NIST cloud computing reference architecture defines five major actors: Cloud Consumer, _____, Cloud Carrier, Cloud Auditor and Cloud Broker.

3. The intermediary that provides connectivity and transference of cloud services between Cloud Providers and Cloud Consumers is called_____.

4. A commitment between a cloud service provider and a client is known as _____.

5. Mobile cloud computing (MCC) is the incorporation of cloud computing into _____ the applications.

Answers:

1. operate

2. Cloud Provider

3. cloud carrier

4. Service Level Agreements (SLAs)

5. mobile device

Descriptive questions

1. What are the cloud architecture design principles? Explain them in detail.

2. List the phases of the cloud computing life cycle (CCLC).

3. Draw a neat sketch of cloud computing life cycle (CCLC).

4. What are the major actors of the NIST cloud computing reference?

5. What do you mean by load balancing approach?

6. Explain the system load and system topology algorithms of the load balancing.

7. Explain the mobile cloud computing (MCC) concepts.

8. What are the benefits of the mobile cloud computing architecture?

9. Draw the neat sketch of mobile cloud computing architecture.

10. Give an overview of Oracle's cloud management model.

CHAPTER 4

Virtualization Technology

"Virtual Reality is better than the 'limited' real world."

~ Mark Zuckerberg, Co-founder, Facebook

Objectives

- To learn about the basic concepts of virtualization which is the back bone of the cloud architecture

- To learn about the classification of virtualization on the basis of techniques and usage

- To know the role of virtualization in building an efficient cloud architecture

Virtualization technologies are the founding concepts behind the successful adoption of the cloud computing paradigm. Virtualization not only upgrades the relation between hardware and software, but also helps utilize their full capabilities. On-demand and shared virtual resources provided through a service architecture is indispensably the primary reason behind omnipotent architecture of cloud. This chapter introduces the basic concepts of virtualization. We will introduce the theory of hypervisor and also discuss a few predominantly used hypervisors.

The following list of the topics covered in the chapter is as follows:

- Understanding virtualization
- Adopting virtualization
- Techniques of virtualization
- How virtualization works
- Types of virtualization
- Virtualization in cloud

Understanding virtualization

With the expansion of computing, Internet and the latest mobile technology, the word *virtual* has experienced a radical change in the last few years. Applications allow us to shop online on virtual stores; virtual guides create vacation tours on the basis of budget and time, and store downloaded movies and songs in our personalized virtual video library. Virtualization is a technology which enables us to create a logical/ virtual object of an actual physical object. It involves distribution of capabilities of a physical machine among many users or environments emulated using software. Any resource such as operating system, storage, computer network, and so on can be virtualized. The spectacle of the technology is that the applications running on top of a virtual machine think that they have their own dedicated operating system and libraries but actually the resources are shared among various applications.

Virtualization technology can be tracked down for its foundations in late 60s but due to some recent developments and technological paradigm shifts like cloud and grid computing, it is now widely accepted. Generations of operating system like batch processing systems also affect the adoption of virtualization and results in development of hypervisors which give multiple users simultaneous access to computers. The actual change happened in 90s when IT sector evolved. The growth of Internet and high-level networking protocols resulted in obsolescing/ incompatibility of most of the applications (Legacy apps) with the existing resource architecture. There was an immediate need for the enterprises to upgrade their IT infrastructure. Acceptance of virtualization in that scenario allowed the IT Industry to run multiple operating system types and versions over multiple partitions of their servers. This resulted in optimized use of resources and ultimately reduced various associated costs like license purchase, infrastructural set up, and cooling cost, and so on.

Adopting virtualization

Virtualization of an object can somehow increase the efficiency of the resource in terms of its utility; for example, the ability to run versions multiple systems and application software on a single computer system simultaneously and software-defined controls for **Storage Area Networks (SANs)** for availability and load balancing. Various organizations are taking advantage by adopting virtualization due to the following factors:

- Cost reduction in terms of limiting the hardware resources, and thereby reducing significant operational and maintenance cost which ultimately reduces the electricity, air conditioning, and cooling costs.

- Increased ubiquity, decreased downtime by increasing isolated instances of resources, and thereby increasing efficiency, uptime and business continuity.

- Easier backup and redeployment by simplified backup procedures not only on virtualized servers but also on virtual machines which can move from one server to another quickly.

- Protecting the environment by safe guarding planet Earth, saving energy and less e-waste generation.

We've discussed about the benefits and adoption of virtualization in business community in detail but there are still a few issues that need to be addressed:

- Proper VM management and proper capacity management is required or else VMs can become uncontrollable and create a virtual bottleneck that can cause disasters on the performance of virtualized system.

- Virtual backups are most prominent IT challenges for the business community and can be very tricky at times which threaten to compromise performance of whole system.

- Additional and unanticipated costs often result when specialized hardware and licenses are required to keep high availability and performance. Burden of VM management, requirement of storage area networks, increased headcount, and so on are a few examples of unanticipated cost.

- Depleted resources occur due to VM and network card saturation and can result in serious performance issues like reduced bandwidth, bogging of I/O intensive operations, and so on.

Techniques of virtualization

The focus of virtualization is to escalate the utilization of underlined hardware resource to its maximum capacity. This results in decreased hardware costs by running multiple virtualized instances in one physical machine and minimizing power consumption.

However, a running application demands exclusive access to the processor and this is the task of the operating system to implement abstraction and make sure that there is no interference between the applications.

This protection is usually implemented as a set of concentric rings as shown in *Figure 4.1*. Also known as privilege level or protection ring, they provide security and fault tolerance by restricting usage of resources to specific privilege levels:

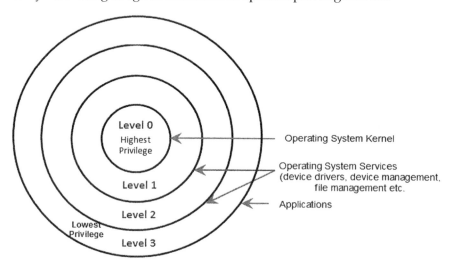

Figure 4.1: Privilege levels of an operating system

Level 0 runs the OS kernel and therefore is the most privileged one whereas in **Level 3**, user programs run and thus it is the least privileged level. Device drivers and other operating system services execute in **Level 1** and **Level 2**. The operating system switches between these levels as per the requirement and the type of the program in execution; for example, when the OS is booted, the CPU usually is in **Level 0**.

Techniques of virtualization can be categorized into the following three categories:

- **Full Virtualization**:

    In full virtualization, primary hardware is replicated and made available to the guest operating system. The guest OS is not aware that it is being virtualized and requires no further modification but the user level code (executed in **Ring 3**) is directly executed on the processor for high performance virtualization. Since, this technique translates kernel code to replace nonvirtualizable instructions with new sequences of instructions that have the intended effect on the virtual hardware, the VMM must be executed in **Ring 0**:

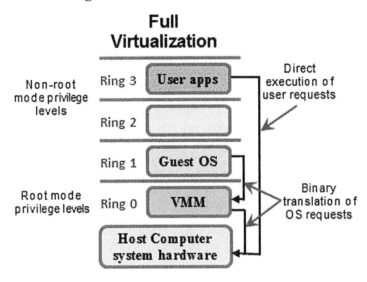

Figure 4.2: Full virtualization

Full Virtualized architecture provides virtualized memory, virtual devices and also virtual BIOS. To run the guest operating system without any modification, a particular technique is used which is known as Binary Translation. VMWare ESXi and Microsoft Virtual Server are examples of full virtualization.

- **Para Virtualization**:

  Para Virtualization is an extension of virtualization which recompiles the guest operating system (**Guest OS**) before installing it inside a virtual machine. It is sometimes also known as OS assisted Virtualization. Paravirtualization improves the communication between the guest operating system and the hypervisor by replacing the non-virtualizable instructions with hypercalls that communicate directly with the virtualization layer hypervisor. Due to this reason, the OS must run its privileged instructions in **Ring 0**. **Ring 3** is for less privileged user applications.

  As paravirtualization modifies operating systems before executing, its compatibility and portability is poor. The open source Xen project is an example of paravirtualization that virtualizes the processor and memory using a modified Linux kernel and virtualizes the I/O using custom guest OS device drivers.

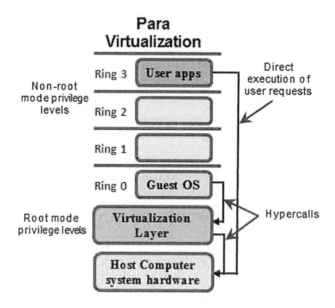

Figure 4.3: Para virtualization

- **Hardware assisted virtualization**:

  As the name suggests, it is a virtualization approach that provides full virtualization using hardware capabilities. The technology is invented by Intel and AMD to improve the performance of processor utilization and to overcome other challenges like memory address resolution and instruction translation.

  Hardware virtualization is actually embedding of VM into the hardware component of a server. The idea is to aggregate small physical servers into one large physical server and use the processor effectively. Since, the OS needs direct access to hardware and memory modules in this approach, it must execute its privileged instructions in **Ring 0**. While user level applications typically run in **Ring 3**. Privileged instructions are executed into a CPU execution mode that allows the VMM to run in a new root mode below **Ring 0**:

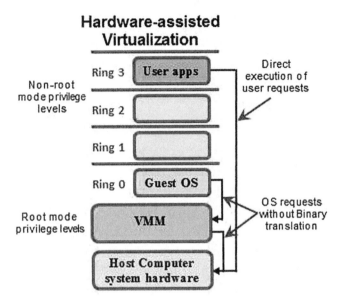

Figure 4.4: Hardware virtualization

Figure 4.2, *4.3*, and *4.4* diagrammatically represents full, para and hardware virtualization on the basis of privilege levels of operating system.

How virtualization works?

The goal of virtualization technology is to create an independent environment for different applications on a single hardware machine. This is done by creating virtual instances of operating systems, applications, etc. designed to run directly on hardware. The technique extends the capabilities of your machine and allows you to run multiple applications (especially operating systems) at the same time over a single hardware configuration. A **Virtual Machine** (**VM**) is application software which is responsible for creating these virtual instances. The end users have the same look and feel on a VM as they would have on the actual physical hardware. These VMs are portable, platform independent and sandboxed from the host system. A host can even run multiple VMs simultaneously on a single hardware configuration. But to create a VM we need substantial processing power, physical memory and network bandwidth.

Figure 4.5 shows the logical architecture of a VM in which multiple guest operating systems run simultaneously on a single host machine:

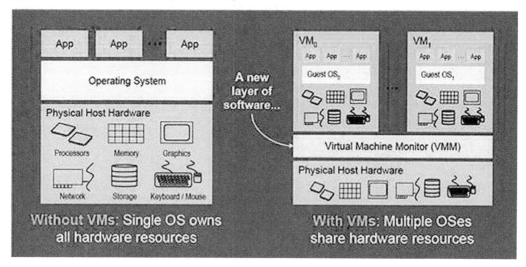

Figure 4.5: Virtual architecture

To properly manage the working of VMs and maintain the integrity of virtual environments, **Virtual Machine Monitor** (**VMM**) or Hypervisor is used. It can be a software agent, a firmware or a hardware device. The physical machine on which the VMM runs is called the host machine and each VM is termed as a guest machine. We would like to discuss some popular VMM/Hypervisors.

XEN

Xen is a Type 1, native or bare-metal hypervisor. It directly runs on the host's hardware and therefore multiple instances of operating systems (either similar or different) can be installed on a single hardware machine. We can consider it as a software virtualization layer that operates over the hardware and manages CPU, memory, and interrupts. It is just the next program that succeeds the execution of the Bootloader program. Xen is an open source project which is used in the AWS Cloud, server virtualization, **Infrastructure-as-a-Service** (**IaaS**), desktop virtualization, security virtualization, and so on.

Figure 4.6 shows the **Xen** hypervisor architecture. You can see that the hypervisor layer is directly installed on **Physical Hardware**. There is no need to pre-install any host operating system to run virtual machines:

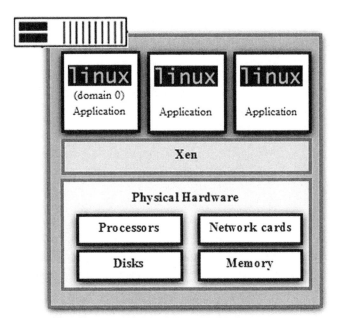

Figure 4.6: Xen hypervisor architecture

The features of Xen are as follows:

- **Memory ballooning**: It is an advance memory management technique in which the hypervisor can claim the unused memory from one guest machine and share it with the other guest machines within a host. It therefore allows the amount of RAM required by guest VMs to exceed the actual amount of physical RAM available on the host.

- **CPU pools**: It is a unique resource management feature of XEN version 4.2. This technique divides the physical cores on the machine into different pools, each with its own customizable CPU scheduler. At runtime, a VM is assigned to one of the pools, but it can further migrate between any other pools through the course of its execution. Since the scheduler is customizable, requests can be made for different scheduling parameters for different VMs.

- **Remus fault tolerance**: It is responsible for high availability in Xen. This is done by recurrently creating live backups of running VMs to the backup server which automatically activates in case of failure.

- **Virtual machine introspection**: It is a security technique in Xen which audits the sensitive memory areas of guest machines using specialized hardware support with minimal overhead.

Kernel-based virtual machine (KVM)

KVM is an open source virtualization layer fused into the mainline Linux kernel. It converts a Linux operated machine into a Type 1, bare-metal hypervisor that can run multiple but isolated virtual environments. Since KVM is integrated in Linux Kernel, modules like memory management, CPU scheduling, input/output (I/O), device management, and so on are already built-in. Each VM is treated as a standard Linux process which is scheduled by a typical Linux Scheduler with virtualized hardware.

Figure 4.7 shows a typical KVM architecture. The KVM module is embedded with the Linux operating system, over which virtual machines run simultaneously with standalone Linux applications.

QEMU is an open source emulator for hardware virtualization. It stands for Quick Emulator and acts as a virtual machine monitor when executed using the KVM kernel module in Linux:

KVM Architecture

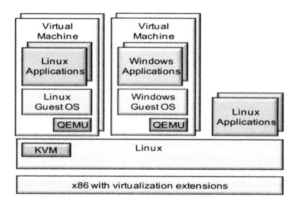

Figure 4.7: KVM architecture

The features of KVM are as follows:

- **Mandatory Access Control (MAC) security**: Mechanisms are implemented for the security of guest machines. VM Security and VM Isolation is provided using enhanced Linux features, namely, **security-enhanced Linux (SELinux)** and **secure virtualization (sVirt)**. (https://www.redhat. com/en/resources/secure-virtualization-with-svirt).

- **Hardware and storage support**: KVM is compatible with a wide variety of Linux certified hardware platforms, local disks and **network-attached storage** (**NAS**) (https://www.redhat.com/en/topics/data-storage/network-attached-storage).

- **Live VM migration**: It is a feature of KVM through which running VMs can be migrated between hosts without service interruption.

VMware

VMware (now a subsidiary of Dell Technologies) is a virtualization software provider based in Palo Alto, California. The company has gained its position among the key virtualization providers in the industry.

VMware classified their products in the following two categories:

- **Desktop applications**: Desktop applications are compatible with almost all operating systems and provide three major applications which are as follows:

- **VMware workstation**: It is a virtualized software package in which multiple instances of operating systems (either similar or different) are installed on a single hardware machine.

- **VMware fusion**: It is a specialized product for Apple's Mac OS X with additional compatibility.

- **VMware player**: VMware player is the free counterpart to VMware workstation.

- **Server applications**: VMware's software hypervisors is based on bare-metal hypervisor ESX/ESXi in x86 architecture and provides three major applications which are as follows:

- **VMware server**: It is a freeware server software used to introduce virtualization over pre-installed operating systems.

- **VMware ESX server**: It is an enterprise-level server that provides improved functionality with lesser system overhead over the VMware server.

- **VMware ESXi server**: It is the same as the ESX Server except that the service console is interchanged with the BusyBox installation. Alternatively, it also operates on a very low disk space as compared to ESX.

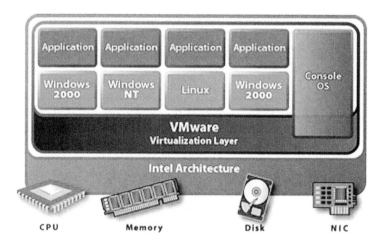

Figure 4.8: VMware architecture

Figure 4.8 shows the architecture of VMware. As mentioned, it requires a console OS to be installed over the hardware. It creates a software-based virtualization layer over which multiple instances of operating systems can be hosted simultaneously. All the instances of the operating systems can be similar or different but they share the single hardware configuration.

The features of VMware are as follows:

- **Fault tolerance**: This feature provides high availability and fault tolerance by creating a copy of a primary virtual machine. The copy becomes active immediately in case of VM failure.

- **Distributed Switch** (**VDS**): It is a virtual switch that can span multiple ESXi hosts. This feature enables a significant reduction of on-going network maintenance activities and increasing network capacity.

- **Host profiles**: This feature saves the record of valid and authenticated hosts. Later, the hosts are auto-deployed using this stored configuration.

VirtualBox

VirtualBox is a free, open-source, pre-built Binaries hypervisor (https://en.wikipedia.org/wiki/Hypervisor) developed by Oracle Corporation (https://en.wikipedia.org/wiki/Oracle_Corporation) for X86 and AMD64/Intel64-based machines. It is a 'type 2 hypervisor' that requires a pre-installed operating system over which it runs. Being a cross-platform virtualization software product, VirtualBox can run on **Windows, Linux, Mac OS, Solaris OS** and all operating systems that exist as shown in *Figure 4.9*. It is a simple but very powerful tool and provides support from desktop machines to cloud environment datacenters:

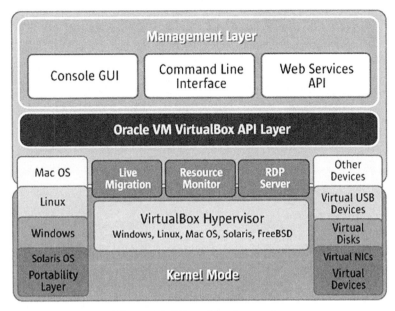

Figure 4.9: VirtualBox hypervisor

The features of VirtualBox are as follows:

- **No specialized hardware**: Unlike Intel VT-x or AMD-V, VirtualBox doesn't have any backward compatibility issues nor does it require any additional hardware resources to run.

- **Hardware support**: In spite of being a Type 2 hypervisor, VirtualBox provides a number of hardware compatibility features like Guest Multiprocessing, USB device support, full **Advance Configuration and Power Interface** (**ACPI**) support, Multiscreen Resolution, PXE Network Boot, and so on.

- **Remote Display Protocol (RDP)**: It is a unique feature of a VirtualBox and is generally used for security purposes. Through RDP, remote access to a running virtual machine is given to a remote desktop client. The clients' need to authenticate themselves using the RDP authentication mechanism before connecting to a server. Winlogon on Windows and **Pluggable Authentication Modules** (**PAM**) on Linux are examples of RDP authentication services.

Citrix

Formerly known as XenServer, Citrix is a virtualization solution provider for application, desktop and server virtualization built over the Xen virtual machine hypervisor. It is a well known for its integration with cloud technologies like **Software-as-a-Service** (**SaaS**) and **Desktop-as-a-Service** (**DaaS**). Citrix offers remote devices to access applications and resources through a centrally located server.

Being an open source and platform independent, the resources can be accessed from anywhere, any time and from any device.

Figure 4.10 shows a Citrix XenServer architecture. The architecture is similar to **Xen Hypervisor**, which is at the heart of Citrix systems:

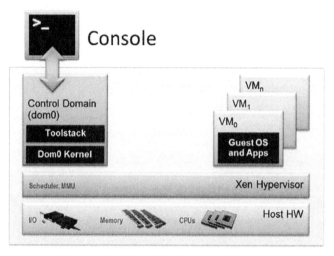

Figure 4.10: Citrix XenServer architecture

The major areas where Citrix is used are:

- **Desktop and application virtualization**: Citrix XenApp provides application virtualization whereas Citrix XenDesktop, Citrix VDI-in-a-Box are tools for desktop virtualization.

- **Desktop-as-a-Service (DaaS)**: Some useful DaaS and business applications include Worx mobile apps for secure email (https://en.wikipedia.org/wiki/Email), browser (https://en.wikipedia.org/wiki/Web_browser), and document sharing and Citrix workspace suite for mobile workspaces.

- **Software-as-a-Service (SaaS)**: Podio (https://en.wikipedia.org/wiki/Podio), a cloud-based collaboration service, and OpenVoice for audio conferencing are SaaS offering by Citrix.

The features of Citrix are as follows:

- **Any device, any time**: Users have simple and secure access to resources regardless of location or device.

- **Single instance management**: Application and server images are stored, maintained and updated once in the datacenter and delivered on-demand.

- **High end security features**: Like encrypted delivery, multi-factor authentication, built-in password management and activity auditing, etc. provide secure cloud infrastructure for delivering resources.
- **Scalability**: XenApp has proved its efficiency to support more than 70,000 users, scale beyond 1,000 servers in a single implementation and ensure 99.999 percent application availability. It also provides intelligent load and capacity management.

Types of Virtualization

We will discuss the different types of virtualization in the following section.

Data virtualization

Availability of right data at the right time is one of the main objectives of virtualization. Data virtualization is analogous to data agility in which an application is allowed to access data irrespective of its technical details, formatting style and physical location. As shown in *Figure 4.11*, data virtualization aligns disparate sources into a single virtual data layer that provides unified access and integration data service. Tools like Red Hat's JBoss, Denodo, and so on fetch data from multiple heterogeneous sources, integrate it and transform it as per the user's need. This ultimately results in faster access of data, less replication and high data agility:

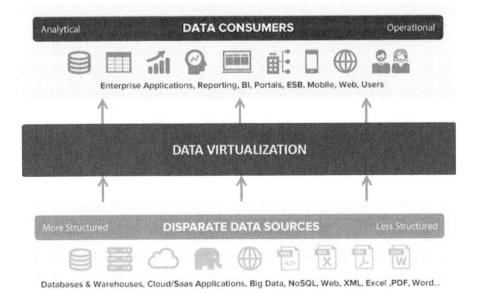

Figure 4.11: Data virtualization

The features of data virtualization are as follows:

- **Modern data integration**: The integration and transformation of data is similar to the traditional **Extract-Transform-Load Model** (**ETL Model**) but leverages modern features like delivery of real-time data, data federation and data agility.

- **Logical abstraction**: This feature introduces the capability of heterogeneous data from varied sources, middleware and applications to easily interact.

- **Data blending**: It is a feature of **Business Intelligence** (**BI**) in which heterogeneous data from multiple sources is combined and fed to the BI tool for analytical queries.

Desktop virtualization

Desktop virtualization is a technique in which the virtualization layer runs on top of a hypervisor and provides desktop provisioning. It is also alternatively called **virtual desktop infrastructure** (**VDI**). We can relate this type of virtualization with the traditional client-server model where a client requests for service from a centralized and remotely located server. In desktop virtualization, VDI is responsible for hosting of the desktop environment in a VM that runs on a centralized or remote server. This is the reason why we also sometimes refer to desktop virtualization as client virtualization:

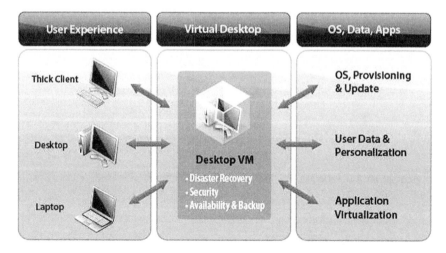

Figure 4.12: Desktop virtualization

Figure 4.12 shows a **Virtual Desktop**, which is a two-facet centralized server. **User Experience (Thick Client, Desktop, Laptop)** on one side and applications (**OS, Provisioning & Update, User Data & Personalization, Application Virtualization**) on the other side. The remote server is responsible for disaster recovery, security, and availability and backup of data.

The features of desktop virtualization are as follows:

- **User's computer dies; the user's desktop does not die**: If a hardware damage occurs, the failed hardware can be quickly replaced and simply reconnected to the virtual desktop.

- **No installations or updates**: Since the operating system and other application software are centrally managed, there is no overhead of installation and regular version updates.

- **Inter device compatibility**: The virtual desktop can be accessed by either a desktop machine or by a tablet or mobile device. Also, multiple users can share a common virtual desktop environment, that is, the desktop or application needs to be installed only once and it will be available to multiple users.

CPU virtualization

CPU virtualization allows a single processor to act as multiple individual CPUs, that is, two separate systems running into a single machine. The objective of CPU virtualization is to enable the users to run different operating systems simultaneously. As represented in *Figure 4.13*, a hypervisor layer is installed over the physical hardware. Multiple virtual machine monitors are installed over the hypervisor to allow the execution of multiple instances of operating systems.

Currently, all prominent CPUs, including Intel (**Intel Virtualization Technology** or **Intel VT**) and AMD (AMD-V) supports CPU virtualization. Since virtualization sometimes requires kernel level and control sensitive instructions which tend to change memory mapping and resource configuration, CPU virtualization is generally disabled by default in BIOS and needs to be enabled manually once using the CPU configuration settings:

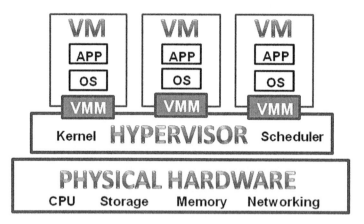

Figure 4.13: CPU virtualization

The features of CPU virtualization are as follows:

- **Virtual processor IDs (VPID)**: These are the unique IDs given to each VM that is currently in the running state. This prevents the CPU from flushing out the data structures from the **transition look-aside buffers** (**TLBs**) at the time of context switching of VMs. VPIDs therefore help in achieving flexibility and quality of service in terms of live VM migration.

- **Descriptor table exiting**: This feature prevents the relocation of key system data structures and thereby protects the guest OS from internal vulnerabilities.

- **Pause-loop exiting**: This feature enables to detect spin locks in the guest software and avoid lock-holder preemption which reduces overhead and improves performance.

- **Extended page table (EPT)**: This technique gives the capability to the guest OS to handle page faults and modify its page tables.

Network virtualization

In network virtualization, hardware and software network resources and their functionalities are encapsulated into a software-based administrative entity. The ultimate result is a virtual network which is highly efficient in terms of utilization with less time overhead.

Figure 4.14 illustrates that network virtualization creates the virtualized combination of available resources by splitting up the bandwidth into channels so that each device or user can have shared access to all the resources on the network. The advantages of multiple instances of virtual networks are as follows:

- Each has a separate control and data plane.

- They coexist together over a single physical network.

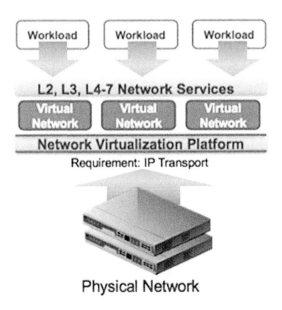

Figure 4.14: Network virtualization

Network virtualization can be classified into the following two classes as follows:

- **External network virtualization**: In this type of virtualization, a single virtual network is created by either a combination or division of multiple local area networks, administered by the software system. VLAN and network switch are the components of this type of virtualization.

- **Internal network virtualization**: This type of virtualization uses a single system to act as a hypervisor (Xen/KVM) to control **virtualized network interface cards** (**VNICs**). Each host can have one or more NICs and each NIC can be a base for multiple VNICs.

The features of network virtualization are as follows:

- **Partitioning**: This feature allows you to create logical network partitions with a programmable control panel so that users can define protocols, network topologies, and functions as per their requirements.

- **Isolation**: This feature is kept among various logical network partitions to avoid any kind of interference and reduce the performance.

- **Abstraction**: This feature hides the underlying complexities and characteristics of network elements from applications and users.

Storage virtualization

Virtualization of storage is nothing but assembling of physical storage from heterogeneous storage devices to form a large pool of memory which is managed centrally as shown in *Figure 4.15*. By allowing the storage to participate in **storage area networks** (**SANs**), we are actually increasing the efficiency, flexibility and load balancing of storage devices. You should not get confused with the technology of **network attached storage** (**NAS**) as SAN is a network of storage devices while NAS is either a single device or a server:

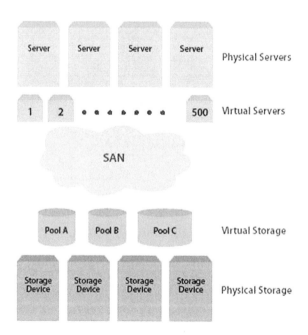

Figure 4.15: Storage virtualization

In 2001, **Storage Network Industry Association** (**SNIA**) has made an effort to describe the important characteristics of storage virtualization. The group first defined storage virtualization as follows:

- The act of abstracting, hiding, or isolating the internal functions of a storage system or service from applications, host computers, or general network resources for the purpose of enabling application and network-independent management of storage or data.

- The application of virtualization to storage services (https://www.sdxcentral.com/directory/organizations/) or devices for the purpose of aggregating functions or devices, hiding complexity, or adding new capabilities to lower level storage resources.

The features of storage virtualization are as follows:

- **Non-disruptive data migration**: This feature allows data to migrate without disturbing the concurrent I/O access.

- **Improved utilization**: Utilization is increased by pooling and migration.

- **Thin provisioning**: Technology dynamically allocates storage capacity to a volume as per the usage requirement, that is, it allows you to tell the application that it has sufficient storage without actually assigning storage to it.

Server virtualization

In the traditional client-server architecture, the server machine runs only one instance of resources. These resources can be processors, operating systems, application software, memory, and so on. The idea of server virtualization is to divide a physical server machine into a number of logically isolated virtual machines and thereby create a number of instances of resources as shown in *Figure 4.16*.

Adopting this approach serves the advantage that rather than deploying number of servers that may not be fully utilized, numerous virtual machines can run on the same physical platform. For example, in a company payroll system, rather than using separate servers for employee database, email server and document maintenance, all these applications can be virtualized onto a single server machine.

A server can be virtualized by any of the following techniques:

- Hypervisor or a VMM is a software layer that exists between the hardware machine and the operating system is used to handle kernel level instructions, queuing and processing client's requests, and so on.

- Paravirtualization is a hypervisor-based virtualization in which the performance of a virtual machine is enhanced by pre-compilation of the guest OS before installing it on the virtual machine. The idea behind paravirtualization is to prepare the machine for virtualization and abstract the underlying hardware resources from the software that uses those resources. Xen and **User Mode Linux** (**UML**) are examples of server virtualization through paravirtualization.

- Hardware virtualization is similar to paravirtualization except that some hardware assistance is provided. AMD—V Pacifica and Intel VT Vanderpool are examples of hardware supported virtualization.

- OS virtualization provides multiple but logically isolated virtual machines that run on the operating system kernel. The technique is also called **shared kernel approach** because all the virtual machines share the same kernel of the host operating system. FreeVPS, Linux Vserver are examples of OS level virtualization:

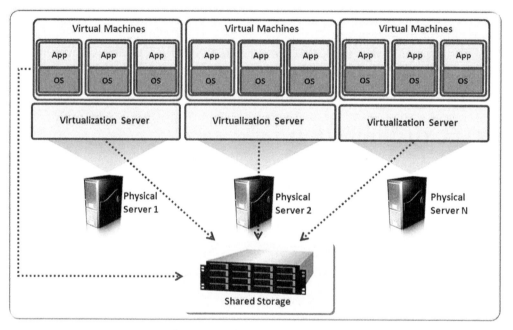

Figure 4.16: Server virtualization

The features of storage virtualization are as follows:

- **Partitioning**: This feature allows multiple virtual servers to run on one physical server at the same time.

- **Isolation**: The virtual servers running on the physical server are completely isolated and don't affect the execution of each other.

- **Encapsulation**: All the information on virtual servers, including boot disks is saved in the file format.

- **Hardware independence**: A virtual server runs as it is after migration to different hardware platforms.

- **Improved business continuity**: Live migration of virtual servers to another physical server results in maintenance of servers without shutting down and hence improves availability and business continuity.

Virtualization in Cloud

The ultimate aim of cloud technology is to be ubiquitous, pervasive, and agile but with an unquenchable thirst for collaboration and sharing of resources. Virtualization plays a very vital role in achieving these objectives and empowering cloud. To convert your ideas into a streamline business, the enterprise needs business applications which are very expensive and come with a complicated software stack. Whenever the new version releases, the updating can cause incompatibility among the stack and break the whole system down. To overcome this problem, virtualization is used. Virtualization not only provides sharing of data but also sharing of infrastructure. Through virtualization, the resources become massively scalable and can be integrated with IT-related capabilities.

The capabilities of virtualization and sharing of infrastructure in the Cloud computing paradigm is fulfilled by three major distribution models, namely, SAAS, PAAS and IAAS.

Google Apps and Cisco WebEx for SAAS, Microsoft Azure, and Google App Engine for PAAS, Rackspace and Amazon AWS for IAAS are some third-party providers that host applications, platform and infrastructure over cloud.

Summary

- Virtualization is a technology which enables us to create a logical/virtual object of an actual physical object.

- Xen and KVM are Type 1, bare-metal hypervisors.

- VMware and VirtualBox are virtual machine monitors and Type 2 hypervisors which require a pre-installed host operating system.

- Citrix is infrastructure virtualization software based on the Xen hypervisor.

- Desktop virtualization, data virtualization, CPU virtualization, storage virtualization, network virtualization and server virtualization are the different types of virtualization.

- The cloud computing paradigm is based on the concepts of virtualization, multi-tenancy, and shared infrastructure which is fulfilled by three major distribution models, namely, SaaS, PaaS and IaaS.

Exercise

Tick the correct option

1. Which of the following is a type of virtualization?

    a. Storage

    b. Desktop

    c. CPU

    d. All of the above

2. Type __ VM is a full virtualization.

    a. 1

    b. 2

    c. 3

    d. All of the above

3. What is the solution for full virtualization?

    a. Processor

    b. Application

    c. Desktop

    d. Hardware

4. Which of the following is an example of a server operating system?

    a. VMware

    b. Virtual Disk

    c. VMware ESXi

    d. VirtualBox

5. Which standard describes the interface of web services?

    a. SOAP

    b. ESB

    c. BPEL

    d. XML

Answers:

1. d. All of the above
2. a. 1
3. d. Hardware
4. c. VMware ESXi
5. d. XML

Fill in the blanks

1. _____control memory and processor resources while virtual machines control their own network and storage resources.

2. The virtual machine can be reverted to the original state through the use of_____.

3. A _____hypervisor runs on top of an operating system to provide resources to the virtual machines.

4. The first commercial x86 hypervisor was released by_____.

5. Desktop virtualization, _____, CPU virtualization, storage virtualization, network virtualization and server virtualization are the different types of virtualization.

Answers:

1. Hypervisor
2. Snapshots
3. Type 2
4. VMware
5. Data virtualization

Descriptive questions

1. Define virtualization. What are its types?
2. Explain paravirtualization. How it is different from full virtualization?
3. What are the limitations of virtualization?
4. Why is Xen a Type 1 hypervisor? Elaborate the major components of Xen with a suitable diagram. How Xen is different from KVM?
5. What are layers of virtualization?

6. What is server virtualization? What are its main features? List some advantages and disadvantages of server virtualization.

7. How the concept of virtualization can be integrated with cloud?

CHAPTER 5

Service oriented Architecture

"Services are inextricably tied to messaging in that the only way into and out of a service are through messages."

~ Microsoft Developer Network

Objectives

- To lay the foundation of service orientation in correlation to cloud
- To discuss the various Service-oriented Architecture (SOA) techniques and components
- To know the reasons behind the need of SOA
- To integrate business process management with the cloud architecture

The following list of the topics covered in the chapter is as follows:

- SOA foundation
- Web services and SOA
- SOA communication, components and infrastructure
- Need of SOA
- Business Process Management (BPM)

SOA foundation

A **service-oriented architecture (SOA)** is a design methodology used to develop software based on interoperable services. Actually, these services are the IT capabilities that are provided to components using a communication network. SOA extents both enterprise and application architecture domains and its real power can be realized when it is applied across heterogeneous environments.

We can simply state that SOA promotes service-orientation through the use of web services. Organizations compliant with SOA are known as the **service-oriented enterprises (SOE)**, where all business processes are composed of and exist as a service.

Due to the following characteristics, SOA stands out to be the choice of developers nowadays and it is a strong pillar for the cloud computing paradigm:

- **Refurbished and reusable**: Services can be reused multiple times for multiple processes.

- **Loosely coupled**: Services are designed to be independent with minimum dependency on implementation.

- **Platform independent**: The base of services in the XML format.

- **Based on standards**: The service design is based on WSDL and SOAP standards.

Web Services and SOA

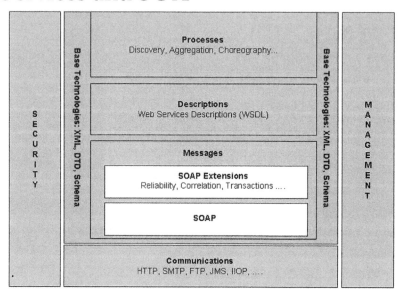

Figure 5.1: Web service administration architecture

Web services are the technical foundations of SOA that include the concept of interoperability. They are independent software accessed over a network through standard protocols. Web services have a prescribed interface on which they are written. There are constraints applied and policies as per the specified service description. Services are described in terms of the messages accepted and generated. *Figure 5.1* represents the basic web service administration architecture.

On the basis of the above service description, SOA as defined by IBM is as follows:

"SOA is a business-centric IT architectural approach that supports integrating your business as linked, repeatable business tasks, or services."

SOA communication

Figure 5.2 shows SOA from a viewpoint of service providers, consumers and the service registry:

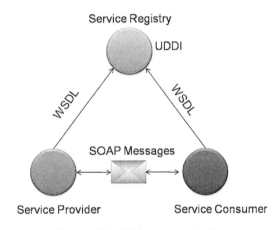

Figure 5.2: SOA communication

- **Service Provider**: It provides all kinds of service-related operations like service registration, service discovery, exception handling, platform independence, interoperability, and so on.

- **Service Consumer**: It is a human or a system that uses service(s) supported by SOA and which has a valid entry in the service registry.

- **Service Registry**: It is the connection between service providers and service customers. Both the service provider and service consumer needs to register themselves to service registry before starting communication. It is just like an information catalog that allows service providers to discover services. The registry is constantly updated with services and their information.

SOA components

There are three core components in a SOA communication model:

1. **Extensible Markup Language (XML)**: Due to open standards and platform-independence, SOA needs a common platform to form a mutual base of understanding. XML is at the core of this infrastructure because:

   - XML is device independent and structured way to represent the content

   - XML is compatible with different data formats in different applications across multiple platforms.

   - XML is text-based which makes it natural, easily representable and flexible.

   - XML is a generic language that underlies a web service. XML namespaces and XML schemas are widely used while creating a web service.

2. **Simple Object Access Protocol (SOAP)**: It is a universally accepted XML based messaging protocol through which a client calls a service remotely. SOAP relies on **Hypertext Transfer Protocol (HTTP)** and **Simple Mail Transfer Protocol (SMTP)** for message negotiation and transmission. A SOAP message consists of three parts:

   - **An envelope**: Contains message content and the method to process it. It is actually a packaging method which indicate start and end of the message.

   - **A Header**: It is an optional part of the SOAP message and contains additional information such as authentication credentials, digital signature, and so on.

   - **Body**: It contains the actual application-defined XML data which needs to be exchanged between the web services.

Other major characteristics of SOAP message is Platform independence, Internet usability, natural language representation and well structured. Figure 5.3 shows a simple SOAP message with elaborated elements.

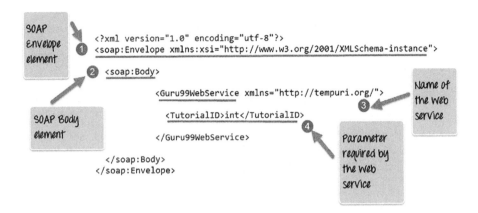

Figure 5.3: SOAP message

3. **Web Services Description Language (WSDL)**: Aka service endpoint, is an XML-based descriptive language. WSDL has three parts:

- **Types**: Written in XML including definitions of both data types and message types.

- **Operations**: Describe actions for the messages supported by a Web service. There are four types of operations:

One-way: Messages sent without a reply required

Request/response: The sender sends a message and the received sends a reply.

Solicit response: A request for a response. (The specific definition for this action is pending.)

Notification: Messages sent to multiple receivers. (The specific definition for this action is pending.)

- **Bindings**: A port is defined by associating a network address with a port type. A collection of ports defines a service. These Services are further bind to a port using SOAP, CORBA **Internet Inter-ORB Protocol (IIOP)**, **Java Message Service (JMS)** and other protocol architectures.

SOA Infrastructure

Applications need the SOA infrastructure and SOA platform for successful execution and organization. The SOA infrastructure comprises three levels as illustrated in *Figure 5.4*:

- **Core**: This level performs core functions which include constructing, seeking and binding of web services. It constitutes the most important components like SOAP, WSDL, and UDDI.

- **Platform**: This level is where the World Wide Web services are developed using some programming languages like J2EE and .NET.

- **QoS**: This level tests if the evolved web service supports value of service.

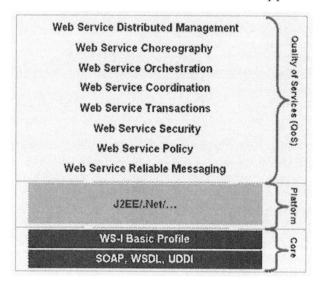

Figure 5.4: SOA infrastructure

Need of SOA

- **Reduced cost**:
- Reengineering and reusability adds value to core investments
- Faster integration, agile and long-term value of interoperability
- **Scalability**:
- Scalable and evolvable systems
- Rapid scale up and scale down as per organizational needs

- **Platform independence and compatibility with heterogeneous environment**:
- Semantic message-oriented interactions
- **Business agility**:
- Build to change
- Build and deployed incrementally
- Loosely coupled

Business Process Management (BPM)

BPM is a dimension of operations management that emphasizes on refining and optimizing business processes through automation. BPM itself is not a technology but enables technologies to operate in such a way that the current processes get aligned to a desired and optimized state. Reengineering and outsourcing are examples of BPM. *Figure 5.5* represents the complete life cycle of a BPM:

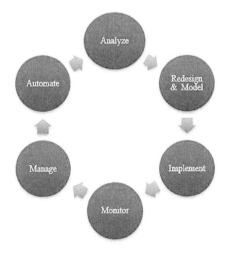

Figure 5.5: Life cycle of BPM

Cloud computing implements BPM using the SaaS model. The business logic is deployed at the application server and data resides over the cloud. BPM can also be employed as a PaaS model after deployment of its middleware capabilities for business processes. In fact, BPM in the cloud can be seen as a combination of BPM PaaS and **BPaaS (Business Process as a Service)** as shown in *Figure 5.6*.

Business Process Management Platform as a Service – BPM PaaS

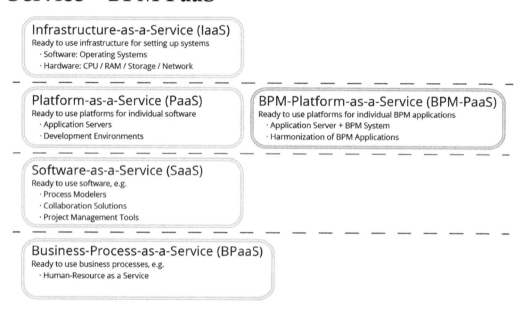

Figure 5.6: BMP stack in cloud computing

BPM PaaS is a complete pre-integrated BPM platform hosted in the cloud and delivered as a service for the development and execution of general-purpose business process application. BPM suites combine the disciplines for managing processes, for example, business rules, SLAs, data, and resources with the enabling technology to facilitate their design and delivery. For example, process modeling, process execution engine, connectivity, and web forms.

Business Process as a Service–BPaaS

BPaaS represents the process outsourcing in which business processes like human resources, payroll, expense management, and so on are provided using the web. Automatic scalability, high standards, on-demand processes are some features of BPaaS. These characteristics can reduce costs and improve the organization's business agility.

Benefits of BPM with cloud:

- It is cost efficient because BPM is delivered through SaaS in the cloud. There is no need to build a large and complicated IT infrastructure.

- It is time efficient because lack of substantial internal infrastructure results in rapid roll out business process management in the organization.

- It is agile in nature and enables the earlier adoption of process management.

- It automates manual flows, load balancing, exception handling and failovers.

Challenges of BPM with cloud:

- High vulnerability to external intruders; therefore, firewalls are required but with expected quality of service.

- Service level agreements are a must to achieve dependable performance.

- Application integration: Many organizations are unwilling to use BPM with cloud until they completely migrate to their data over cloud.

Summary

- A Service-oriented Architecture (SOA) is a design methodology used to develop software based on interoperable services.

- SOA promotes service-orientation through the use of web services.

- Web services are the technical foundations of SOA.

- Web services are self-contained software capabilities that can be accessed via network protocols.

- Web services are independent software that can be accessed over a network through standard protocols.

- Service Provider, Service Consumer and Service Registry are the core components of SOA communication.

- XML, SOAP and WSDL are the building blocks of a SOA message.

- BPM is refining and optimizing of business processes through automation.

- Cloud computing implements BPM using the SaaS model. It can be seen as a combination of BPM PaaS and BPaaS.

Exercise

Tick the correct option

1. What are the core components of a web service?
   a. XML and XML Schema
   b. SOAP and HTTP
   c. WSDL and XML
   d. ESB and WS-Policy

2. What is true in case of SOA and BPM?
   a. Tasks can be rearranged with user interference
   b. Business rules can be dynamically changed
   c. New services can be created at runtime
   d. None of the above

3. How services communicate with each other in SOA?
   a. Using XML messages
   b. Using common data and communication model
   c. Using the ESB (Enterprise Service Bus) layer
   d. Integration of business logic between services

4. Which is not the part of the BPM stack in cloud computing?
   a. BPaaS
   b. BM-PaaS
   c. IaaS
   d. SaaS

5. Which is the Need of SOA?
   a. Adaptivity
   b. Scalability
   c. Robustness
   d. None of these

Answers:

1. c. WSDL and XML

2. a. Tasks can be rearranged with user interference

3. a. Using XML messages

4. b. BM-PaaS

5. b. Scalability

Fill in the blanks

1. In SOA, _____are developed, maintained and owned by multiple stakeholders.

2. _____is a methodical set to advance a company's enterprise processes.

3. SOA infrastructure comprises three levels: Core, Platform and_____.

4. BPaaS stands for _____.

5. _____are the technical foundations of SOA.

6. A _____is a design methodology used to develop software based on interoperable services.

Answers:

1. Services

2. BPM

3. QoS

4. Business Process as a Service

5. Web services

6. Service-oriented architecture (SOA)

Descriptive questions

1. Define SOA.

2. State the core components of SOA used in communication model.

3. What is BPM? Illustrate the lifecycle of BPM.

4. What are web services? How are they important in SOA?

5. With a suitable diagram, represent the elements of a SOA message.

6. How BPM is integrated with cloud? List the benefits and challenges of this integration.

7. Explain the difference between BPaaS and BPM-PaaS.

CHAPTER 6

Cloud Security and Privacy

"Cloud computing is often far more secure than traditional computing."

~ Vivek Kundra, former federal CIO of the United States

Objectives

- To discuss succinctly security challenges threatening the survival of the cloud ecosystem
- To describe the characteristics of a cloud CIA security model
- To identify and discuss cloud security threats and mitigation approaches
- To discuss cloud computing security architecture as well as user layer, service provider, virtualization, and data center-related security issues
- To identify and discuss privacy issues associated with the cloud and potential mitigation strategies
- To discuss how the performance of cloud services can be monitored and managed
- To identify and discuss legal-related issues with the use of cloud computing and services
- To discuss issues concerning risk management in the cloud, the requirements, framework and processes for cloud consumers

- To discuss the requirements, architecture, mechanisms and challenges associated with business continuity and disaster recovery in a typical cloud ecosystem

- To discuss the components, types and significance of practices regarding cloud service level agreements

- To discuss the various types of cloud vendors

- To identify and discuss some basic techniques to provisioning **Quality of Service (QoS)** in cloud as well as the performance, economic, security, and quality assurance dimensions of quality of cloud services

- To succinctly discuss the basic types and stepwise approaches to migrating a typical local server to the cloud

- To identify and discuss the techniques and evaluation approaches to trust management in a cloud ecosystem.

This chapter discusses the key fundamental concepts of cloud security and privacy. It identifies basic cloud threats and discusses the corresponding mitigation approaches and emphasizes on the CIA security model. It provides an explicit narrative of a prototype cloud computing security architecture with its composite layered structure. Furthermore, it presents and discusses some performance monitoring and management solutions for cloud systems. Legal issues related to cloud computing, risk management, business continuity and disaster recovery, threats in the cloud, cloud vendors, step by step procedures and requirements to successfully migrate a local server to the cloud are also extensively discussed in this chapter. Issues of quality of cloud services, cloud service level agreements and trust management in the cloud are also discussed and form the concluding part of this chapter.

The topics that are covered in this chapter are listed as follows:

- Cloud security – Issues and challenges

- The cloud CIA security model

- The cloud computing security architecture

- Cloud computing model security threats

- Privacy issues in the cloud and mitigation strategies

- Performance monitoring and management of cloud services

- Legal issues in cloud computing

- Risk management in cloud computing

- Business continuity and disaster recovery

- Threats in cloud

- Cloud service level agreements (SLA) practices

- Cloud vendors

- Issues of quality of cloud services

- Migration of local server into cloud

- Trust management in cloud

Cloud security

Let us discuss cloud security issues and challenges.

Security issues and challenges threaten the survival of the cloud ecosystem. These include but are not limited to data breaches, data loss, network security, data locality, data access, system vulnerabilities, account hijacking, malicious insider, and advanced persistent threats among others. These challenges are briefly discussed as follows:

- **Data breaches**: Data breach occurs when an unauthorized third-party maliciously gains access to data at rest in a cloud infrastructure or data in transit for compromising its integrity. The attractive targets are the cloud data and file servers that hold massive volume of data. How much severe the attack is depends on the confidentiality nature of the data being attacked. However, the impact of the attack depends on the type of the compromised data. This could range from financial data (for example, credit card information), personal data, trade secrets, health information and government critical data to intellectual properties of a person or an organization.

- **Network security**: Network security problems often arise when an elastic cloud infrastructure is incorrectly configured or experience a malicious-denial-of-service attack or unauthorized access leading to data leakage. To mitigate against leakage of sensitive information, appropriate measures must be put in place to secure the data, the transmission medium and the network. Hence, a strong network traffic encryption can be implemented to secure the network against malicious intrusions and extrusions.

A brief list of some cloud security threats and mitigation approaches is presented in the following table:

Cloud security threats	Potential defense mechanisms
Spoofing identity	<ul><li>Authentication</li><li>Encrypt sensitive data</li><li>Do not store sensitive data like password</li></ul>
Data tampering	<ul><li>Authorization</li><li>Hashes</li><li>Message authentication codes</li><li>Tamper-resistant protocols</li><li>Digital signatures</li></ul>
Repudiation	<ul><li>Digital signatures</li><li>Time stamps</li><li>Audit trails</li></ul>
Information disclosure	<ul><li>Authorization</li><li>Encryption</li><li>Protect sensitive data</li><li>Privacy-enhanced protocols</li><li>Do not store sensitive data</li></ul>
Denial of Service (DoS)	Authentication Authorization Throttling Filtering **Quality of Service (QoS)**
Elevation of privilege	Run with least privilege

Table 6.1

- **Data locality**: Cloud service consumers are not aware of where their data is stored due to virtualization. However, legal implications of using, sharing and storing of data exist and vary from one country to another based on relevant laws and policies regarding intellectual property.

- **Data access**: Data accessibility is the ability of cloud service customers to be able to gain authorized access to their subscribed services anywhere and at any time. However, strong identity management and access control schemes must be implemented for user authentication before access to the massive cloud resources is granted.

- **System vulnerabilities**: Vulnerabilities of the system are exploitable program bugs in the operating system that can be exploited by attackers to gain full access to the host computer. Vulnerable systems are prone to a denial-of-service attack, advanced persistent threat and malicious user's attack. When participating in a network, the attacker leverages on these vulnerabilities to distribute different kinds of malware. The zombies are made to send fake traffic which in turn floods the network, thereby making real data, applications or other resources in cloud unavailable to legitimate users. To mitigate this, appropriate security fixes and overhauls should be periodically conducted.

- **Account hijacking**: This involves the stealing and using of the account details of a legitimate user for disreputable purposes using techniques like fraud and phishing. The credential hijackers could easily compromise the availability, integrity and confidentiality of the cloud services. A multifactor authentication mechanism should be enabled to mitigate the sharing of account credentials between users and cloud services.

- **Malicious insiders**: These are past or present malicious insiders like system administrators, former employees, business partners or a third-party contractors with high-level of access to potentially private, sensitive information and critical systems leading to a serious data breach.

- **The advanced persistent threats**: This is a stealthy computer network attack in which multiple assault code are injected into a vulnerable system at entry points while participating in a targeted network such that certain malicious individuals gain unauthorized access and remain undetected over a long period of time.

- **Permanent data loss**: This can be due to natural disaster, total hardware failure, unintentional cancellation by clients or support staff at the service providers' end or psychological militant assault. The cloud service provider must make adequate mitigation plans against data loss regardless of any form it takes. Regular backup routines to remote locales can help in this regard.

- **Shared technology, shared dangers**: Vulnerability and misconfigured components or weak isolation properties of a cloud services' component in a shared multi-tenant cloud system can be leveraged upon by attackers to cause data breach due to compromised cloud data security. Best practices should be employed for data management and client implementation to guide against shared technology vulnerabilities.

- **Compromised credentials and broken authentication**: Many cloud applications are equipped towards clients' collaborations, thereby releasing open cloud administrations to pernicious clients. These clients can use assault code, including email spam, DoS assaults and computerized click extortion, and so on to gain unauthorized access to critical data, control and management functionalities of the cloud services. Attackers can inject malicious software to attack the cloud services, modify data and service management/control parameters or sniff data in transit.

- **Hacked interfaces and Application Programming Interface (API)**: APIs and user interfaces are the fundamental backbones of cloud system connections and synergy among clients and the elastic computing systems. Cloud APIs' **Internet Protocol (IP)** addresses expose the association between clients and the cloud, so securing APIs from corruption or human mistakes is pertinent to cloud security. A special security requirement for the APIs needs to be designed to allow for access via encrypted keys, which are used to authenticate the API user so as to guide against accidental and malicious random attempts.

Cloud CIA security model

Due to the multi-tenancy structure of the cloud computing system, cloud data is highly vulnerable to a number of security threats. However, the level of vulnerability of the cloud resources depends on the cloud delivery model used by a cloud service consumer. The major challenges of cloud resources are **confidentiality, integrity and availability (CIA)**.

Data confidentiality

Data confidentiality refers to the ability to share sensitive data between a number of users without violating the privileges granted by the data owner to each of the targeted user. A streamlined concept of data confidentiality is data privacy. Data privacy means that the data owned by an individual will never be disclosed to any other. However, privacy is much easier to manage than confidentiality because sharing is precluded. In public clouds, the cloud service provider is solely responsible for securing the cloud service consumer's data. Confidentiality of data is enforced using virtualization, job scheduling and resource management. However, attackers can gain full access to the host and via cross-VM side-channel attacks; they can extract information from a target VM on the same machine.

Data integrity

Data integrity refers to the process of ensuring that cloud users' data is protected from unauthorized modification, thus assuring that the stored data has not been manipulated in any way by any unauthorized parties. To maintain data integrity, the cloud service provider must ensure that access restriction to data in transit or data in storage is enforced against third parties.

Data availability

This characteristic indicates that rightful owners of data, in this case, cloud service consumers, can seamlessly gain access to their data, and they are not denied access erroneously or due to malicious attacks by any entity. It could also refer to the cloud data server or virtual machine uptime and the capability to operate continuously. However, a **DS (DoS)** attack is the main threat to data availability.

The following table provides an overview of the CIA threats and their significance to the cloud service delivery models:

Potential threats	Description of the threat
Confidentiality	
Malicious insider threats: • Malicious cloud consumer • Malicious cloud provider • Malicious third-party user (supporting either the cloud provider or consumer organizations)	The threat of malicious insiders accessing cloud service consumer's data in the cloud is greater as each of the delivery model can introduce the need for multiple internal users: • SaaS: Cloud consumer and provider • PaaS: Application developers and test environment managers • IaaS: Third-party platform consultants
External attacker threats: • Remote software attack of cloud infrastructure • Remote software attack of cloud applications • Remote hardware attack against the cloud • Remote software and hardware attack against cloud user organizations' endpoint software and hardware • Social engineering of cloud provider users and cloud customer users	The threat from external attackers is most profound in public clouds. However, all types of cloud delivery models are affected by external attacks, especially private clouds where user endpoints can be targeted. Cloud service providers with large data stores hosting sensitive data like personal information, sensitive government or intellectual property, credit card details, and so on are highly susceptible to group attacks, with significant resources, attempting to access and retrieve sensitive data. This includes the threat of hardware attack, social engineering and supply chain attacks by dedicated attackers.

Potential threats	Description of the threat
Data leakage: • Failure of security access rights across multiple domains • Failure of electronic and physical transport systems for cloud data and backups	A threat from widespread data leakage using the same cloud provider could be caused by human error or faulty hardware leading to information compromise.
Integrity	
Data segregation: • Erroneously-defined security perimeters • Erroneously-configured virtual machines and hypervisors	Effective segregation of system resources is key to maintaining data integrity against threats to the cloud hosting environments such as public clouds are configured to share computing resources among customers.
User access: • Poor identity and access management procedures	Implementation of poor access control procedures creates many threat opportunities to cloud customer data. Unauthorized third party or administrators can gain remote access to administer customer cloud services and can cause intentional damage to their data sources.
Data quality: • Introduction of faulty application or infrastructure components	Faulty or misconfigured components required by another cloud user could potentially impact the integrity of data of other cloud consumers sharing the same infrastructure.
Availability	
Change management: • Customer penetration testing affecting other cloud customers • Infrastructure changes on cloud provider, consumers and third-party systems impacting cloud consumers	Necessary change management within all cloud delivery models could introduce threats and negative effects due to software or hardware changes to the existing cloud services.

Potential threats	Description of the threat
DoS threat: • Network bandwidth distributed DoS • Application and data denial of service • Network domain named service denial of service	Internal and external threat agents could inject application or hardware components that can cause a denial of service.
Physical disruption: • Disruption of cloud providers' Information Technology services through physical access • Disruption of cloud consumers' Information Technology services through physical access • Disruption of third-party WAN providers' services	Cloud service providers are expected to exhibit technical expertise in securing large data center facilities and have considered resilience among other availability strategies. Mitigation strategies against disruption of cloud services of any kind should be a top concern of any cloud service provider.
Exploiting weak recovery procedures: • Invocation of inadequate disaster recovery or business continuity processes	The threat of inadequate recovery and incident management procedures being initiated is heightened when cloud users consider recovery of their own in-house systems in parallel with those managed by third-party cloud service providers. If these procedures are not well tested, then the impact on the recovery time may be significant.

Table 6.2

Cloud computing security architecture

The security architecture of cloud computing is the most critical and fundamental determinant of the level of security that would be experienced in the entire cloud computing ecosystem. Currently, there is no globally accepted official standard for the cloud security architecture; however, reliable cloud security architecture must be designed to uphold optimal protection of the cloud ecosystem and the associated functionalities in an efficient manner. A typical cloud security architecture is represented in *Figure 6.1*. It is a four-layered architecture which is made up of the user, the service provider, the virtual machine, and the datacenter:

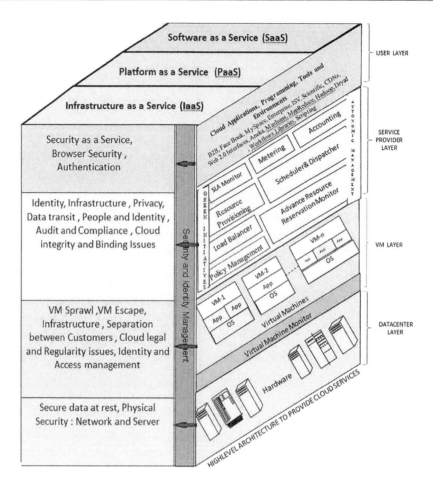

Figure 6.1: A prototype security architecture of cloud computing

The user layer consists of several components, including programming, cloud applications, tools, and environments. Examples of such cloud applications include **Facebook**, **B2B**, **CDN**, **Aneka**, **Enterprise**, **Mashups**, **Web 2.0 Interfaces**, **Scientific** and **MapReduce**, and so on. However, common security implementations at the user layer include, but are not limited to, **Browser Security**, **Authentication** and **Security-as-a-Service**.

At the service provider layer, the important constituent components include resource provisioning, **SLA Monitor**, **Scheduler & Dispatcher**, **Metering**, **Load Balancer**, **Accounting**, **Policy Management** and **Advance Resource Reservation Monitor**. Security concerns in the service provider layer include **Data transmission**, **Privacy**, **People and Identity**, **Infrastructure management**, **Audit and Compliance**, **Cloud integrity and Biding Issues**. Furthermore, the virtual machine layer is composed of several instances of virtual machines, operating systems and monitoring applications.

Virtual machine layer security considerations include cloud legal and regulatory issues, **VM Escape**, **VM Sprawl**, **Infrastructure**, **Identity and Access management** as well as separation between customers and others. Lastly, the data center which is the infrastructure layer is composed of the servers, storage, memory, the CPU and other cloud service resources, typically denoting an **Infrastructure-as-a-Service (IaaS)** layer. However, key security concerns in this layer are physical security, **Secure data at rest**, and **Security: Network and Server**.

User layer security

Security-as-a-service, browser security and authentication are discussed in this section.

Security-as-a-service

Security-as-a-service is a service-oriented security mechanism for protecting the user layer of the cloud computing ecosystem. It consists of two broad approaches.

In the first approach, the consumer, the provider and established information security vendors can solicit or provision security-as-a-service when required. With the second approach, security is provided as a cloud service by the cloud service provider in conjunction with information security companies like the anti-malware vendors delivering SaaS to filter email messages.

Browser security

A standard web browser is an application used by cloud consumers to access their subscribed services anywhere and at any time. To ensure security of browsers, a number of policies have been proposed of which the most dominant ones are the **transport layer security (TLS)** for host authentication and data encryption, and the Legacy **Same Origin Policy (SOP)** involving scripting of web pages for access and usage rights. It makes read or write operations privileges possible if the content emanates from the same origin and disallows such privileges for updates on content evolving from different origins. By *Origin*, we mean 'the same application', which is easily identified by the domain name, protocol and port in a web. However, TLS offers the functionalities to protect data during transport and authenticate the server's domain name in web applications. *Attacks on Browser-based Cloud Authentication* is one of the security concerns with browser-based protocols in cloud computing which occurs when the browser is incapable of generating cryptographically-valid XML tokens. To mitigate this, browser security APIs can be updated with recent enhancements of XML encryption and signature.

Authentication

In the cloud ecosystem, user authentication is the primary objective of an access control mechanism due to wide range of accessibility to cloud data via the internet.

This is because authentication is the most frequently targeted attack focal point in hosted and virtual services. Until now, a number of mitigation strategies against authentication attacks have been developed. An example of the authentication standard adopted in the cloud is the **Trusted Platform Module (TPM)**. TPM is commonly available and a more reliable authentication scheme than the password login verification check. It uses an IF-MAP standard to authorize users in real-time communication between the cloud provider and the consumer. This standard offers a means to revoke, modify and reassign the user's cloud access while authenticating client nodes and other devices participating in the cloud's active transaction.

Service provider security issues

It is the responsibility of the cloud service provider to ensure that the public cloud provisioned to a consumer meets all organizational security and privacy requirements. The cloud service provider is expected to provide safety standards required to protect the organization's data, applications and other components as well as a presentation of a guarantee on the fail-safe potential and effectiveness of the safety standards provided to secure organizational data and applications into the cloud.

Identity and access management

Identity and access management (IAM) involves the **Authentication, Authorization and Auditing (AAA)** of users accessing cloud services. To manage IAM, a static *trust boundary* is created, monitored and controlled in most organizations for applications that reside within the organization's perimeter. The systems, network and applications make up the trust boundary in a private data center. However, the private data center perimeter is secured via network security controls that include **virtual private networks (VPNs)**, **intrusion prevention systems (IPSs)**, **intrusion detection systems (IDSs)** and multifactor authentication. For a dynamic trust boundary, such as in the cloud, in which the organization's application, system and network boundary extend into the service provider domain, application security, user's access control mechanism, trusted sources with user activity monitoring, accurate attributes, strong authorization, authentication based on roles or claims, identity federation, **single sign-on (SSO)**, and auditing must be put in place to enforce strict IAM.

Privacy

Privacy is a critical challenge in cloud computing. Regulations on storage, usage, management and access to individual information vary across the world and some stringent restrictions are enforced by a number of countries regardless of where the data is stored. A cloud service provider must ensure strict compliance with service level agreement on data privacy concerns of the organization because non-compliance or a potential mistake made might come with very great consequences and the costs might be very huge to manage. However, an effective assessment strategy must be formulated to cover identity management, data protection, secure operations, privacy, and other issues related to security and legal aspects.

Securing data in transmission

Encryption techniques are often employed to secure data in transmission. Securing data in transmission literally means that the data is sent to the correct destination only via authentication and integrity check, not intercepted or modified during transmission using **secure socket layer** (**SSL**)/TLS protocols to verify. Integrity and confidentiality of data in transmission from/to the cloud provider can be enhanced by using access control mechanisms like authentication, authorization, auditing of accessed resources, and ensuring that internet-facing resources are available at the cloud provider's end. A possible attack during active data transmission is *Man-in-the-middle attack*. This is a cryptographic attack that occurs when an attacker is able to intercept the communication's path between the users and attempts to interrupt and change communications.

User identity

A cloud computing ecosystem supports large enterprises and diverse communities of users which make user identity a critical part of the cloud security architecture. Most cloud service providers often hire privileged users as administrators. A cloud service provider must ensure stringent requirements to monitor the activities of privileged users. This may include but not limited to background checking, physical monitoring and logging activities. To synchronize and manage authentication and authorization with the enterprise back-end or third-party systems, identity federation and rapid on-boarding capabilities must be initiated. This will provide the capability for the users to easily and efficiently use single sign-on logons for both the cloud and internally-hosted applications.

Audit and compliance

After a number of organization's requirements have been mutually agreed upon by both the consumer and provider of a cloud service and reported in a SLA document, audit and compliance strategies must be established to ensure that the internal and external processes are duly executed based on the documented requirements and business objectives, laws and regulations and internal corporate policies. These policies and procedures must be well checked and monitored for compliance reasons. The **cloud service providers** (**CSPs**) are responsible for the monitoring, evaluation and demonstration of the degree of compliance with regulatory requirements, coordination of external auditing and internal policy requirements in addition to the customers' business and organization's objectives.

Cloud Integrity and Binding Issues

An important requirement in the cloud computing ecosystem is to coordinate and maintain instances of virtual machines (IaaS) or explicit service execution modules (PaaS). For any user request, the cloud system is responsible for determining a free-to-use instance of the implementation type for the requested service such that the new instance is accessed by communicating the address to the requesting user. *Cloud Malware Injection Attack* is a typical attack aimed at injecting a malicious service performance module into a legitimate instance of a virtual machine. This is mainly done to modify unauthorized data and gain full functionality changes or blockings. This attack is adaptive as it can create its own malicious service implementation module (PaaS or SaaS) or virtual machine instance (IaaS).

Flooding attacks

A cloud computing environment provides a dynamic adaptation of hardware requirements to the actual workload by using virtual machines. However, a common security challenge to the availability and accessibility of the hardware resources is the DoS. A DoS attack occurs when a host is visited with heavy requests emanating from multiple computers to prevent it from responding to reasonable requests in a timely manner. A flooding attack causes the server's hardware resources to become completely exhausted such that the same hardware system is unable to perform any intended tasks. This can lead to non-availability of resources or services in the cloud computing environment.

Accounting and accountability

Accounting and accountability is a significant cost-effective motivator to adopt cloud services. As customers are charged based on the actual usage of cloud services, a flooding attack on a cloud service can drastically increase the bills of cloud usage. As a result, the customer running the flooded service is additionally billed for the workload caused by the attacker.

Security issues in virtualization

A **virtual machine** (**VM**) is a software implementation of a physical machine that executes programs and processes users' data. Extending virtual machines to public clouds can cause the enterprise network perimeter to grow.

Virtual machine escape

VM escape is a security situation which occurs when a total system failure is experienced due to improperly configured virtual machines. The other potential risk associated with virtualization is *Rogue Hypervisors*. A hypervisor is a component of the virtual machine that enables host isolation and resource sharing. It is a key component for managing risk in a VM. However, Rogue hypervisors is the guest operating system running in a virtual environment like a traditional operating system and managing input/output processes to hardware and network traffic, hijacking the functions of the hypervisor. *Increased Denial of Service Risk*: The threat of DoS attacks is no different in virtualized systems as being experienced in physical systems. The denial of service risks continues to grow tremendously in virtualized systems, the host or an external service because virtual machines share the host's resources such as disk, processor, memory, I/O devices, and so on.

VM security recommendations (best practices security techniques)

Hardening the Host Operating System involves moving the vulnerabilities from the operating system of the host system to the operating system of the virtual machine. *Limiting Physical Access to the Host* is an attempt to use the physical host security to protect the hardware of the virtual machine to keep intruders away from attacking the hardware. *Using Encrypted Communications* is to provide secure communications via cryptography techniques like **Secure Shell (SSH)**, **Transport Layer Security (TLS)**, **Secure HTTP (HTTPS)** and encrypted **Virtual Private Networks (VPNs)**, and so on between the client domain and host domain and/or from administrations to host systems. *Disabling Background Tasks* is to schedule traditional server operating systems to execute after long hours with a number of low-priority processes. *Updating and Patching* is the mechanism of effective patching and updating of systems in standards' organizations. The patching process is undermined by the creation of virtual machines. *Implementing File Integrity Checks* is a verification process of the files for accurate consistency retention. *Securing VM Remote Access* is the management of remote access to VM systems located on a server. The use of strong authentication techniques, including one-time passwords, use of encrypted communications (SSH, MAC address, VPNs or IP address filtering only), public/private key pairs, strong passwords and two-factor authentication should be employed.

Separation between users

Separation between a cloud provider's users to avoid intentional or inadvertent access to sensitive information is a great concern. The cloud service provider must ensure to use strong virtual network separation technologies and conduct VM integrity and hardware-based verification of hypervisors.

Cloud legal issues

A cloud provider must be aware of strong policies that address regulatory and legal issues and each cloud consumer is expected to consider issues like legal discovery and compliance, data retention and destruction, data security and export, and auditing when preparing a service level agreement with a cloud service provider.

Datacenter (infrastructure) security issues

It is pertinent to capture the datacenter security solutions and products as a constituent part of the complete cloud security architecture and not just deployed to be more effective.

Securing data-storage

Cloud data storage' security concerns include the manner in which data is accessed and stored, notification requirements, audit requirements, compliance, issues involving the cost of data breaches and damage to brand value. Sensitive and regulated data must be identified and properly segregated. Data privacy protection and compliance management are critical at the cloud service provider's end. This can be achieved via encryption. Extra caution must be made between the cloud consumer and the cloud service provider to share the encryption keys securely. With data-at-rest, the economics of cloud computing are such that PaaS-based applications and SaaS use a multi-tenancy architecture. Data-at-rest can be secured via cryptographic encryption and self-encrypting. Self-encrypting provides automated encryption with minimal cost or performance impact. Software encryption is less secure and slower because the encryption key is highly prone to being copied off the machine without detection.

Network and server

Server-side protection: Virtual servers and applications are required to be secured in IaaS clouds physically and logically. An example is the virtual firewalls which are often used to isolate teams of virtual machines from different hosted teams like production systems from development systems or development systems from different cloud-resident systems.

Securing the hybrid cloud

A hybrid cloud is a composite cloud infrastructure consisting of a private cloud composed with another organization's public cloud or vice versa. Both composite clouds are distinctive entities along the standardized or proprietary technology that fosters unified service delivery and interdependency. However, possibility of leaks or holes between the hybrid infrastructures is a security issue that requires attention. Furthermore, the availability of the hybrid cloud computed by the supply levels for each of the distinct clouds also raises a concern. If the availability level of either cloud system drops, the notion of hybrid tendency diminishes proportionately. Hybrid cloud service providers must ensure that each consumer's virtual domains are properly isolated such that no probability exists for data or transactions to leak from one tenant domain into another. This can be achieved by configuring trusted policy-based security zones or virtual domains. Intrusion detection and prevention systems can also be designed to detect data leakages, intrusions and extrusions (the misuse of a client's domain to mount attacks on third parties) into a client's trusted virtual domains as data management gets out of the customer's management window.

Privacy issues in the cloud and mitigation strategies

Sensitive information that must be held private include:

- **Personally identifiable information (PII)**: These are information that have close connections with the name or address of any individual which could be used to identify or locate people or information that can be potentially correlated with the other information to identify an individual (for example, postal code, credit card number, **Internet Protocol** (**IP**) address).

- **Sensitive information**: These are private information that can be used to describe a person or way of life. These include health records, religion or race, sexual orientation, union membership, and so on. The other information that may be considered sensitive include personal financial information and job performance information. PII considered to be sensitive include the collection of surveillance camera images in public places or biometric information.

- **Usage data**: Usage data is data that is collected from computer devices like printers and behavioral information such as viewing habits for digital content, users' recently visited websites or product usage history.

- Unique device identities: The other types of information that can be uniquely traceable to a user device are IP addresses, **Radio Frequency Identity (RFID)** tags, and unique hardware identities.

To mitigate the risks relative to information security and privacy, the following questions need to be addressed:

1. Who are the stakeholders involved in the transaction or communication?

2. What are their roles and responsibilities?

3. Where is the data kept?

4. How is the data replicated?

5. What are the relevant legal rules for data processing?

6. How will the service provider meet the expected level of security and privacy?

The main privacy risks and stakeholders are as follows:

- **The cloud service user**: Being forced or persuaded to be tracked or give personal information against their will, or in a way in which they feel uncomfortable.

- **Organization using the cloud service**: Failure to comply with business policies and legislation, credibility and loss of reputation.

- **Developers of cloud platforms**: Exposure of sensitive information stored on the platforms (potentially for fraudulent purposes), loss of reputation and credibility, lack of user trust, legal liability and take up.

- **Cloud service providers**: Loss of reputation, legal non-compliance, 'function creep' using the personal information stored on the cloud.

- **The data subject**: Exposure of personal information.

Performance monitoring and management of cloud services

Performance monitoring and management of cloud services offer the basis to evaluate the quality-of-service and adoption benefits of cloud services and to correctly assess the current resource demands of an application. Simply put, performance monitoring delivers the basic knowledge required to make scaling decisions confidently. In this section, we will discuss five cloud monitoring and management solutions such as Amazon CloudWatch, Private Cloud Monitoring Systems, Cloud Management System, runtime Model for Cloud Monitoring and Flexible Automated Cloud Monitoring Slices:

- **Amazon CloudWatch**: Amazon CloudWatch is a proprietary monitoring solution for **Amazon Web Services** (**AWS**). This solution makes easy management of basic metrics such as storage and processing possible. Furthermore, it offers various types of statistics and self-configuration. It is designed specifically for managers and users of Amazon clouds and AWS products only. Examples of similar commercial proprietary cloud monitoring solutions include Rackspace cloud monitoring, AccelOps, Zenoss, CopperEgg, and Monitis.

- **Private Cloud Monitoring Systems (PCMONS)**: PCMONS is an open source monitoring solution developed for private clouds. It uses an integration layer to grant homogeneous access to managers (administrators, services providers, cloud service brokers, and so on) and users (cloud service consumers) that manipulate resources in a cloud. It is specifically developed for uniform monitoring of infrastructure, regardless of the type of hosted resource(s) in a cloud. An advantage of using PCMONS is its ability to integrate with other monitoring solutions complementing its performance. However, it can only be manually configured to monitor private clouds that undermine its autonomy and scalability.

- **Cloud Management System (CMS)**: CMS leverages on RESTful Web Services to provide monitoring services. The REST serves as a technology for designing monitoring elements. As a result, CMS is able to integrate with other technologies, services and solutions that use REST. It also supports integration with other monitoring solutions via the REST interfaces.

- **Runtime Model for Cloud Monitoring (RMCM)**: RMCM is designed to monitor resources through abstract models which allow possible homogeneous handling of heterogeneous resources. In this way, a unified mechanism to access different resources like virtual systems and platforms in the same manner is provided. RMCM is a 3-tier composite cloud monitoring model described as *model for operators*, *model for developers*, and *model for users* due to its flexibility to generate customized models depending on the request of each agent that integrates a cloud. However, it requires a constant update of monitoring resources in order to maintain the model consistency. Similar to PCMONS, RMCM also requires manual installation and configuration of specific agents which compromises cloud monitoring requirements such as migration, scalability and autonomy.

- **Flexible Automated Cloud Monitoring Slices (Flex-ACMS)**: Flex-ACMS is a composite and comprehensive cloud monitoring solution resulting from a rich integrated set of monitoring solutions. Unlike PCMONS and RMCM, Flex-ACMS can be automatically configured to provide dynamicity and flexibility to cloud providers, which in turn, offers improved operational efficiency of cloud providers such as in billing and SLA. However, Flex-ACMS is configured by cloud administrators based on rules defined to indicate the metrics that must be monitored on each cloud slice and check monitoring solutions that need to be used to monitor each slice.

Legal issues in cloud computing

A number of key legal issues that should be agreed upon by the cloud service consumer and the service provider are as follows:

- **Governing law and jurisdiction**: This is often liable and governed within the service provider's country. In the same vein, disputes arising from any legal contract are always under the jurisdiction of the courts of the service provider's country. This can be amended if the cloud service consumer wishes to move any legal jurisdiction to their home country and in some cases when the service provider is a large multinational, this may be possible. Such a provision can be removed from a contract and you can allow a legal debate to decide when or if such a situation arises.

- **Data location**: Issues related to data storage locations must be addressed directly within the contract by the cloud service provider and the customer. Although maintaining data across multiple geographical locations provides a greater level of security, concerns usually grow over time relative to export controls leading to legislation against extraterritorial storage.

- **Privacy and confidentiality**: Most often, data are used for a specific purpose for which they are collected. However, contracts governing data outsourcing need to ensure data usage specifically for the required service, and non-disclosure of data by the third party without authorization. This needs to be expressed explicitly within a contract to ensure that enforcement is not compromised.

- **Data security**: Independent specific security standards should be used to replace relative cloud service providers envisioned *reasonable* or *industry-standard* security provisions in the contract to realize greater level of security. The meaning of *reasonable* or *industry standard* is relative and can lead to serious argument and misinterpretation over time between the cloud provider and the cloud consumer. However, the independent security standards adopted must be updated and audited from time to time. Also, any contract must contain a requirement on the service provider to inform of data or security breaches.

- **Data access for E-discovery**: This contract is expected to exhibit the architecture of the service being provided. The contract must also specify the format used for data storage and available tools for data access if any e-discovery requirements arise. Some services fail to provide such tools, turning e-discovery into a complex and time consuming task.

- **End-users responsibility**: In a situation where the cloud subscriber makes end users of the service to abide to the terms and agreements of the cloud service provider and customer, a liability of the third-party usage of the system is placed with the cloud consumer. An alternative would be to enforce an agreement between third parties and the service provider for compliance of the service providers' terms and conditions.

- **Inappropriate and unauthorized usage**: In an attempt made by the service providers to place the responsibility of monitoring and preventing inappropriate and unauthorized usage of the provided service with the customer, the customer should ensure that the service contract limits the liability to the customer not authorizing or knowingly allowing prohibited usage of the service since the service resides in the cloud and outside the control of the customer. These contracts should also include a requirement for the customer to inform the service provider of all material breaches and other unauthorized or inappropriate usage of the service. Caution must be exercised by the customer to report material breaches rather than unauthorized usages.

- **End-users' account suspension**: Service providers can suspend the customer's end-users' account at their will on the violation of some terms and conditions. It is preferable for the customer to restrict the service provider's right of suspension to material or significant violations that compromise the security of the vendors' system.

- **Emergency security issues**: Service providers may have legislation laws inserted to suspend without notice, a provisioned service, in the event that an unethical use of such a service causes an emergency issue. In the consumer's best interest, what constitutes an emergency issue should be clearly defined with the service provider so as to limit the flexibility and/or discretion of the service provider if any emergency occurs.

- **Service suspension and termination**: Service providers have the reserved right to suspend a service or to even terminate a service in the event of specified events. While such conditions are practical and legitimate from the service provider's point of view, the service consumer must ensure that the service contract offers a time-window opportunity to rectify the situation, rather than an immediate denial of service (except for extreme emergencies), and to provide the consumer some reasonable period of time to make alternative arrangements for service provision. The service provider must ensure that if such an event occurs, the customer's data is made available in a usable format for a specified amount of time after service termination. Finally, the contract must oblige the service provider to return or destroy any customer data once the service termination is complete.

- **Data ownership**: The service contract between the service provider and the consumer is expected to explicitly state that all data is the property of the customer and the service provider does not acquire any licenses or rights to the customer's data based on the transaction. The restriction of any security interest in the customer's data by the service provider should also be noted.

- **Publicity**: The service provider may request to use the customer's name, logos or trademarks for the service providers' own advertisement purpose; while this can be occasionally granted, cloud service consumers must request that an approval be sought regarding the use of any of their associated brand or limit the use to the customer name without implying an endorsement.

- **Service Level Agreements (SLAs)**: Guarantees for the service provision need to be detailed to provide for the minimum amount of uptime, the process, and the timescale associated with correcting the downtime. Consequences for falling outside the agreed SLAs need to be precise and detailed.

- **Disclaimer of warranty**: The service contract is expected to guarantee that the provided service operates correspondingly to its specifications without breaching the rights of any third party as a basic minimum requirement. If these kinds of warranties are absent in a service contract, an enforceable assurance of the service functionalities is not possible, or the service provider even has the authority to provide the service. If a service failure event occurs or a liable action is taken against the cloud consumer, without such warranties, the consumer will not have any legal recourse against the service provider.

- **Customer indemnification**: Some service provider contracts require indemnification for the service provider in the event of illicit third-party actions, together with the consumer's actions. The cloud service consumer must ensure that this liability is not voluntarily accepted, although it does not constitute adopting an extra liability as the customer is liable to face legal action over the third-party content.

- **Vendor indemnification**: Service provider contracts rarely outline any indemnification that benefits the customer, despite legal protection being essential in a minimum of two scenarios—third-party intellectual property rights infringement and a breach or unauthorized disclosure of sensitive customer data. In both the scenarios, the responsibility lies solely with the service provider, and defending or remedying the situation can prove extremely costly. Care must be taken by the cloud service consumer to ensure that the prospective service provider is ready to accept liability in either scenario before a decision is being made.

- **Contract modifications**: The cloud service consumer must ensure that the rights of the service providers to modify services as required must be made limited to those services that would not expose the consumer to service deterioration even if the service providers reserve the right to modify their services as they deem them fit.

- **URL terms incorporation**: Beyond advertised contract terms advertised on the service provider's website and other related avenues, legal information should rather be maintained within the confines of the service contract. In the case where service providers cannot provide this, an advanced and individual notice of such a change should be incorporated, with the option of termination of service provided to the customer without penalties, if such amendments are materially detrimental to the requirements of the customer.

- **Automatic renewal**: It is expected of a service contract to provide advanced notice of any changes to terms and conditions in the renewal, and automatically renew with the option of termination on short notice within a specified period of time after the automatic renewal.

Data security in cloud

Risk can be referred to as a statistical concept associated with uncertain outcomes of business activities in the future. According to TechTarget, risk management is defined as *the process of identifying, assessing and controlling threats to an organization's capital and earnings*. Major sources of such threats can include but are not limited to strategic failures, market disruptions, accidents, legal liabilities, natural disasters, financial uncertainty, data-related risks, and **Information Technology (IT)** security threats. However, the subject of risk management in cloud computing is an IT security threat concern. More often than not, the need to identify and mitigate threats to digital assets takes the lead priority in most digitized organizations.

The other definitions of risk management are as follows:

- The process of *identifying, quantifying,* and *managing* the risks that an organization faces (Lexicon).

- The process of *evaluating* the chance of loss or harm and then taking steps to *combat* the potential risk (your dictionary).

- The process of *identifying any potential threats* that may occur during the investment process and doing anything possible to *mitigate* or *eliminate* those dangers (my accounting course).

- The practice of *identifying potential risks* in advance, *analyzing* them and taking precautionary steps to *reduce/curb* the risk (economic times).

- The identification, analysis, assessment, control and avoidance, minimization or elimination of unacceptable risks (business dictionary).

All these definitions have several key attributes in common which unify the concept of risk management. These include a process of *identifying, analysis/quantifying/ evaluating/assessing,* and *managing/combating/mitigating/eliminating/reducing/curbing/ minimizing* of risk.

Security and privacy risks are the major challenges of the cloud platform due to sensitivity of some stored information. Basic trade-offs to be considered before adopting cloud services for organizational use include the cloud model, the type of data involved, type of cloud service considered, the cost savings, the system's criticality/impact level, the service type, and any associated regulatory requirements. These trade-offs are required to measure the degree of risk involved in using a cloud service. Most often, the integrity, confidentiality and availability of the stored data in the cloud are threatened, compromised and exploited by malicious entities due to its vulnerabilities.

Risk management is a very crucial activity that must be wholly integrated into every process of an organization. It should be implemented at three major classical risk-related levels of an organization:

- The organization level (tier 1)

- The mission and business process level (tier 2)

- The information system level (tier 3)

Risk management is a routinely executed practice with an associated set of organized activities to identify and mitigate risks in order to intensify tactical and strategic security. This includes the implementation of *risk assessment, risk mitigation* strategy and *risk control* procedures for onward observation and continuous management of the security level of the information system throughout the **system development**

life cycle (SDLC). In a cloud ecosystem, acceptable risk is evaluated by cloud actors relative to the level of their risk tolerance to the cloud ecosystem overall risk.

High-level risk elements of the cloud security ecosystem are as follows:

- Each cloud actor must be assigned risk management responsibilities which can further be extended to their senior executives, leaders and representatives.

- Establish and disseminate tolerance for risk in the entire cloud ecosystem via SLA.

- Each cloud actor is required to continuously inspect, identify and understand security risks arising from the use of any cloud-based service.

- Prompt information sharing and accountability are required by the cloud actors on security issues, risk management plans and solutions.

The cloud risk management framework

A **Risk Management Framework** (**RMF**) provides a controlled and organized approach that embodies information security and risk management activities into the system development life cycle in a cloud ecosystem is shown in the following table:

Risk assessment (analyze cloud environment to identify potential vulnerabilities and shortcomings)	**Step 1:** • Categorize the information system and the information processed, stored, and transmitted by that system based on a system impact analysis. • Identify performance, operational, security and privacy requirements.
	Step 2: • Select, based on the appropriate security requirements, the initial set of security controls for the information system (referred to as baseline security controls). • Streamline and adjust the baseline security controls with respect to the organizational evaluation of risk and the conditions of the operational environment. • Develop a systematic approach for the continuous monitoring of security control effectiveness. • Document all the controls in the security plan. • Review and approve the security plan.

Risk treatment (design mitigation policies and plans)	Step 3: • Implement the security controls and describe how the controls are employed within the information system and its environment of operation.
	Step 4: • Assess the security controls using appropriate assessment procedures as documented in the assessment plan. The assessment determines if the controls are implemented correctly and if they are effective in producing the desired outcome.
	Step 5: • Authorize information system operation based on the determined risk resulting from the operation of the information system and the decision that this risk is acceptable. The assessment is performed considering the risk to organizational operations (including mission, functions, image, or reputation), organizational assets, individuals, and other organizations.
Risk control (risk monitoring-surveying, reviewing events, identifying policy adjustments)	Step 6: • Monitor the security controls in the information system regularly, including assessing control effectiveness, logging system and environment operational changes, conducting security impact analyses of these changes, and reporting the security state of the system to designated organizational officials.

Table 6.3

Risk management process for cloud consumers

A greater influence over processes and systems helps organizations to accept risks more comfortably. A high level of control helps organizations to evaluate alternatives, set priorities, and make sound decisions best suited in the face of an incident. For a cloud consumer to adopt a cloud-based system successfully, the cloud-specific requirements of the system, deployment model, the architectural landscape for the cloud service and the cloud actors' responsibilities in ensuring a secured cloud ecosystem must be well understood.

In addition, for business and mission-critical processes, cloud consumers should:

• Identify all cloud-specific, risk-associated security and privacy controls

- Make necessary request for Service Agreements and SLAs from the cloud brokers and providers and brokers regarding security and privacy controls in the cloud via contractual means wherever applicable

- Assess the execution and effectiveness of the adopted security and privacy controls

- Regularly monitor all identified security and privacy controls

A risk management process can help to leverage between the offerings of opportunities of cloud computing adoption and its associated security risks. On the other hand, risk assessment can help to determine the readiness of an organization to trust their data, business operations and business continuity, which are prone to insecure transmission, storage and processing, to a cloud provider.

Requirement for risk management in ISO/IEC 27001

It is required for an organization to define and apply an information security risk assessment process that:

- Establishes and maintains information security risk criteria

- Ensures consistent output of risk assessments

- Identifies respective information security risks and risk players

- Analyzes consequences and possibilities of the risks

- Evaluates and prioritizes the risks for mitigation

There is a category of risks associated with the adoption of cloud services that include data privacy, availability, service provisioning, malicious activities, and regulatory compliance risks.

Data privacy risks in the cloud

Data privacy risks include those associated with access control, internal segmentation, sub-contractors, data ownership, e-discovery, data censorship and encryption. Let us discuss them in detail as follows:

- **Access control**:

    When an organization decides to move corporate data and/or documents to an external cloud environment, there is a high tendency that individuals working in the service provider organization may have access to the data in a bid to provide support to the provisioned service.

To manage this risk, potential cloud consumers can request the cloud service provider to:

- Grant data/files access to only personnel

- Run background checks on such personnel

- Maintain proper records of approval and removal of internal access to the data

- Review and monitor data access

- Conduct essential training for internal staff on data protection requirements

- **Internal segmentation**:

  This is a data disclosure risk of likely occurrence between two or more organizations when the vulnerabilities associated with improper structuring and configuration of the data architecture of a cloud service exposes the data of one organization to another in a multi-tenant cloud environment.

  To manage this risk, potential cloud consumers can request the cloud service provider to:

- Practice internal walls/segmentation between the data of different organizations

- Audit data storage to ensure effective implementation of internal barriers

- Monitor the cloud provider for compliance to these risk mitigation strategies

- **Sub-contractors**:

  A number of cloud service providers with multiple layers of cloud services usually engage in subletting cloud provisioning to support the services of other cloud providers. Should it arise that the original cloud service provider sub-contracts one or more of the cloud services being provisioned to an organization to another service provider, the organization must enforce that its cloud services' regulatory compliance requirements be met by the sub-contractors through appropriate contract language/terms with the original cloud service provider. The organization must also ensure it identifies all sub-contractors associated with provisioning of its cloud services in order to be able to track their level of compliance adherence.

To manage this risk, the organization is required to:

- Discuss how to provide the identities of all sub-contractors with the cloud service provider in order to monitor their compliance status.

- Reach a contractual agreement with the service provider to ensure that the serial service providers associated with the organization's cloud service provisioning adhere to compliance requirements.

- Ensure that the service provider puts a vendor management program in place to track the compliance of its vendors.

- Monitor the service provider's compliance with the vendor management program requirements.

- **Data ownership**:

  Most cloud service providers usually place ownership claims, usage and redistributable rights over consumers' data being hosted. To manage this risk, the organization can:

- Emphasize on the primacy of its data ownership rights and ensure it is acknowledged by the service providers.

- Contractually bind the service provider to use organization data within the agreed limit.

- Contractually bind the service provider to return and delete the organization's data when the period of their contract terms expires.

- **E-Discovery**:

  Organization data hosted by a cloud service provider is potentially prone to e-discovery and disclosure risk and as such compromised by legal actions targeting the service provider, any of its associated service providers or customers. To manage this, the organization can:

- Contractually bind the service provider to inform the organization of any required legal disclosure that may compromise the organization's data via e-discovery.

- Make internal arrangements to tackle e-disclosure needs if it arises.

- **Data censorship**:

  Unacceptable delays on the part of an organization (cloud consumer) are often experienced when changes are required to be made to an organization's data when the cloud providers hold the right to audit and censor any data to the host. To manage this risk, the organization can:

- Contractually identify and assess conditions for such activities to hold any supported process from the service provider.

- Request to be notified of such activities by the service provider.

- **Encryption**:

  Some uncommon cloud services are hyped to meet specific regulatory requirements, including data encryption however, it could be very expensive to encrypt data-at-rest. To address this risk, the organization can:

- Adopt the use of encryption-free cloud data services only.

- Select and validate such that a cloud service provider is encryption compliant and with appropriate encryption controls that are often assessed.

- Ensure that the appropriate key management practices for encryption support are available.

Availability risks

- **Service degradation**:

  The external services offered by a cloud provider are provided via internet connections. More often than not, these services suffer from congestion and outages, or malicious attacks emanating from a diversion of resources as a result of an attack on the service provider, an attack on one of their service providers or by a successful penetration and use of the service itself as the tool for further attacks on other sites.

To address this risk, the organization can:

- Ensure cloud services are only used for applications that are not affected by degradation of service.

- Use alternate carriers to obtain redundant lines to the service provider to secure alternate connecting lines to the service.

- Implement relevant and sustainable alternatives for services during periods of service degradation.

- **Service outage**:

  In case service outages arise. To address this risk, the organization should do the following:

- Validate that the provisioned service by the service provider has sufficient capacity and multiple service sources to reduce outages

- Establish a SLA with the service provider on the minimum acceptable availability performance levels with contractual penalties for non-compliance

- Ensure that the established level of service availability is proportional to business productivity

- Validate that the service provider executes a proactive backup program and recovery plan

- Validate that the service provider recovery plan is tested regularly

- Confirm the availability of alternative service options at moments of non-availability of service

- Implement relevant and sustainable alternatives for services during an outage

Service provisioning risks

- **Service changes**:

  Possibility is high that an organization might me unable to gain access to its data or to its cloud services on a short notice peradventure due to failure, acquisition, and discontinuity of a service or change in business models at any time.

  To manage this risk, the organization can do the following:

- For possible event of service changes, contractually demand for a specified minimum period of prior notice.

- Confirm the availability of alternative service options that can be used on needs.

- Keep an updated internal copy of the data for emergency use.

- **Cost changes**:

  Due to possible cost changes to cloud services over time, the essence of cloud adoption might become jeopardized.

  To address this, the organization should do the following:

- Ensure that the service contract contains information regarding the service costs and potential changes.

- Assess the cost/benefit/risk trade-offs of the relationship during each contract renewal.

- **Malicious activity risks**:

  The fact that the cloud service providers operate in the open internet makes their cloud environments and services rich targets for attacks through their website portals. This challenge is further aggravated by the web support and administration tools made available to the customers as mostly defined in a normal business model through the web portal, making these tools more vulnerable to attacks as they can be accessed by attackers.

To manage this risk, the organization can do the following:

- Ascertain that the service provider adheres to recommended security best practices in the development of its web application, including code reviews and appropriate application security fundamentals at each level of its cloud infrastructure.

- Ascertain that appropriate vulnerability and penetration tests are conducted on a regular basis and any issues identified are addressed promptly by the cloud provider.

- Ensure that proper auditing of these tests is conducted by the service provider to confirm that the tests are operationally effective.

- **Regulatory compliance risks**

- **Audit records:**

  As a matter of policy, certain cloud providers do not provide internal operational reports of the systems supporting their cloud services to their external customers. This makes it very difficult for customers to obtain auditable records for the systems provisioned for their solicited services. Significant variability exists for the audit tools of individual service providers and thus requires evaluation as a possible requirement for compliance with regulatory requirements.

To address this risk, the organization should do the following:

- Establish an understanding with the service provider on standing modalities to ensure that supporting systems are audited and verified. This can either be through an internal audit conducted by the organization's audit team or through a third-party verification using SSAE 16 SOC 1 and SOC 3 reports, which must be included in the contract agreement.

- Request copies of the past relevant service provider SAS 70/SSAE 16 reports or maintain regular audits of the provider.

- Maintain contractually mandate appropriate audit reports to meet the organization's needs.

- **Storage location:**

  A cloud service provider may choose to store or transfer an organization's data on servers located outside the region of a legal jurisdiction or country where the organization is located, and this may not be acceptable based on regulations guiding the operations of the organization.

To checkmate this risk, the organization can do the following:

- Make its legal and regulatory requirements accessible to the service provider to understand the data storage restrictions and policies that exist in the organization.

- Contractually commit the service provider to matters regarding storage location restrictions as it legally affects the organization.

- **Lack of breach notice**:

  Sometimes, cloud service providers may breach an organization's regulatory compliance requirement while the concerned organization is unaware for some time after the breach has occurred.

To address this risk, the organization can do the following:

- Allocate cloud resources only to such data applications with no regulatory compliance requirements.

- Contractually commit a cloud service provider to report immediately of the event of a possible breach.

Business continuity and disaster recovery

A disaster is an unforeseen event in a system lifetime. It can be caused by natural disaster (earthquake, climate change or tsunami), human errors or hardware/ software failures. This in turn can lead to serious financial loss or even death. As a result, the major objective of **Cloud Disaster Recovery** (**DR**) is to provide an organization with automated and reliable approach (es) to data recovery and failover in the event of a man-made or natural catastrophe. A model of a disaster recovery system is presented in *Figure 6.2*.

The definitions of Cloud Disaster Recovery are as follows:

- Techopedia defines cloud disaster recovery as *a service that enables the backup and recovery of remote machines on a cloud-based platform.*

- Techtarget defines cloud disaster as a backup and restore strategy that involves storing and maintaining copies of electronic records in a cloud computing environment as a security measure.

Cloud DR is an **Infrastructure-as-a-Service** (**IaaS**) solution that provisions backup and recovery for critical dedicated server machines hosting enterprise-level data applications, (for example, Oracle, MySQL), located on a remote offsite cloud server.

A cloud disaster recovery system is often structured in a distributed computing, centralized storage manner to ensure ready availability of application and the security of data. Disaster recovery can be categorized into three levels based on different requirements. These include data-level, system level and application-level disaster recovery.

Data-level disaster recovery is the most fundamental among all others and guarantees the security of the application data. System level disaster recovery disaster makes recovery for operating system of application server as short as possible. System level disaster recovery ensures recovery occurs in real-time relieving the users of the feel that any disaster occurred.

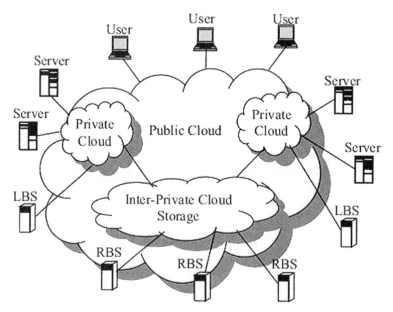

Figure 6.2: A model of a disaster recovery system

Disaster recovery requirements

Five major requirements, including **Recovery Point Objective (RPO)**, **Recovery Time Objective (RTO)**, performance, consistency and geographical separation are discussed in this section. These requirements are influenced by factors like actual cost of system downtime or data loss, correctness and application performance:

- **Recovery Point Objective (RPO)**: The RPO of a DR system depicts the point in time of the most recent backup prior to the event of a disaster or failure. RPO is affected by a business decision, either to allow a *no data loss* for some applications via a continuous synchronous replication process with RPO=0, while on the other hand, it permits some level of data loss for some other applications, which could range from a few seconds to days as the case may be.

- **Recovery Time Objective (RTO)**: The RTO is an impertinent business decision that determines the duration it takes an application to be restored back online in the event of a failure. This includes the required time for failure detection, configure any required servers in the backup site (virtual or physical), initialize the failed application, and perform the network reconfiguration required to reroute requests from the original site to the backup site so the application can be used. The application type and backup technique determine the process to be executed next. Such processes may include the verification of the integrity of state or performing application specific data restore operations and require careful scheduling of recovery tasks to be done efficiently. It should be noted that a very low RTO ensures continuous running of business such that an application seamlessly continues to run despite a disaster.

- **Performance**: Disaster recovery service must allow a minimal impact on the performance of each application being protected under failure-free operation for it to be useful. The impact of DR on performance can be direct or indirect. Direct impact involves operations like synchronous replication that allows application write not to return until it is committed remotely. However, with indirect impact, disk and network bandwidth resources are consumed which could have otherwise been used by the application.

- **Consistency**: This ensures that an application regains a consistent state after a failure occurs. To achieve this, the DR mechanism often requires application-specific settings that guarantee proper replication of all relevant state of the application on the backup site. Similarly, the DR system assumes a consistent copy of the pertinent state of an application to be made available on disk, and leverage on a disk replication scheme to create consistent copies at the backup site.

- **Geographic separation**: This ensures that both the primary and backup sites are located at separate geographical locations such that they are not affected by a single or similar disaster at the same time. This requirement is challenged by higher WAN bandwidth costs due to increased distance and greater network latency.

Mechanisms for cloud disaster recovery

These are additional requirements that must be met for DR to be provisioned as a cloud service. These include network reconfiguration, security and isolation, virtual machine migration and cloning:

- **Network reconfiguration**: Cloud platforms allow a flexible reconfiguration of the network setup for an application after it is restored online in the backup site to ensure business continuity. Two possible network reconfiguration processes to achieve this include modification of **Domain Network Service (DNS)** or updating routes to redirect traffic to the failover site, especially for public internet facing applications. However, a strong collaboration between cloud platforms and network service providers will make this a success.

- **Security and isolation**: Cloud platforms must provide leverage, mechanism and guaranteed assurances that potential disasters will not impact the performance of applications running in the cloud. Security concerns to be addressed include the privacy of storage, network, and the virtual machine resources being used. Likewise, clouds must guarantee that the performance of applications running in the cloud will not be impacted by disasters affecting other businesses.

- **Virtual machine migration and cloning**: Although not currently supported, cloud platforms are expected to allow VM migration in or out of the cloud. This can be made possible as cloud exposes additional hypervisor level functionality to customers while optimizing migration techniques for the WAN environment. Virtual machine migration and cloning is very important for the following two reasons:

- Provides simplified failback procedure for moving an application back to its original site after a disaster has been managed.

- It can be used to improve planned maintenance downtime.

Disaster recovery as a service

Disaster recovery as a service is perceived as a future low-cost service designed after the cloud computing nomenclature is expected to offer flexible replication be it physically or virtually. This phenomenon allows recovery of data center infrastructures and critical servers to be replicated in the cloud as a service. The architecture is configured with pre-built options to support virtual recovery environments characterized by network connectivity, security and server failover. In the event of a disaster, provisioned backup and applications can be executed on DR services until the backup to the primary site is obtained. *Table 6.4* presents a comparative analysis of both traditional and service-oriented disaster recovery approaches:

Traditional disaster recovery	Disaster recovery as a service
This requires a secondary physical DR site and thus translates into further costs of manpower requirements, site maintenance, and operational costs, additional data center space, connectivity and servers.	This only makes a virtual machine replica of physical or virtual servers available at the primary data center. Additional cost attraction is only for storing the replica and application data in a suspended mode as well as data replication from primary to secondary site for data synchronization. If a disaster occurs, virtual machines are brought online to substitute for the primary site.
A physical DR site is operated when an actual disaster occurs. It takes more time to bring the DR site live leading to huge data loss.	The DR site can be brought online within minutes after the event of a disaster translating to data loss of a little timeframe.
It requires manual connection if the connectivity is unavailable to commence site operations.	It is triggered seamlessly regardless of geographical location using the internet.

Table 6.4

The cloud disaster recovery architecture

In a two-zone cloud DR configuration, **Zone "A"** and **Zone "B"**, each zone replicates the other such that if a zone experiences a downtime as a result of disaster, then the other becomes active. Each zone has its own internal **System Architecture (SA)** similar to the other. The **zone "A"** has an **Active Load Balancer** and **zone "B"** has a **Passive Load Balancer** as shown in *Figure 6.3*. However, the components of the cloud disaster recovery architecture are discussed as follows:

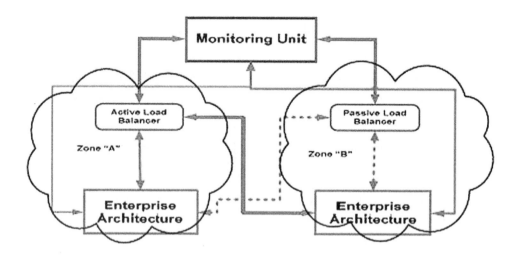

Figure 6.3: Disaster recovery architecture with cloud computing

- **Active Load Balancer**: The primary function of a load balancer is to ensure fair distribution of the system's work load. The load balancer is also responsible for citizen request identification and evaluation to include the type and volume of requests and confirms if the available resources can serve these requests or not. If the available resources are not adequate to manage the citizen's request, then it signals the monitoring unit to provision additional resources to the system architecture. This reflects the scalability features of cloud computing. **Active Load Balancer** also synchronizes with SA in **zone "B"**.

- **Passive Load Balancer**: This is the same as **Active Load Balancer** except that it is in the passive mode. It becomes active within 5 to 10 minutes when **zone "A"** experiences a downtime due to a disaster.

- **Monitoring Unit**: This unit manages the activities and states (good/compromised) of both **zone "A"** and **zone "B"** to improve efficiency and reliability of service. It gets resource constraints' feedback from the load balancer and verifies the request. If additional resource(s) are truly required, it responds with the appropriate resource back to the load balancer to execute accordingly. It is responsible for the switch in the active role between **zone "A"** and **zone "B"** depending on their internal states. If **zone "A"** experiences a disaster or found to have been compromised, then it is taken down and **zone "B"** is made active and vice versa.

Challenges of the cloud disaster recovery

Some common challenges of the cloud disaster recovery are discussed as follows:

- **Dependency**: Customers are totally dependent on cloud service providers due to lack of control over the system and the data as the data backup is on premises of service providers.

- **Cost**: Cloud service providers annually charge differently for interrelated DR systems as a service operation which annuls the initial cost savings expectation of the consumers. These costs include the initializing cost, a form of a liquidated annual cost, ongoing cost (storage cost, data transfer cost and processing cost), and disaster cost (charges for recovered disasters and associated cost of unrecoverable disasters).

- **Failure detection**: A failure detection time is expected to be very short so that the system downtime can be adequately managed on time. Hence, it is highly expedient to report a failure immediately when it is detected to facilitate quick DR and reduce system downtime.

- **Security**: Cyber terrorism attacks and natural disasters are major problems. Mechanisms must be developed to protect important data and ensure its recovery in the case of a disaster.

- **Data storage**: Storage single point of failure and data loss are critical challenges to store data in cloud service providers' DR solutions. To manage this, the following are suggested as potential solutions:

- **Local backup**: An alternative backup plan can be made for both data and complete application at the customer's end using a Linux box and seamlessly updated through a secured channel. In case of a disaster, the local backup can be leveraged upon for recovery purposes.

- **Geographical Redundancy and Backup (GRB)**: With this approach, two cloud zones are located at different geographical locations and ones synchronously mirrored as a replication of the other. A monitor is deployed to detect the disaster at each zone. However, it is expensive and unaffordable.

- **Inter-Private Cloud Storage (IPCS)**: This approach provisions three different geographical backup locations for business data storage such that each backup location is dedicated to backup only one of the servers, **local backup server (LBS)** or **remote backup server (RBS)**.

- **Resource management**: Improved technologies for hardware and software application management must be deployed for seamless critical data DR services. Examples include the use of the fastest disk technology, changing dirty page threshold and replacement of risky devices by determining factors like heat dissipation, power consumption, and carbon credit utilization, and so on from time to time.

Threats in cloud

A number of threats in the cloud include but are not limited to the following:

- **Data breaches**: This security incident occurs when an unauthorized intruder accesses, copies or transmits private, confidential or sensitive data belonging to a person or organization. Data breaches are often a result of simple human error, poor security practices, targeted attacks, and application vulnerabilities.

- **Data loss**: This is often experienced due to hard drive failure, malware attacks, natural disasters (for example, earthquakes and floods), power failure and human errors (accidental file deletion by a cloud administrator) leading to corrupt or unavailability of data. Data must be backed up in multiple geographically-spanned locations so that in case of a data loss, a similar copy can be obtained from a remote location for replacement.

- **Malicious insiders**: These are past or present malicious insiders like a system administrator, former employee, business partner or a third-party contractor with high-level of access to potentially private, sensitive information and critical systems leading to a serious data breach.

- **Denial of Service (DoS)**: A DoS attack originates from a source machine only and is designed to deny legitimate users access to their privileged/subscribed cloud services, data or application, by making these resources and services available.

- **Distributed Denial of Service (DDoS) attack**: Unlike DoS that originates from a single system to attack a cloud service, on the other hand, a DDoS attack locates vulnerable systems (zombies/slaves) participating in a network, whose collection is termed as a botnet, and the attacker leverages on these vulnerabilities to distribute different kinds of malware. The zombies are made to send fake traffic which in turn floods the network, thereby making real data, applications or other resources in cloud unavailable to legitimate users.

- **Vulnerable systems and application programming interfaces (APIs)**: Cloud APIs represent gateways which can be well exploited by an attacker to gain considerable access to cloud resources. Similarly, cloud APIs commonly used by subscribers to access cloud services are also sometimes exposed by cloud service providers. A special security requirement is that the APIs need to be designed to allow access via encrypted keys, which are used to authenticate the API user to guide against accidental and malicious random attempts.

- **Weak authentication and identity management**: Potential vulnerabilities are exploited by attackers when organizations allocate designated permissions to job roles of their users. Hence, attackers could masquerade as legitimate operators, users or developers to gain unauthorized access to critical data, control and management functionalities of the cloud services. As such, attackers can inject malicious software to attack the cloud services, modify data and service management/control parameters or sniff data in transit.

- **Account hijacking**: This involves the stealing and using of the account details of a legitimate user for disreputable purposes using techniques like fraud and phishing. The credential hijackers can easily compromise availability, integrity and confidentiality of the cloud services. A multifactor authentication mechanism should be enabled to mitigate the sharing of account credentials between users and cloud services.

- **Shared technology vulnerabilities**: Vulnerability and misconfigured component or weak isolation properties of a cloud services' component in a shared multi-tenant cloud system can be leveraged upon by attackers to cause data breach due to compromised cloud data security. Best practices should be employed for data management and client implementation to guide against shared technology vulnerabilities.

- **Lacking due diligence**: Lack of due diligence entails the failure of a cloud consumer to evaluate the CSPs for availability of cloud services with best practices resulting in application security problems. Due diligence involves verification of the availability of appropriate security controls, standards and accreditations such as DCS, HIPAA, ISO 9001 and PCI owned by CSPs to meet standard service requirements of the customers.

- **Advanced Persistent Threats (APT)**: An APT is a very hard-to-detect adaptive program that penetrates the cloud infrastructure of an organization to steal data via techniques such as direct hacking, use of unsecured third-party APIs, spear phishing, attack code on USB devices, and penetration through the network. This can be mitigated via frequent infrastructure monitoring, advanced security controls and rigid process management.

- **Abuse of cloud services**: Poorly secured cloud service deployments, fraudulent account sign-ups via payment interfaces, and free cloud service trials expose cloud computing models to malicious attacks.

- **Metadata spoofing attack**: The metadata of cloud service contains information of the user about different services, including location of different network components, format of data or security requirements. This information can be modified by attackers to redirect users to a different place, a concept similar to DNS poisoning.

Security techniques for threats protection

To mitigate against the threats discussed in the previous section, the following security measures must be taken into consideration to secure the cloud:

Protection from Data Breaches:

- Encrypt sensitive data before the actual storage on cloud and in the network using some efficient key management algorithm.
- Implement proper isolation among virtual machines to guide against information leakage.
- Ensure proper access controls are implemented against unauthorized access.
- Conduct a risk assessment of the cloud environment to identify the storage of sensitive data and its transmission between various services and networks.
- Use attributed-based encryption to secure data before storage such that only users with access attributes and keys can access the data.
- Use fine-grained and scalable data access control.

Protection from data loss:

- Maintain backup of all cloud data for replication purpose in the event of data loss.
- Protect data backup to maintain data metadata security properties such as integrity and confidentiality.

Protection from account or service hijacking:

- Monitor network traffic and nodes in cloud to detect malicious activities via network security features like the **intrusion detection systems (IDS)**.
- Ensure proper implementation of identity and access management to avoid unauthorized access to account credentials.
- Implement multi-factor authentication for remote access using at least two credentials.

- Audit all users' privileged activities along with their associated information security events.

Protection from DoS:

- Identify and implement all the basic security requirements of cloud network, applications, databases, and other services.

- Verify and close every potential loop hole that can be exploited by attackers by testing applications after designing.

- Prevent DDOS attacks by having extra network bandwidth, using **intrusion detection system (IDS)** that verify network requests before reaching the cloud server, and maintaining a backup of IP pools for urgent cases.

- Secure cloud from DDOS using IDS in a virtual machine such that when an intrusion detection system detects an abnormal increase in inbound traffic, the targeted applications are transferred to VMs hosted on another data center.

Protection from insecure Interfaces and APIs:

- Developers should design APIs via the principles of trusted computing.

- Cloud providers must ensure that APIs implemented in the cloud are designed securely and checked before deployment for possible flaws.

- Implement strong authentication mechanisms and access controls to secure data and services from insecure interfaces and APIs by following the **Open Web Application Security Project (OWASP)**.

- Customers must analyze the interfaces and APIs of cloud providers before migrating their data to cloud.

Protection from malicious insiders:

- Limit the hardware and infrastructure access to the authorized users only.

- Service providers must implement and enforce strong access control and segregation of duties in the management layer to restrict administrator access to only their authorized data and applications.

- Audit employees routinely for possible suspicious behavior.

- Make the employee behavior requirements a part of legal contract and take appropriate action(s) against anyone involved in malicious activities.

- Implement appropriate encryption in storage and public networks.

Protection from abuse of cloud services:

- Identify malicious customers via strict initial registration and validation processes.

- Make policies that allow the protection of critical organizational assets a part of the SLA between the user and service provider.

- Ensure the network monitoring process is comprehensive enough to detect malicious packets.

- Install all the updated security devices in the network.

Protection from insufficient due diligence:

- Organizations should fully understand the scope of risks associated with cloud before migrating their business and critical assets to it.

- Service providers must disclose the applicable logs and infrastructure such as a firewall to consumers to take measures for securing their applications and data.

- The provider must set up requirements for implementing cloud applications and services using industry standards.

- A cloud provider must conduct risk assessment using quantitative and qualitative methods periodically to check the storage, flow and processing of data.

Protection from Shared Technology Vulnerabilities:

- A hypervisor must be secured to ensure proper functioning of other virtualization components and implementing isolation between VMs.

- Create and use baseline requirements for all cloud components in the design of the cloud architecture.

- A service provider should monitor the vulnerabilities in the cloud environment and release patches to fix those vulnerabilities periodically.

Cloud service level agreements (SLA) practices

A SLA is a formal and legal contract document containing a set of well-negotiated objectives, purpose, terms and conditions of business engagements between the cloud service providers and the cloud users which has been mutually agreed to. A SLA also contains details of the cloud services to be rendered, benefits and drawbacks of the cloud, responsibilities, cloud deployment and security challenges as well as guarantees and warranties of the services. This makes the pros and cons of the cloud adoption realities more transparent to prospective cloud consumers and serves as a common ground for interactions between cloud consumers and cloud service providers with both participating parties having a clear understanding of their pre-defined responsibilities, the mutually-agreed terms and conditions. These agreements might include but not limited to *what cloud services will be offered*, *the mode of service delivery* and who will be responsible for the execution, monitoring, reporting failures, security, and privacy responsibilities.

Components of a cloud SLA

A typical cloud service level agreement is composed of a service guarantee, service guarantee time period, service guarantee granularity, service guarantee exclusion, service credit, and service violation measurement and reporting:

- **Service guarantee**: This establishes the metrics which a cloud provider seeks to achieve within a service guarantee time period. Such metrics include cloud service performance quality evaluation parameters like disaster recovery, response time, availability and fault resolution time, and so on. When these metrics are quantified and associated with a value, then a service guarantee emerges. Examples of a service guarantee includes response time (< 40ms), fault resolution time (within 30 minutes of detection), availability (98.7%), and so on, and a decline by the service provider from meeting up with the service guarantee will add up as a service credit to the cloud consumer.

- **Service guarantee time period**: This is the acceptable period of time required for a service guarantee to be met. It could be on monthly, daily or hourly basis and as well could be based on some other arrangements like the time span since the last system update was made, and so on.

- **Service guarantee granularity**: This typifies the resources scale on which a provider defines a service guarantee. This granularity can be on per instance, per data center, per service, on per transaction basis or a service guarantee granularity can also be calculated as a collection of the concerned resources like transactions or instances.

- **Service guarantee exclusions**: These are the potential possibilities and likely events that are not included in the service guarantee metric calculations. These exclusions might typically include instances like downtime due to a scheduled maintenance or abuse of the service by the cloud service consumer.

- **Service credit**: This is the accrued amount in favor of the cloud consumer or brought forward towards future payments for new services if a service guarantee is violated by a cloud service provider.

- **Service violation measurement and reporting**: This identifies true violations of a service guarantee by defining how and who is responsible for measuring and reporting of such violation(s), respectively.

Types of SLAs

Service level agreements can be multilevel, customer level, or service level based on the customer or the service.

- **Customer-based SLA**: This is an agreement with the entity personal group which covers all services used by the users.

- **Service-based SLA**: This is an agreement between the cloud service provider and all registered users using the service.

- **Multilevel SLA**: This kind of SLA consists of different levels with each containing the conditions of different customers using the same service.

- **Customer level SLA**: This document contains records of all service level management problems related to a group of certain users.

- **Service level SLA**: This document contains records of all service level management problems related to a specific service for some group of users.

Significance of SLAs:

- It provides concise and transparent understanding of the cloud services and the cloud service providers.

- It presents a list of all available services a service provider could provide with an associated detailed specification and description of each service.

- It provides detailed information regarding business requirements and objectives in a transparent manner, including the respective expected responsibilities of the cloud consumers and the cloud service providers.

- It showcases critical privacy and security management policies for the cloud environment.

- It offers service-oriented monitoring of performance, service quality, responsibilities, and priorities.

- It presents the service management requirements in a transparent manner if an event of a cloud service failure occurs.

Cloud vendors

Some of the common cloud vendors include Salesforce, RackSpace, IBM, AT&T and HP:

- **Salesforce**: In March 1999, Marc Benioff, Dave Moellenhoff, Parker Harris and Frank Dominguez started Salesforce.com as a company having specialty in **Software-as-a-Service (SaaS)**. It has its headquarters in San Francisco,

California and regional headquarters in Tokyo, Singapore and Dublin with over 2,100,000 subscribers, a customer base of 82,400 and translated services in over 16 languages. Services provided by Salesforce.com include sales cloud, service cloud and social chatter via its advanced **Customer Relationship Management (CRM)** system and CRM products.

- **RackSpace**: RackSpace is an IT hosting company that started off as an application development company. It is currently located in San Antonio, Texas, USA with data centers in Illinois, Hong Kong, Virginia, Australia, the United Kingdom, Texas and Hong Kong. RackSpace runs an intensive and managed service-level business models intended for different businesses and are strongly supported via a ticket system, live chat, e-mail and telephone. The intensive service level is characterized by 'proactive' support with numerous proactive services provided and customer-centered technical renditions. However, the managed service level is characterized by 'on-demand' support and proactive services with flexibility such that the customer can contact Rackspace for additional support when needed. The present Rackspace's cloud computing system started with white-labeling hosting services in 2006 under the name Mosso Inc. By 2008, Rackspace became a Slicehost, virtual servers' provider and Jungle Disk provider for online backup software and services. By 2012, Rackspace could implement OpenStack computing for their cloud servers' products. Other add-on services rendered include block storage, server monitoring, databases and virtual networking.

- **International Business Machines (IBM)**: The IBM cloud structure was initiated as physical hardware platforms of cloud having built-in support for virtualization. The cloud technologies of IBM combine mainframes with virtualization, with profound success on the development of virtual machines in 1960. By 2007, IBM started building enterprise-level clouds. However, the IBM SmartCloud solutions have been experiencing massive adoption since 2011. IBM cloud solutions, software and services are currently subscribed by over 20 million active end-user customers globally. IBM cloud services are enumerated as follows:

- **Design and build**: Basically, design and build a cloud and then migrate to cloud.

- **Secure and manage**: Secure customers' cloud and manage their IT security and infrastructure with cloud.

- **Store and virtualize**: Store customers' data in the cloud and virtualize their infrastructure with cloud.

- **Recovery**: Back up and recover your critical business data based on requirements.

- **AT&T Synaptic**: AT&T is a successor of the old Southwestern Bell company, a telephone company owned by Alexander Graham Bell dated to as far back as 1982. Today, AT&T offers a **Platform-as-a-Service (PaaS)** cloud service platform, a complete integrated development environment to build and deploy custom applications in no time, execute them reliably and manage them easily across the full application lifecycle. The AT&T PaaS platform is characterized by cloud-based self-service tools, high performance and low per-user pricing model. The AT&T PaaS cloud-based, self-service tools include:

- An online sign up for AT&T PaaS

- Virtual resources provisioning

- Quick creation and setup of a development environment

The unparalleled advantages of adopting the AT&T PaaS platform include:

- Elimination of long procurement cycles

- Reduction in expenditure for capital equipments

- Speedy development with 50 pre-loaded, customizable templates

- Seamless development of applications without any coding required

- Quick automation, modification and support for a wide range of business activities

- Supporting non-traditional developers to build applications

- **Hewlett Packard (HP)**: HP inaugurated cloud services offering in 2011 and provisioned HP Cloud Object Storage, HP Cloud content delivery network and HP Cloud Compute as publicly available in 2012. Furthermore, the **HP Cloud Services Enablement for Infrastructure-as-a-Service (HP-CSE-for-IaaS)** solution is a pre-integrated, end-to-end solution for communications service providers that enables them to create a complete compute services-on-demand offering to support the businesses of their customer base. HP-CSE-for-IaaS is a composite solution containing the HP Cloud Service Automation, HP Aggregation Platform for SaaS and HP BladeSystem Matrix servers. The **HP Cloud Service Automation (HP CSA)** software runs on the HP-CSE-for-IaaS platform to enhance the deployment of the successful private cloud architecture.

    Basically, HP CSA provides a unified and consistent approach to the complete lifecycle management of the critical IT processes and resources in both public and private cloud environments, including application and infrastructure provisioning, monitoring, patching, and compliance. HP Cloud services solutions include web and mobile applications, Big Data processing, Collaboration-as-a-Service, Enterprise Application Migration,

Backup-as-a-Service, Data Archival-as-a-Service, PC and Mobile Backup and Synchronization as well as Test & Development Converged Cloud. In the same vein, HP Cloud services products include HP Cloud Compute, HP Cloud Block Storage, HP Cloud Object Storage, HP Cloud Identity Service, HP Cloud **Content Delivery Network** (**CDN**), HP Cloud Application Platform-as-a-Service, and HP Cloud Relational Database for MySQL.

Issues of Quality of Cloud Services

Quality of Services (**QoS**) depicts a considerable level of performance expected of a service provider in terms of the utility derived from the cloud service being provided to a cloud service consumer. The utility derived is fundamental and highly dependent on the type of cloud service and application, the business objectives and regulatory requirements of the cloud service consumers. Quality of cloud services depicts the level of minimum expected satisfaction derived from the use of cloud services (including the platform, application or infrastructure) based on reliability, performance, availability, and compliance with customers' business requirements provisioned by a cloud service provider or broker. Cloud QoS can be evaluated along with performance utility features, economic, security and quality assurance dimensions. Performance quality evaluation measures of the cloud services are summarized and presented in *Table 6.5*. In Tables (*6.6, 6.7 and 6.8*), the economic, security and general quality assurance evaluation parameters are presented, respectively:

Measures	Description	Metrics
Communication	This measures the quality of the efficiency of the connection and data transfer between internal service instances, different cloud services, or between the external consumer and the cloud.	Packet loss frequency
		Connection error rate
		MPI transfer bit/byte speed
		MPI transfer delay
Computation	This represents the computing task and/or data processing in the cloud.	CPU load (%)
		Benchmark OP (FLOP) Rate
		Instance efficiency (% CPU peak)

Measures	Description	Metrics
Memory	This defines the efficiency in the rate of use of temporarily stored information contained in slow-accessed hard disk drive.	Mean hit time (s)
		Memory bit/byte speed (MB/s, GB/s)
		Random memory update rate
		Response time (ms)
Time	This specifies the time taken to run a project to completion without violating quality requirement constraints.	Computation time
		Communication time

Table 6.5

The following table represents the economic quality features of cloud services:

Measures	Description	Metrics
Cost	This is the total cost associated with the use of a cloud service. It is evaluated to reflect the economic benefits of adopting cloud to drive business objectives over a period of time.	Total cost ($)
		FLOP cost (cent/FLOP, $/GFLOP)
		Supported users on a fixed budget
		Component resource cost ($)
		Price/performance ratio
		Cost over a fixed time ($/year)
Cloud (rapid) elasticity	This quality attribute describes the degree of on-demand flexibility of a cloud service to workload changes via dynamic provisioning (scaling-up) and de-provisioning (scaling-down) of public cloud infrastructure resources on a pay-as-you-grow or pay-per-use model. It also significantly typifies the speed of responses used to adjust workload.	Boot time (second)
		Suspend time (second)
		Delete time (second)
		Provision (or deployment) time (second)
		Total acquisition time (second)

Table 6.6

The following table represents security quality requirements:

Measures	Description	Metrics
Data security	This attribute refers to a consolidated set of technologies, policies, controls, and systems employed to protect data, applications components and other infrastructure of cloud systems.	Is SSL applicable
		Communication latency over SSL
		Auditability
Authentication	This attribute is responsible for the verification and management of valid identities of both users and devices on the cloud.	Meaning
		Sensitivity
		Effectiveness
		Confidentiality

Table 6.7

The following table shows general quality assurance requirements for cloud services:

Measures	Description	Metrics
Availability	This phenomenal attribute depicts the ability to access cloud services, data and tools anytime and anywhere.	Flexibility
		Accuracy
		Response time
Scalability	This depicts the ability to enhance the resizable computing power of the service provider's system by adding more workload without affecting the system's performance.	Average of assigned resources among the requested resources
Reliability	This is a critical measure of the system's capability to continuously provision a service with an acceptable degree of efficiency without malfunctioning.	Service constancy
		Accuracy of service
		Fault tolerance
		Maturity
		Recoverability

Measures	Description	Metrics
Efficiency	This is a measure of the performance level derived from the use of the least amount of resources to provide a service relative to energy, time, cost expended, and level of resource utilization with the highest utility after the service runs into completion.	Utilization of resource
		Ratio of waiting time
		Time behavior
Reusability	This measures the degree to which a resource, a component, an application or a system may be reused in a number of other programs or applications.	Readability
		Coverage of variability
		Publicity
Composability	This refers to a measure of interoperability characteristics.	Service Modularity
		Service interoperability
Adaptability	This measures the capacity of a solution, an application, a service or a system to be modified for new utilization by other services, applications or systems.	Completeness of variant set
		Coverage of variability
Usability	This is the potential degree to which a service could be used by particular consumers to meet their business objectives based on ease-of-use and consistency.	Operability
		Attractiveness
		Learn ability
Modifiability	This depicts the ease with which a cloud service and/or associated component(s) can be modified to improve performance, correct errors or adapt to a changed and different environment rapidly and cost-effectively.	**Mean Time To Change (MTTC)**

Measures	Description	Metrics
Sustainability	This depicts the environmental effect of the cloud service employed. It measures how well the needs of a customer are satisfied and how the social and environmental performance of the entire cloud service has been significantly improved.	**Data Centre Performance per Energy (DPPE)** parameter
		Power Usage Efficiency (PUE)

Table 6.8

Techniques for providing QoS to the cloud applications

A number of standard techniques to achieve QoS of cloud applications include scheduling, admission control and dynamic resource provisioning:

- **Scheduling**: Cloud service scheduling can be system level or user level. System level scheduling addresses resource management issues in cloud computing data centers. The system level scheduling ensures that several multiple requests from the users are scheduled to available physical machines in the data center dynamically. This might involve the use of auction-based schedulers to manage the demand, allocation, de-allocation, and reallocation of cloud resources. On the other hand, user level scheduling manages service issues arising between a cloud service consumer and the cloud service provider with respect to the provisioned service(s). It might require a re-evaluation of the service level agreement previously contracted between the service provider and the consumer.

- **Admission control**: At the admission control time, this mechanism offers the service provider a huge capacity to consider the basic computational and networking resources and extra potential resources' requirements that would be needed to drive flexibility of service runtime towards optimal service performance.

- **Dynamic resource provisioning**: This involves the selection, deployment and run-time management of software (load balancers, file and database servers) and hardware resources (network, CPU, storage, and so on) for ensuring guaranteed satisfaction of cloud service performance to the end-users. This is a fundamental QoS requirement ensuring that cloud workloads are provisioned with appropriate resources. Parameters for resource provisioning include response time, cost, revenue maximization, fault tolerance, reduced SLA violation, and reduced power consumption.

Migration of a local server into cloud

Migration of a local server (database, file and other resources) into the cloud is a pretty good idea due to the profound benefits that cloud computing offers. Consequentially, cloud computing comes with some challenges which must be considered before making a decision of what goes into the cloud and what stays behind. Therefore, the first initial step of migrating an organization's resources into the cloud starts by conducting a preliminary checklist of some important definitions of needs and requirements with its associated risk factors, followed by extensive planning and then migration.

Preliminary checklist/planning for migration

Some important preliminary considerations when planning to migrate traditional computing infrastructures into the cloud include the following:

- Identify all potential benefits for moving from the existing computing infrastructure to cloud services.

- Confirm that the traditional computing infrastructure suits cloud-based services.

- Prepare a cost/opportunity and risk evaluation model to guide decision making about where, when, and how cloud computing services can be adopted.

- Develop a standard guideline and blueprint to optimize the current computing resources for migration to the cloud services (public/private).

- Identify which current computing resources can/cannot be migrated into the public cloud based on the organization's data privacy policy, risk-mitigation and/or legal reasons.

- Identify and prepare in-house technical how-to competencies that will be needed to manage effective adoption of cloud services.

- Appoint a cross-functional team to continually monitor which new services, providers, and standards are available, and to determine if they affect the blueprint.

- Assess technical problems that must be tackled when migrating any current resource (data/application) into a cloud environment.

- Confirm that the current networking/computing environment is ready for migration into a cloud environment.

Migration steps

After a successful preliminary planning, the following are the basic steps required to migrate data, application and business services into a cloud environment. This is depicted in *Figure 6.4*:

- **Analyze business requirement**: The prospective cloud service consumer must clearly define and analyze the purpose of migrating an application, data, a component or a legacy system into a cloud computing environment. This is best achieved by establishing the overall business goals and objectives and how the migration can help to achieve them. Furthermore, the prospective cloud service consumer should analyze the data attributes and requirements and understand how the proposed migration to a different computing environment is liable to threaten the integrity of sensitive data for migration:

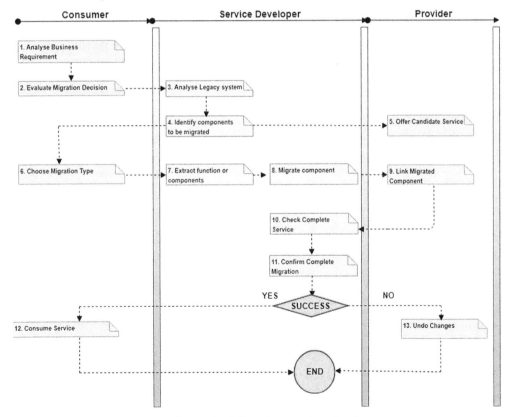

Figure 6.4 Migration steps to cloud

- **Evaluate migration decision**: At this stage, the significance, purpose, goals, scope and limitations for migration of projects, including data, application and other components into the cloud are defined and assessed. Migration into the cloud space are often justified by cost savings, scalability, enhanced productivity and capabilities to adapt functionality to new markets, and so on. Business requirements must be defined by the potential cloud service consumer and how these requirements have an impact on the realization of the organization's goals and objectives must be identified and understood before a final migration decision is made.

- **Analyze legacy system**: This requires due diligence in analyzing, understanding and documenting the existing system, its associated components and all the related and associated documentation and information regarding the system implementation. For *black box* systems, where there is no access to the underlying source program, the inputs, system responses and the outputs must be analyzed and documented. For *white box* systems characterized by available and accessible source code, reverse engineering can be employed to break down the system into data and functions. Furthermore, the system is broken down along with the dimension of the type of functions where each function is mapped functionally to specific business objective(s) and requirements. The decision on which of the legacy system functions to migrate into a cloud environment becomes easier to make.

- **Identify component(s) to be migrated**: Having identified the functions to migrate in the previous step, the next step is to identify components to migrate and their associated configurations. Examples of such components include a function, database, an application layer, an algorithm or the whole legacy system. However, efforts should be made to ensure due privacy and security preservation of the components via data encryption or other encoding techniques.

- **Offer candidate service**: This is a necessary step to identify already deployed services in cloud environments which can readily serve as a migration solution based on the consumer's business requirements, including the expected security level as contained in contracts and SLAs. To achieve this, a service search can be performed either by the prospective consumer or a cloud service broker. Furthermore, retrieved services must be compared with the expected cloud service behavior that matches the consumer's business requirements by analyzing the input, the output and the performance level with the expected results. It is vividly possible not to find a service that meets the requirements, or an incomplete service, or a service that perfectly meets the expected solutions.

- **Choose migration type**: In a bid to choose the migration type, it is important that the prospective cloud service consumer validates the identified components, the service candidate (provided there is any) and the required resources for the migration. In addition, the consumer is expected to specify the type of migration that meets the business requirements and fulfills its objectives. If a candidate service that meets business requirements is found, the consumer should analyze the rules for the contract for services.

- **Function or component**: At this stage, the cloud service provider locates and extracts each component that has been identified by the prospective cloud service consumer for its migration via loose coupling and high modularity approaches.

- **Migrate component**: At this level, the data and source code of the current system is backed up for reuse if the need to rollback changes is made to a component during migration. Depending on the migration type, this also involves the development of appropriate interfaces, function prototyping and conversion as well as mapping of the data schema to the new datastore.

- **Link migrated component**: At this stage, the software solution is deployed into the cloud system. Its configuration as a service from the cloud service provider's environment is tested. Furthermore, connections and configurations are established to synchronize the contracted services to the service consumer environment. More often than not, a cloud service carrier is engaged to securely transport all the migrated components to the provider systems.

- **Check complete service**: The migrated legacy system, applications, solutions, components and data are verified, validated and tested at the cloud service provider's environment to ascertain that the migrated services and resources exhibit the correct behavior after the migration. This helps to confirm that the functionality of the migrated system is available and accessible in the new system environment. The other important quality analysis to conduct unit test, integration test, acceptance test, and pilot test before the control of functionalities of the system is transferred to the new system.

- **Confirm complete migration**: Having confirmed that the migrated services are functioning as expected, the quality assurance test should be conducted relative to the predefined standards and business requirements of the organization. Appropriate documentation related to the service implementation, configuration settings and all changes made during the migration must be made.

- **Consume service**: The service consumer should use the service as expected, evaluate the quality of the service periodically and also understand the new processes and necessary changes made to the initial organization procedures due to the migration.

- **Undo change**: The cloud service consumer may use a backup copy of all migrated services, applications and data to reverse the entire migration process if it is discovered that the migration process violated the minimum acceptable quality standards required or if the entire migration failed.

Types of migration for cloud-enabled applications

There are basically four types of cloud-enabled migrations which are Type I, Type II, Type III, and Type IV discussed as follows:

- **Type I**: Replace component(s) with cloud offerings. This is the least invasive type of migration, where one or more (architectural) components are replaced by cloud services. As a result, data and/or business logic have to be migrated to the cloud service. A series of configurations, rewiring and adaptation activities to cope with possible incompatibilities may be triggered as part of this migration. Using Google App Engine Datastore in place of a local MySQL database is an example of this migration type.

- **Type II**: Partially migrate some of the application functionality to the cloud. This type entails migrating one or more application layers, or a set of architectural components from one or more layers implementing a particular functionality to the cloud. Using a combination of Amazon SimpleDB and EC2 instances to host the auditing data and business logic for HIC is an example of such a migration.

- **Type III**: This is a classic migration in which the entire software stack of the application is migrated to the cloud. This type of migration makes encapsulation in virtual machines and execution in the cloud possible.

- **Type IV**: This type of migration is also known as **Cloudify the application**. It typifies a complete migration of the application, data and business logic to the cloud as well as the associated functions and components to manage possible incompatibilities. However, the application functionality is implemented as a composition of services running on the cloud.

Trust management

Trust is one of the most concerned challenges straining rapid adoption and growth of cloud computing. A key technical solution requires trust to be critically managed at all levels of the cloud computing adoption lifecycle. Trust management is the assurance component for establishing and maintaining successful relational exchanges among all stakeholders in a cloud environment. In a highly competitive and distributed service environment, cloud service(s) consumers are uncertain about trustworthiness and dependability of cloud service providers. As a result, trust management procedures assist potential cloud service consumers to reliably identify trustworthy cloud providers, and to devise effective means to manage the trust relationships among business partners in cloud environment. The trust level is derived from the analysis of the cloud service rating feedback supplied by trading partners after a transaction is completed successfully. Accumulation of these trust values generated from past transactions can be used to provide important reference points to potential consumers in the future. Positive trust values increase trust level and strengthens relationship and dependability of the cloud service consumer on the quality of services of the cloud service provider.

Trust management evaluation attributes

A **Trust Management (TM)** system should be able to measure the degree of truthfulness of cloud-services via the following attributes:

- **Data integrity**: This includes service requirements such as privacy, data security, and accuracy.

- **Security**: Cloud service providers must put up mechanisms to protect their consumer's personal information and data securely.

- **Privacy**: The cloud service providers should maintain privacy of sensitive information of their customers for continued trustworthiness and integrity.

- **Credibility**: This is the degree of quality of a cloud service provided to a cloud service consumer by a cloud service provider.

- **Turnaround efficiency**: This includes both the actual and the promised turnaround times. The actual turnaround time is the time expended from the start of a cloud consumer application for a service and the provisioning of this service. On the other hand, the promised turnaround time is the expected duration of time by the cloud service provider for a service to run to completion.

- **Availability**: This measures the degree of uptime and accessibility of resources, services or components provisioned by a cloud service provider.

- **Reliability/success rate**: This defines the degree of compliance of a cloud service provider to provide mutually agreed upon services based on the consumer's business requirement specifications and duration.

- **Adaptability**: This reflects redundant provisioning of data storage and processing facilities to manage potential single point of failure events.

- **SLA**: This is an official document that clearly specifies technical and functional descriptions to be complied by the cloud service provider.

- **Customer support**: This is the actual support (technical, feedback, security, and so on) offered by the cloud service provider to its consumers.

- **User feedback**: This is a post-service experience scoring by a cloud consumer on the performance and quality of service(s) being rendered by the cloud service provider.

Cloud trust management techniques

Trust management techniques are classified into four techniques, namely, policy-based, recommendation-based, reputation-based, and prediction-based:

- **Policy-based trust management**: With this technique, a set of policies is adopted to evaluate trust. Each policy is used to control the authorization level and to specify a minimum expected trust threshold to authorize the access. The trust thresholds can be obtained via either the trust results or credentials. Result-based thresholds are retrieved via a monitoring and auditing approach (using the SLA), entities credibility approach (which measures the qualitative and quantitative features of the cloud services being provisioned) and the feedback credibility approach (that specifies a set of parameters to measure the experience of the cloud service consumers). In credential-based threshold, credentials are issued following standards like **Security Assertion Markup Language (SAML)** and **Simple Public Key Infrastructure (SPKI)**. The major disadvantage is that it does not consider the value of past interactions and history of the participants. The policy-based trust management approach supports all the cloud service deployment models.

- **Recommendation-based trust management**: In this approach, recommendations are requested by an inquiring entity from some participants with previous interactions and knowledge about the trusted parties. However, recommendations can be explicit or transitive in nature. Explicit recommendation occurs when a cloud service consumer directly recommends a particular cloud service to their established trusted contacts. Similarly, a transitive recommendation occurs if a particular cloud service is trusted by a cloud service consumer if at least one of their trusted contacts trusts the cloud service. The main disadvantage of this model is that the degree of satisfaction for recommendation of a service is based on the perspective of the entity and might not encompass other relevant attributes of the cloud service that may be important to the prospective consumer. Recommendation-based trust management supports all the cloud service deployment models.

- **Reputation-based trust management**: This approach follows a community-based (social network-based) aggregation of opinions on trust towards an entity. Normally, an entity with the highest reputation trust value is usually trusted by many other entities. One benefit of this approach is the wider perspective of past consumers from many different situations about the performance of the cloud service provider. On the other hand, it requires a large number of entities to provide their opinion and additionally, such entities are expected to be familiar with the attributes being evaluated. In the same vein, trust feedback sources are usually unknown due to a large sample space. Examples of some reputation-based trust management systems include Amazon and eBay. This approach also supports all the three cloud service deployment models.

- **Prediction-based trust management**: In this approach, a trust threshold is computed based on the similarity of the capabilities and interests between two entities. This is commonly determined using similarity measurements like cosine similarity to establish possibility of trust between the entities. This approach is the most appropriate in situations with limited or no prior information about the cloud service's previous interactions. However, it does not guarantee accurate trust evaluation results.

Summary

- Cloud security issues and challenges include but are not limited to data breaches, data loss, network security, data locality, data access, system vulnerabilities, account hijacking, malicious insider, and advanced persistent threats.

- The cloud security architecture spans four layers which are the user layer, the service provider layer, the virtual machine layer and the data center layer.

- Cloud monitoring and management solutions include Amazon CloudWatch, private cloud monitoring system, cloud management system, runtime model for cloud monitoring, and flexible automated cloud monitoring slices.

- Legal issues in cloud computing can involve phenomenon such as data location, governing law and jurisdiction, privacy and confidentiality, data security, data access for e-discovery, end-users' responsibility, inappropriate and unauthorized usage, end-users' account suspension, emergency security issues, service suspension and termination, data ownership, publicity, service level agreements, disclaimer of warranty, customer indemnification, vendor indemnification, contract modifications, incorporation of URL terms, and automatic renewal.

- Risk management is defined as 'the process of identifying, assessing and controlling threats to an organization's capital and earnings.'

- Data privacy risks in the cloud include those associated with access control, internal segmentation, sub-contractors, data ownership, e-discovery, data censorship, and encryption.

- Cloud disaster recovery is an IaaS solution that provisions backup and recovery for critical dedicated server machines hosting enterprise-level data applications, (for example, Oracle, MySQL), located on a remote offsite cloud server.

- Five major cloud disaster recovery requirements include Recovery Point Objective (RPO), Recovery Time Objective (RTO), performance, consistency, and geographical separation.

- Mechanisms for cloud disaster recovery include network reconfiguration, security and isolation, virtual machine migration, and cloning.

- Threats undermining the survival and performance of the cloud computing ecosystem include but are not limited to data breaches, data losses, malicious insiders, Denial of Service (DoS) attacks, Distributed Denial of Service (DDoS) attacks, vulnerable systems and APIs, weak authentication and identity management, account hijacking, shared technology vulnerabilities, lacking due diligence, advanced persistent threats, abuse of cloud services, and metadata spoofing attack.

- A Cloud Service Level Agreement (SLA) is a formal and legal contract document containing a set of well negotiated objectives, purpose, terms and conditions of business engagements between the cloud service providers and the cloud users which has been mutually agreed to.

- A typical cloud service level agreement is composed of a service guarantee, service guarantee time period, service guarantee granularity, service guarantee exclusion, service credit, and service violation measurement and reporting.

- Types of service level agreements can be multilevel, customer level, service level, customer-based or service-based.

- Some of the common cloud vendors include Salesforce, RackSpace, IBM, AT&T and HP.

- Quality of cloud services depicts the level of minimum expected satisfaction derived from the use of cloud services (including the platform, application or infrastructure) based on reliability, performance, availability and compliance with the customers' business requirements provisioned by a cloud service provider or broker. Cloud QoS can be evaluated along with performance utility features, economic, security, and quality assurance dimensions.

- A number of standard techniques to achieve QoS of cloud applications include scheduling, admission control and dynamic resource provisioning.

- The basic orderly steps required to migrate data, application and business services into a cloud environment are Business Requirement Analysis, Migration Decision Evaluation, Legacy System Analysis, Identification of component(s) to be migrated, Offering of Candidate Service, Choosing Migration Type, Function or Component, Migration of Component, Linking of Migrated Component, Checking Complete Service, Confirming Complete Migration, Consumption of Service and Undo Change.

- The four basic types of cloud-enabled migrations are Type I, Type II, Type III, and Type IV.

- Trust management evaluation attributes include data integrity, security, privacy, credibility, turnaround efficiency, availability, reliability/success rate, adaptability, SLA, customer support, and user feedback.

- Trust management techniques are classified into four, namely, policy-based, recommendation-based, reputation-based, and prediction-based.

Exercise

Tick the correct option

1. Potential defense mechanism to repudiation include all of the following except
    a. Digital signatures
    b. Time stamps
    c. Audit trails
    d. Filtering

2. Authentication, authorization, throttling, and filtering are potential defense mechanisms for
    a. Data tampering
    b. Repudiation
    c. Information Disclosure
    d. Denial of Service

3. The user layer of the cloud security architecture consists of the following except

    a. Authentication

    b. Security-as-a-Service

    c. Infrastructure

    d. Browser Security

4. Origin in browser security means

    a. Different browser

    b. Same application

    c. Source browser

    d. Origin application

5. Cloud monitoring requirements are all of the following except

    a. Migration,

    b. Scalability

    c. Portability

    d. Autonomy.

6. Which of the following is related to RESTful Web Services?

    a. CMS

    b. PCMONS

    c. RMCM

    d. CloudWatch

7. When an unauthorized intruder accesses, copies or transmits private, confidential or sensitive data belonging to a person or organization, this phenomenon is known as

    a. Data loss

    b. Data access

    c. Data breach

    d. Data hack

8. A cloud service level agreement is composed of all of the following except

   a. Service guarantee

   b. Service guarantee time period

   c. Service guarantee granularity

   d. Service guarantee inclusions

9. BladeSystem matrix servers are products of which cloud vendor?

   a. IBM

   b. HP

   c. Salesforce

   d. RackSpace

10. Customer relationship management is associated with one of the following cloud vendors.

    a. IBM

    b. HP

    c. Salesforce

    d. RackSpace

11. HP Cloud Services Enablement for Infrastructure-as-a-Service is made up of all of the following except

    a. HP Cloud Service Automation

    b. HP CloudAutumn Matrix server

    c. HP Aggregation Platform for SaaS

    d. HP BladeSystem Matrix server

12. One of the following can be used to enhance the deployment of a successful private cloud architecture.

    a. HP Cloud Service Automation

    b. HP CloudAutumn Matrix server

    c. HP Aggregation Platform for SaaS

    d. HP BladeSystem Matrix server

13. Packet loss frequency is associated with which of the cloud QoS measures?

    a. Computation

    b. Communication

    c. Memory

    d. Transport

14. Maturity is associated with which of the cloud QoS measures?

    a. Adaptability

    b. Usability

    c. Reliability

    d. Efficiency

15. Power usage efficiency is associated with which of the cloud QoS measures?

    a. Sustainability

    b. Modifiability

    c. Reliability

    d. Reusability

16. Cosine similarity is associated with none of the following trust management except

    a. Reputation-based

    b. Prediction-based

    c. Recommendation-based

    d. Policy-based

17. Amazon and eBay are examples of which trust management?

    a. Reputation-based

    b. Prediction-based

    c. Recommendation-based

    d. Policy-based

18. Which of the following cloud-enabled migration is also known as Cloudify?

    a. Type I

    b. Type II

    c. Type III

    d. Type IV

19. Techniques for provisioning quality of service to the cloud applications include all of the following except:

    a. Admission control

    b. Scheduling

    c. Handoff

    d. Dynamic resource provisioning

20. 'Mean Time to Change' is associated with

    a. Modifiability

    b. Usability

    c. Reusability

    d. Sustainability

Answers

    1. d. Filtering

    2. d. Denial of Service

    3. c. Infrastructure

    4. b. Same application

    5. c. Portability

    6. a. CMS

    7. c. Data Breach

    8. d. Service guarantee inclusions

    9. b. HP

    10. c. Salesforce

    11. b. HP CloudAutumn Matrix server

    12. a. HP Cloud Service Automation

13. b. Communication

14. c. Reliability

15. a. Sustainability

16. b. Prediction-based

17. a. Reputation-based

18. d. Type IV

19. c. Handoff

20. a. Modifiability

Fill in the blanks

1. _____ refers to the ability to share sensitive data between number of users without violating the privileges granted by the data owner to each of the targeted user.

2. When a browser is incapable of generating cryptographically-valid XML tokens, such an attack is known as _____.

3. _____ involves the scripting of web pages for access and usage rights.

4. _____ uses IF-MAP standard to authorize users in real-time communication between the cloud provider and the consumer.

5. _____ is a typical attack aimed at injecting a malicious service performance module into a legitimate instance of a virtual machine.

6. _____ is a component of the virtual machine that enables host isolation and resource sharing.

7. _____ is the economics of cloud computing and a multi-tenancy architecture used in SaaS.

8. _____ can be referred to as a statistical concept associated with uncertain outcomes of business activities in the future.

9. _____ is the degree of quality of a cloud service provided to a cloud service consumer by a cloud service provider.

10. The resources scale on which a provider defines a service guarantee is known as _____.

11. _____ allows credentials to be issued following standards like Security Assertion Markup language (SAML) and Simple Public Key Infrastructure (SPKI).

12. _____ occurs when a cloud service consumer

directly recommends a particular cloud service to their established trusted contacts.

13. _____ is an official document that clearly specifies technical and functional descriptions to be complied by the cloud service provider.

14. _____is derived from the analysis of cloud service rating feedback supplied by trading partners after a transaction is completed successfully.

15. _____ reflects redundant provisioning of data storage and processing facilities to manage a potential single point of failure events.

16. _____ is the assurance component for establishing and maintaining successful relational exchanges among all stakeholders in a cloud environment.

17. _____involves the selection, deployment and run-time management of software and hardware resources for ensuring guaranteed satisfaction of cloud service performance to the end-users.

18. The speed of response to adjusted workload is known as _____.

19. _____ is a document that contains the records of all service level management problems related to a group of certain users.

20. _____ measures the quality of the efficiency of the connection and data transfer between internal service instances, different cloud services, or between external consumer and the cloud.

Answers:

1. Data confidentiality
2. attacks on browser-based cloud authentication
3. The legacy same origin policy
4. Trusted Platform Module (TPM)
5. Cloud Malware Injection Attack
6. Hypervisor
7. Data-at-rest
8. Risk
9. Credibility
10. Service guarantee granularity
11. credential-based threshold

12. Explicit recommendation

13. Service level agreement

14. The trust level

15. Adaptability

16. Trust management

17. Dynamic Resource Provisioning

18. cloud elasticity OR rapid elasticity (any one is correct)

19. Customer Level SLA

20. Communication

Descriptive Questions

1. List and describe any five cloud security threats with their associated potential defense mechanisms.

2. Differentiate between Advanced Persistent Threats and Account Hijacking.

3. What do you understand by the Cloud CIA Security Model?

4. With the aid of a well-labeled diagram, succinctly discuss your understanding of the cloud computing security architecture.

5. An example of an authentication standard adopted in the cloud is the Trusted Platform Module (TPM). Briefly discuss the phenomenal characteristics of this mitigation strategy.

6. Differentiate between hypervisors and rogue hypervisors in a cloud computing environment.

7. List and discuss any four points that must be held private in a cloud ecosystem.

8. List and discuss any three cloud performance monitoring and management solutions.

9. List and discuss any six legal issues associated with the cloud.

10. Define the broad term 'risk management' and discuss the high-level risk elements of the cloud security ecosystem.

11. Discuss your understanding of the cloud risk management framework.

12. Differentiate between data privacy risks and availability risk in the cloud with sufficient examples.

13. List and discuss any five major requirements for disaster recovery in a cloud system.

14. State any three differences between Traditional Disaster Recovery and Disaster Recovery as a service.

15. What are the common challenges associated with disaster recovery in the cloud?

16. Discuss with vivid examples any five security techniques often used for protection against threats in the cloud.

17. Discuss what you understand by Cloud Service Level Agreements, its components and types.

18. With the use of tabular diagrams only, differentiate between performance and economic quality evaluation measures of cloud services.

19. List the important preliminary considerations when planning to migrate traditional computing infrastructures into the cloud

20. With the aid of a well-labeled diagram, discuss the basic migration steps to a cloud.

21. What do you understand by trust management in the cloud?

22. Discuss any six trust management evaluation attributes.

23. List and discuss any four trust management techniques in the cloud.

CHAPTER 7

Cloud Computing Applications

"Cloud is about how you do computing, not where you do computing."

~ Paul Maritz, CEO of VMware

Objectives

- To learn about the basic concepts of the popular cloud computing applications

- To discuss the Google App Engine (GAE) in detail with services and architecture

- To learn about the Dropbox Cloud, Apple iCloud, Microsoft Windows Azure Cloud and Amazon Web Services (AWS) Cloud

- To learn about the various Google Apps: Gmail, Google docs, Google Calendar, Google Drive, Google Cloud Datastore

As technology makes noteworthy developments throughout the modern world, the most essential driving force is unquestionably a greater computing capacity with cloud computing serving as a significant element to this hi-tech progression. This Chapter lays emphasis on cloud computing, complemented by numerous applications and platforms that deliver cloud services. Additionally, prevailing companies along with their cloud computing products, cloud storage, and virtualization technologies are briefly explored.

In this chapter, we will cover the following topics:

- Introduction to Cloud Computing applications
- Google App Engine (GAE)
- Google Apps, Dropbox Cloud and Apple iCloud
- Microsoft Windows Azure and **Amazon Web Services (AWS)** Cloud
- Comparison of various cloud computing platforms—Dropbox, Google Drive, Amazon Cloud Drive and Apple iCloud Drive

Introducing cloud computing applications

Cloud computing is a rapidly emerging technology. With this technology, everyone using the World Wide Web can enjoy flexible computing power on-demand. As this alleviates the pressure on organizations investing in and maintaining costly computer hardware and software, it has become the new standard of computing. There are many firms that provide cloud environments for development, management, and provision of software.

Primarily, cloud computing allows people to use their PCs as well as various portable devices to access high-level computing power using an array of software and hardware infrastructure via a wide area network, without having to understand the cloud architecture. Numerous cloud service providers exist, but the top six cloud computing platforms are Google, Dropbox, Apple, Microsoft, and Amazon, and so on.

The following diagram shows the dominant cloud computing service providers:

Figure 7.1: Cloud service providers

There are three cloud service models, namely, **Software-as-a-Service (SaaS)**, **Platform-as-a-Service (PaaS)**, and **Infrastructure-as-a-service (IaaS)**. As the basic service provided by each cloud vendor is discussed, reference will be made to either SaaS, PaaS, or IaaS.

All three types of cloud service models—IaaS, PaaS and SaaS have been covered in Chapter 2.

Google App Engine

Web applications are created daily and circulated over the Internet for public consumption. Accordingly, environments for building, hosting, and running custom applications are needed by web app developers. **Google App Engine (GAE)** provides a fully managed application development platform (PaaS) that enables software developers to run on programming languages such as Java, Ruby, and Python written code on Google infrastructure.

Like other cloud platform service providers, GAE supports well-known web programming languages with an array of software development tools that allow developers to effortlessly create, deploy, and maintain their web applications. This allows developers to be more versatile while focusing on writing their code without being concerned with the underlying computing hardware and system software that their apps run on. Moreover, GAE is highly flexible and can automatically scale up or down when encountering fluctuations in web traffic and high data storage needs.

When considering costs, it is important to understand that there are no set up fees and no recurrent expenses when using GAE. The computing resources (storage and bandwidth) used by the hosted applications are measured in gigabytes and billed at reasonably modest rates. All web apps are allowed a maximum of 500 MB of free storage and enough processing power and bandwidth to support about 5 million page views per month. Anything above this threshold must be paid for based on the exact storage or bandwidth usage.

Google App Engine Services: GAE has a variety of services that function seamlessly to form the whole environment structure. These include:

- **Application environment**: This service allows developers to build web applications that can handle substantial amount of data traffic.

- **Sandbox**: This service permits the hosting of a developer's web app in a safe online environment and can only be viewed via the Internet through the URL by making an HTTP or HTTPs request.

- **Python runtime environment**: This service provides the means to understand various programming languages and execute the code written in them.

- **Datastore**: This service utilizes **Structured Query Language (SQL)** to offer a vast database repository to store and manage collections of data in virtual machine logs, scripts, and configuration files.

- **Google account**: This service authorizes clients to access all Google applications using a single Google account.

- **URL fetch**: This service permits the hosted web app's scripts to communicate with other apps or access various computing resources on Google's network infrastructure to issue HTTP and HTTPs requests and receive responses.

- **Mem Cache**: This service speeds up datastore queries in order to increase performance and decrease chances of session malfunction.

- **Image manipulation**: This service provides users with basic image editing capabilities.

GAE architecture: Developers utilize GAE to streamline the creation and deployment of web apps. These applications use the auto scaling computing power of an app engine as well as the integrated features like distributed in-memory cache, task queues and datastore to create dynamic applications rapidly and effortlessly as compared to stand-alone software development environments.

The following diagram shows the Google App Engine standard environment:

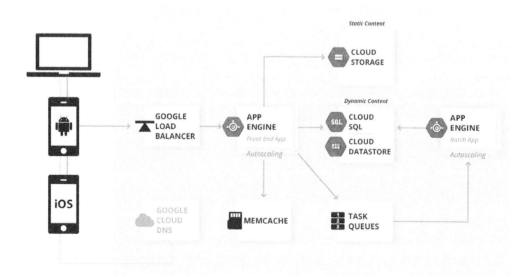

Figure 7.2: Google App Engine architecture

Google Apps

More prevalent in today's online computing environment, software is often provided to end users as a recurring service from vendors (SaaS). This service provision is commonly referred to as 'Apps' which is an abbreviated form of 'Applications'. Though they are one and the same, Apps are technically different because they are web-based (only accessible via the Internet) and can be launched on any PC or mobile device irrespective of its underlying operating system. This is a key advantage of the ubiquitous computing that cloud computing provides. Google, one of the leading online information service providers, offers a suite of SaaS services known as Google Apps.

Gmail

Gmail is a free web-based messaging system developed by Google. Not only does Gmail provide basic email service, but it also offers file sharing, video chatting, Google search, scheduling, and so on. This App can be accessed through any web browser irrespective of the user's geographic location as long as an Internet connection is present. After creating a google account, a user can access their Gmail and many other Google apps:

The following diagram shows a Google account being created:

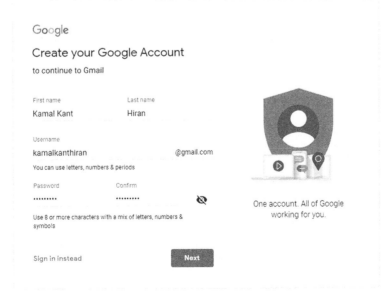

Figure 7.3: Google's account creator page

Google Docs

Google Docs is a free web-based document management.

The SaaS app allows users to create, edit, and view presentations, word documents, and spreadsheets. This app is compatible with a majority of word processing and presentation applications. One of its key features is the ability for users to simultaneously work on the same document which is extremely advantageous in collaborative work.

How to use Google Docs: The following is a brief description of a typical instance of Google Docs. Note: You must first create a google account to access Google Docs.

Starting a new document: On your PC or mobile device, click on the document type icon on the home screen at docs.google.com. The document will open and all edits will be saved in the Google Drive.

Editing and formatting: On your PC or mobile device, open a document in Google Docs. You can edit and format the document in the same manner as you would do on any standard desktop word processing document such as MS Word.

Sharing and working with others: You can share files and folders with people and choose whether they can view, edit, or comment on them.

The following diagram shows a snapshot of a Word document in Google Docs:

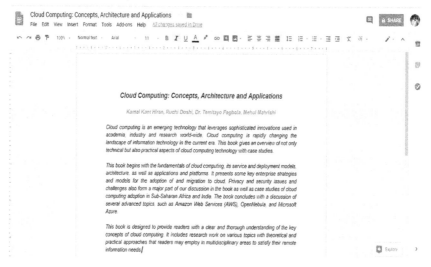

Figure 7.4. Google Docs Word Processing

Google Calendar

Google Calendar is a free time management and SaaS app that allows users to create and modify calendars in order to keep track of their personal and professional events. A snapshot of Google Calendar is shown in the following diagram:

Figure 7.5. Google Calendar

Google Drive

Google Drive is a free file storage SaaS that allows users to store and access files located in the cloud. This app is revered as one of the most resourceful cloud storage services because of its ability to synchronize stored files across all the user's PCs and mobile devices. Another key advantage of using Google Drive is that it seamlessly integrates with the entire ecosystem of Google SaaS apps.

How to use Google Drive: The following is a brief description of a typical instance of Google Drive. Remember, you must first create a google account in order to access Google Drive.

- **Accessing Google Cloud Storage**: On your PC or mobile device, click on the **My Drive** tab on the home screen at drive.google.com. 15 GB of free storage space is allotted. Extra space must be paid for.

- **Uploading files**: Click on **New Folder** to create a new cloud storage folder for specific files. Then, click on **Upload Files** to begin uploading various files from your PC or mobile device. You can even create new Google files from the drop-down list provided in this menu.

- **Sharing, editing, and organizing files**: To share a document after you've uploaded it, click on the vertical ellipses at the top-right corner of the screen and click on the **Share** tab. Type the designated email address of the recipient(s) in the text bar and follow any additional prompts. To edit the document, click on the **Open with Google Docs** icon at the top-middle section of the document window and select the applicable app. As you edit the document, your changes will instantly be saved in the cloud.

Note: Mobile devices usually have a GUI interface in which icons are tapped to access these apps. Check with the mobile device's OS app store to download the specific App.

A snapshot of Google Drive is shown in the following screenshot:

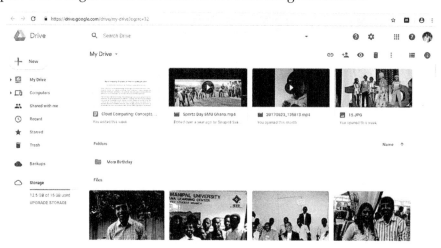

Figure 7.6: Google Drive

Google Cloud Datastore

Google Cloud
Datastore

Google Cloud Datastore is an extremely scalable, fully managed NoSQL database service (PaaS) used to store and retrieve non-relational data for use in big data analytics and real-time web applications.

Features of Google Datastore:

- **Atomic transactions**: Cloud Datastore can perform a set of operations where every transaction is regarded as 'atomic', which means that either all the executed operations succeed or none of them occur.

- **High availability of reads and writes**: Cloud Datastore runs in secure Google data centers with a redundancy system design that ensures that in the event of any problem arising from one or more failed computing resource, retrieval of stored data as well as non-interrupted cloud service provision is certain.

- **Massive scalability with high performance**: Cloud Datastore automatically manages scaling using a combination of indexes and query constraints so that queries scale with the size of user query result sets and not the size of user data sets.

- **Flexible storage and querying of data**: Cloud Datastore runs an SQL-like query language and maps logically to object-oriented and scripting languages.

- **Balance of strong and eventual consistency**: Cloud Datastore ensures that entity queries constantly receive consistent data with every other query ultimately following that same consistency. This allows applications to run smoothly while handling large amount of data and users.

- **Encryption at rest**: Cloud Datastore automatically encrypts each bit of data prior to it being written to the disk and automatically decrypts the data when read by an certified/licensed user.

- **Fully managed with no planned downtime**: Google manages the Cloud Datastore with no interruptions in the service.

- **Google Cloud Datastore versus relational databases**: Although the Cloud Datastore contains a lot of the same characteristics as conventional databases, as a NoSQL database, it contrasts from them because it defines relationships between data objects rather than relating them using tabular columns and rows. This means that entities that are similar do not necessarily need to have a consistent set of properties.

What really distinguishes Datastore from relational databases is its ability to autonomously scale extremely large sets of data, thereby permitting applications to sustain optimal performance as they receive extreme levels of web traffic.

The following table shows the comparison between Cloud Datastore and Relational Database:

Concept	Cloud Datastore	Relational Database
Category of object	Kind	Table
One object	Entity	Row
Individual data for an object	Property	Column
Unique ID for an object	Key	Primary Key

Table 7.1

Dropbox Cloud

Dropbox

Dropbox is a cloud storage service (SaaS) that allows users to store practically any kind of file on remote cloud servers with the ability to share these files in a synchronized format across all PCs or mobile devices. It is one of the prevailing online storage solutions used mainly for small businesses.

Like most cloud applications, Dropbox runs on an array of both desktop and mobile operating systems. A basic Dropbox account is free and includes 2 GB of storage space. Additional space can be purchased on a subscription basis. To access the storage service, users need to install the Dropbox app on various devices which prompts an automatic appearance of a dedicated Dropbox folder on the device's desktop. Then, all you have to do is save 'drop' whatever files you would like to back up in it in the same manner you would do on a local file system. The application immediately uploads the data/files to the **Amazon Web Services** (**AWS**) cloud.

On dropping items into the Dropbox folders, the app immediately synchronizes the data within these dedicated folder(s) across all your devices so that they appear to be in the identical folder (with the exact contents). The uploaded files can then be accessed from the installed application on the devices or through an online control panel as long as there is an internet connection present. The user only needs to log in to his/her Dropbox account to manage, upload, download, or share files.

To share files and folders, a user can make URL requests for them from the Dropbox website and send them to others who have Dropbox accounts. When files or folders are shared, they instantly appear in the folder system of all the recipients who have the authority to access and if need be, edit the files.

The following screenshot shows a Dropbox account being created:

Figure 7.7: Dropbox user account creation

Apple iCloud

The iCloud, provided by Apple, is a cloud-based storage suite system that allows Apple device users to securely store documents, media files, and application data on dedicated Apple servers. As files are put on each iOS powered device, iCloud automatically synchronizes all the data amidst the range of a user's Apple devices that are connected to the Internet. A typical example of this synchronization is when someone takes photos with his/her iPhone. If the phone is connected to the internet, as each photo is taken, it is immediately uploaded to the iCloud in which he/she can view the exact photos using his/her MacBook or iPad, assuming that either of these devices is also connected to the Internet. Also, if an iPad owner downloads some songs from iTunes, as each song is downloaded, it will immediately be ready for listening on his/her iPod if it is connected to the internet. Even games or other applications that are downloaded are synchronized across other Apple devices owned by that particular user.

Apple devices can integrate various kinds of application data, including contacts, calendars, documents as well as various multimedia files. This seamless integration is intended to provide easy back up and access to files. However, a notable limitation of iCloud is that it is does not support cross-platform compatibility with other mobile operating systems such as Google's Android and Windows Mobile. Nonetheless, it does support the standard Windows PC platform.

The following screenshot shows the iCloud log in screen:

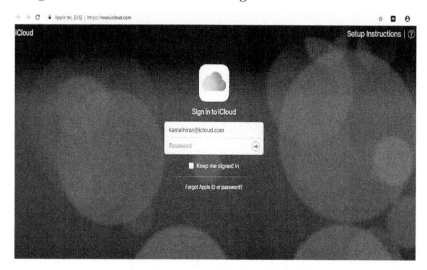

Figure 7.8: Apple iCloud user sign in

Microsoft Windows Azure Cloud

Windows Azure is the Microsoft version of the cloud computing application development environment (PaaS). Azure provides developers with a development platform to create, test, manage, and deploy new web-based apps or to improve existing applications with cloud-based capabilities. Azure also makes provision for users to utilize virtual machines (IaaS) of both Microsoft Windows and Linux operating systems for a broad spectrum of reasons.

The following diagram illustrates the five core elements that Azure encompasses:

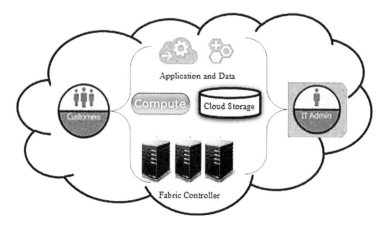

Figure 7.9. Windows Azure main components

The main components of Windows Azure are discussed in more detail as follows:

- **Compute**: Azure compute can run multiple instances of various types of applications. Each instance is comprised of a pair of *Roles*. The first is a *Web Role*, which is responsible for real-time screenshot captures shown to users as they view files or work on documents. The other role is a *Worker Role* which does real-time processing of data.

- **Cloud Storage**: Storage comprises blobs, tables, and queues. Blobs are types of files; tables serve as key-value-pair type data storage slots, and queues integrate Web Roles and Worker Roles for a fluent user experience.

- **Fabric controller**: Fabric controller, also referred to as an Application Fabric, takes care of verification and data transport among Windows Azure applications and hardware resources like servers.

- **Content Delivery Network (CDN)**: The CDN stores copies of a blob at server farms closer to the user's geographical location. For example, if a video recording of breaking news is uploaded to Windows Azure from a cloud facility in France, a user who tries to watch that video on Bing from somewhere in the US won't get the benefit of the CDN since that blob isn't yet cached in North America. Others watching the video on Bing in Western Europe will see better performance as using the cached copy allows the video to load more quickly.

- **Connect**: Running applications in the Microsoft cloud is essential. But connecting to the on-premises environments with Windows Azure is advantageous. Windows Azure Connect is designed to help do this. By providing IP-level connectivity between a Windows Azure application and machines running outside the Microsoft cloud, it can make this arrangement more efficient.

Azure Cloud Storage types: The foundation of Microsoft Azure Storage is, undeniably, the storage types to select from. There are five storage solutions in Microsoft Azure which can be segmented into two groups by their design and function.

The first storage subdivision is available via the REST APIs (Application Programming Interface) which means storage resources may be accessed from within a service running in Azure, or directly over the Internet from any application that can send an HTTP/HTTPS request and receive an HTTP/HTTPS response. REST APIs offer programmatic access to blobs, tables, and queue services which facilitate file storage, scalability, and communication.

The second subdivision exclusively enhances the environment of Azure Virtual Machines which means that Azure virtual networks of scalable computing resources can easily be connected to a firm's existing network on-demand. These virtual machines offer organizations more flexibility of virtualization for application development, testing, deployment, file storage, and disk storage with support for Linux, Windows Server, SQL Server, Oracle, IBM, and SAP.

The following flow diagram shows the Azure Cloud Storage types:

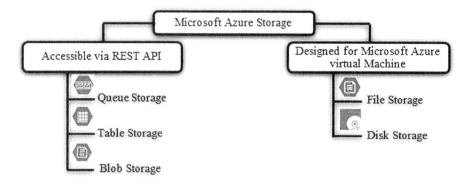

Figure 7.10: Microsoft Windows Azure Storage types

REST APIs

Blob Storage: BLOB is an acronym for **Binary Large Object**, which is essentially a file. Blob storage is utilized for storing large amount of unstructured data which can be stored in three ways:

- **Block Blob**: To store files at 4.77 TB per file
- **Append Blobs**: To store logs or metadata which require perpetual updating
- **Page Blobs**: To store HDD and SSD disks

Table Storage: Table storage is optimized for storing highly scalable, structured NoSQL (non-relational) data in a tabular form to be used in big data analysis.

Queue Storage: Queue storage is intended to connect decoupled and independent components of an application by automatically creating backlogs of asynchronous messages to process from Azure web roles to Azure worker roles.

Virtual machines

Disk Storage: Disk storage is a service that allows users to create **virtual hard disks** (**VHDs**) to be accessed from a virtual machine to be used as the user's local drive.

File Storage: File storage is designed to support the storage of files that can be accessed from various virtual machines.

Amazon Web Services (AWS)

Amazon, the most prominent online retailer, has established the most dominant data center infrastructure consisting of a vast array of virtualized computing resources. It rents portions of theses virtual cluster of computers through the internet as **Amazon Web Services (AWS)**, which is a cloud computing platform provided to individuals, companies, and governments on a paid subscription basis. AWS is made up of numerous remote computing services which form its all inclusive cloud computing platform, but its most recognized services are **Amazon Elastic Cloud Computing (EC2)** and **Amazon Simple Storage Service (S3)**.

The following diagram shows the comprehensive nature of AWS:

Figure 7.11: Amazon Web Services cloud platform

Amazon Elastic Compute Cloud (Amazon EC2)

It is a web application service that provides adjustable computing capacity in the cloud. It provides web-scale computing for developers. Amazon EC2's intuitive web service interface allows users to acquire and configure computing capabilities effortlessly, providing them with complete control over Amazon's impressive computing resources in the form of on-demand access to server instances (applications). Like other cloud providers, AWS only charges customers or the resources that they actually use.

Amazon EC2 provides the following features:

- Amazon Elastic Block Store
- Multiple locations

- Elastic IP Addresses

- Amazon Virtual Private Cloud

- Amazon Cloud Watch

- Auto Scaling

- Elastic Load Balancing

- High Performance Computing (HPC) clusters

- VM Import

- **Amazon Elastic Block Store (EBS)**: EBS provides highly available block-level storage volumes for Amazon EC2 application boot partition instances by keeping instance data persistently on a file system even in the event of a component failure.

- **Multiple locations**: Amazon EC2 provides the capacity for users to place computing resources in multiple locations called **Availability zones** to safeguard against failures in other geographic regions and provide low-latency network connectivity.

- **Elastic IP addresses**: Elastic IP addresses are static IPv4 addresses that are intended to protect against any failure of an instance by rapidly remapping the instance IP address to another functioning instance's IP address within the user's AWS account.

- **Amazon Virtual Private Cloud (VPC)**: VPC permits organizations to securely integrate their on-premise infrastructure to a set of dedicated AWS compute resources through a **Virtual Private Network** (**VPN**) connection, while seamlessly facilitating their existing security protocol systems to include AWS resources.

- **Amazon Cloud Watch**: Amazon Cloud Watch monitors AWS, hybrid, and on-premise applications and hardware utilization, operational performance, network traffic, and other metrics in real time.

- **Auto scaling**: Auto scaling automatically increases or decreases AWS EC2 computing capacity depending on conditions defined by the user's setting stipulated within the Amazon Cloud Watch parameters.

- **Elastic Load Balancing**: Elastic Load Balancing automatically distributes inbound application traffic across multiple AWS EC2 instances which allows applications to achieve better fault tolerance irrespective of the amount of incoming application traffic.

- **High Performance Computing (HPC) clusters**: HPC clusters are comprised of numerous distinct nodes (servers), sometimes filling an entire data center with a lot of power-hungry racks which leverage parallel processing techniques for running advanced applications efficiently, consistently, and swiftly.

- **Virtual Machine (VM) Import/Export**: VM Import allows users to import VM images from your existing environment to Amazon EC2 instances and export them back to your on-premises environment.

Amazon Simple Storage Service (S3)

It is a web storage service that users can leverage to store and retrieve any quantity of data on-demand, anywhere as long as they are connected to the internet. It offers users access to the same data storage infrastructure that Amazon utilizes in its own international network of web sites.

Cloud computing continues to evolve. Cloud-based systems have infiltrated a wide variety of businesses and industries as more and more people discover the technology's potential to revolutionize economic, political, and social relations. In the not too distant future, cloud platforms will be capable of addressing a majority of the world's data problems while delivering better platforms and infrastructure environments to host and manage data and applications. Accordingly, when organizations migrate to the cloud better equipped, they will be in this dynamically integrated world.

The following table shows the comparison of various cloud computing options:

	Dropbox	**Google Drive**	**Amazon Cloud Drive**	**Apple iCloud Drive**
	Dropbox	Google Drive	amazon web services	iCloud
Area of specialization	Compatibility with other services	Collaboration	Personal use	Apple device users
File size restriction	None with Dropbox apps	5TB	2GB (No file size limit with desktop apps)	15GB
Free storage	2GB	15GB	No	5GB
Extra free storage	Yes	No	No	No

Paid plan	$10/month 1TB	$2/month 100GB, $10/month 1TB	$12/month for unlimited photos, $60/year for unlimited files. *Free storage with Amazon Prime subscription	$.99/month 20GB, $3.99/month 200GB
OS supported	Windows, Mac, Android, iOS, Linux, Blackberry, Kindle Fire	Windows, Mac, Android, iOS	Windows, Mac, Android, iOS, Kindle Fire	iOS8, Yosemite, Windows 10 or later

Table 7.2

The following table shows the challenges between **Amazon EC2** and **Windows Azure**:

Challenges	Amazon EC2	Windows Azure
Availability	Zones, Regions, Elastic IP Address with Guaranteed Network Availability: 99.5%	Fault-tolerance, Geo Replication, REST and managed APIs for storage with Guaranteed Network Availability: 99.5%
Resource Scaling	Free auto-scaling enabled by CloudWatch	Paid, based on configuration file specified by the user
Data Deletion	Delete objects in Amazon S3 and delete items and attributes in Amazon SimpleDB	Remove all reference with garbage collection
Data Lock-in	Use Gluster to move between public, private and hybrid clouds	No feature to support moving between clouds
Data Security	Security applied within multiple levels. Encryption can be done by users.	Security mechanisms applied at different layers. Security in SQL Azure is similar to that in SQl server.

Table 7.3

Summary

- Cloud computing is a rapidly emerging technology. Many organizations are now using cloud computing applications and platforms to store their information in the form of online services which are very reliable and highly available.

- Numerous cloud service providers exist, but the top five cloud computing platforms are Google, Dropbox, Apple, Microsoft and Amazon, etc.

- Google App Engine (GAE) provides a fully managed application development platform that enables software developers to run on programming languages such as Java, Ruby, and Python written code on Google infrastructure.

- GAE is Google's stimulating application development and hosting platform in the cloud.

- GAE is highly flexible and can automatically scale up or down when encountering fluctuations in web traffic and high data storage needs.

- Google, one of the leading online information service providers, offers a suite of SaaS services known as Google applications such as Gmail, Google docs, Google Calendar, Google Drive, and Google Cloud Datastore.

- Gmail is a free web-based messaging system developed by Google.

- Google Docs is a free web-based document management.

- Google Calendar is a free time management and SaaS app that allows users to create and modify calendars in order to keep track of personal and professional events.

- Google Drive is a free file storage SaaS that allows users to store and access files located in the Cloud.

- Google Cloud Datastore is an extremely scalable, fully managed NoSQL database service (PaaS) used to store and retrieve non-relational data for use in big data analytics and real-time web applications.

- Dropbox is a cloud storage service (SaaS) that allows users to store practically any kind of file on remote cloud servers with the ability to share these files in a synchronized format across all PCs or mobile devices.

- Apple iCloud, provided by the Apple multi-national company, is a cloud-based storage suite system that allows Apple device users to securely store documents, media files, and application data on dedicated Apple servers.

- Microsoft Windows Azure Cloud provides developers with a development platform to create, test, manage, and deploy new web-based apps or to improve existing applications with cloud-based capabilities.

- BLOB is an acronym for Binary Large Object, which is essentially a file.

- Amazon Web Services (AWS) is made up of numerous remote computing services which form its all inclusive cloud computing platform, but its most recognized services are Amazon Elastic Cloud Computing (EC2) and Amazon Simple Storage Service (S3).

- Amazon EC2 is a web application service that provides adjustable computing capacity in the cloud.

- Amazon S3 is a web storage service that users can leverage to store and retrieve any quantity of data on-demand, anywhere.

Exercise

Tick the correct option

1. Which of these companies is not a leader in cloud computing?

   a. Google

   b. Amazon

   c. Intel

   d. Microsoft

2. Which is not a major cloud computing platform?

   a. Apple iCloud

   b. IBM Deep Blue

   c. Microsoft Azure

   d. Amazon EC2

3. Which of the following is a cloud platform by Amazon?

   a. Azure

   b. AWS

   c. Cloudera

   d. All of the above

4. Amazon EC2 provides virtual computing environments known as?

    a. Chunks

    b. Instances

    c. Messages

    d. None of the above

Answers:

1. c. Intel

2. b. IBM Deep Blue

3. c. Cloudera

4. b. Instances

Fill in the Blanks

1. GAE is software that facilitates users in running web applications on _____ infrastructure.

2. Google Drive provides _____ of cloud storage space for free.

3. Windows Azure has five main parts: Compute, Storage, the _____ _____, the CDN, and Connect.

4. Amazon offers many different cloud services. The most central and well-known of these services are Amazon _____ (EC2) and Amazon Simple Storage Service (S3).

5. Amazon Cloud Watch is a web service that provides monitoring for AWS cloud _____ and applications.

Answers:

1. Google

2. 15 GB

3. Fabric Controller

4. Amazon Elastic Cloud Computing (EC2)

5. Resources

Descriptive Questions

1. State the use of Google App Engine and list Google App Engine Services.

2. List any three Google cloud applications.

3. Name and briefly explain the main components provided by Windows Azure.

4. Explain in brief how to use Google Drive.

5. State the benefits offered by Apple iCloud.

6. What is Google Cloud Datastore? List the features of Google Datastore.

7. Differentiate between Cloud Datastore and Relational Database.

8. Write short note on the following:

   a. BLOB

   b. AWS

   c. Amazon Simple Storage Service (S3)

9. Differentiate between various cloud computing platforms—Dropbox, Google Drive, Amazon Cloud Drive, and Apple iCloud.

10. Differentiate between Amazon EC2 and Windows Azure based on their main features.

CHAPTER 8

Cloud Computing Technologies, Platforms and Services

"The cloud is more than a technology - It's a generation shift."

~ Mark Hurd, CEO of Oracle

Objectives

- To learn about the basic concepts of high-performance computing techniques in the cloud computing model

- To discuss the base layer and concepts behind the development and application of cloud computing tools

- To know about the various open source cloud platforms like Eucalyptus, OpenNebula, Open Stack and Nimbus

- To understand the Apache Hadoop architecture

- To discuss the major components and their roles in the Apache Hadoop ecosystem

The cloud paradigm presents new opportunities for software vendors, developers and programming communities by using cloud-based IDE for their development process. Development tools like Amazon Toolkit for Eclipse, Cloud9 IDE with integrated support for Microsoft Azure and Cloud Foundry supports the ability to collaborate during development.

In this chapter, we will discuss the base layer and concepts behind development and application of such tools. We have tried to cover the specific study of Apache Hadoop with MapReduce models, Open Stack Cloud Platform and OpenNebula Cloud Platform which are open source frameworks for sensing a cloud environment.

In this chapter, we will cover the following topics:

- High-performance computing with cloud technologies
- The Eucalyptus cloud platform
- The OpenNebula cloud platform
- The Open Stack cloud platform
- The Nimbus cloud computing platform
- The Apache Hadoop ecosystem

High-performance computing with cloud technologies

We can easily discriminate cloud with cloud technologies. Cloud is a collection of IT capabilities and services like software (SaaS), platform (PaaS), IT infrastructure (IaaS), virtualized security services, virtualized storage, and so on whereas cloud technologies are various runtime frameworks like Apache Hadoop, Amazon S3, MapReduce, and so on. The inception of commercialized cloud like Amazon EC2, Microsoft Azure and Google App Engine introduce the latest pay-per-use model which is fairly easy and provides quick resource provisioning. In addition to these, accessibility to open source cloud and virtualization stacks like Eucalyptus, OpenNebula, Xen and KVM hypervisor allows ease of building and maintenance of private clouds with dynamic provisioning of resources.

Cloud technologies are the first choice for solving data intensive problems because they provide better quality of services and ability to handle large data sets. **Parallel Virtual Machine (PVM)** and **Message Passing Interface (MPI)** communication protocols are used by most of the **High performance computing (HPC)** applications because they allow the programmers to focus on algorithms rather than communication overheads. But many studies exhibit that due to network virtualization in cloud, performance of MPI communication is degrading.

The MapReduce programming model is another construct available to users for communication in parallel programs especially for composable applications. Similarly, Microsoft Dryad supports parallel applications that resemble **Directed Acyclic Graphs (DAGs)** in which the vertices represent computation unit and the edges represent communication channels between different computation units.

Message Passing Interface (MPI)

The **Message Passing Interface** (**MPI**) is a HPC library used to establish information flow between various nodes and clusters. Open MPI is the most popular and commonly used protocol for communication in parallel programming. It is an open source, language-independent and portable implementation that uses the message-passing paradigm to share the data in the distributed memory architecture.

Figure 8.1 shows the basic message passing interface. High-performance processors (sometimes called as **processing elements**) are connected to each other via high-speed interconnect. Each processor has its private memory module.

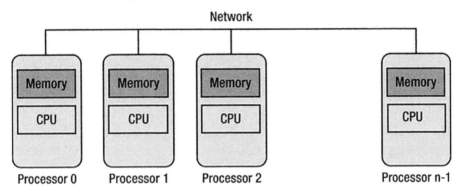

Figure 8.1: Message Passing interface

MPI optimizes CPU utilization for tightly coupled problems like climate modeling, car crash simulation, and so on. Some prominent features of MPI are point-to-point communication, derived data types, parallel I/O operations, and so on.

MapReduce programming model

MapReduce is a linear programming model consisting of two main tasks—Map and Reduce. The Mapper task executes one record at a time and Reducer aggregates the results. Both the tasks can be used for large data sizes and are highly scalable. MapReduce breaks down the large data sets into key-value pairs and may sound like very restrictive programming, but many state-of-the-art algorithms in image analysis or machine learning are written using this technique.

Composable applications: The functional blocks of an application can be decoupled from the composable applications.

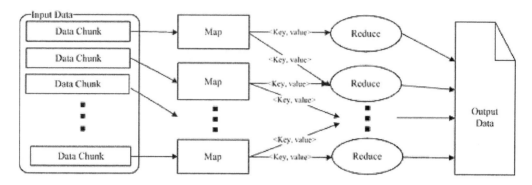

Figure 8.2: MapReduce programming model

CGL-MapReduce is an extension of the MapReduce programming model which proposes significant improvements like faster intermediate data transfer, support long-running map/reduce tasks and support for iterative MapReduce computations. Another advantage of CGL-MapReduce is that it eliminates the overhead of file-based communications used by Hadoop and Dryad.

Dryad and DryadLINQ

Dryad is a distributed execution engine for coarse-grained data parallel applications. It combines the MapReduce programming style with data flow graphs to solve the computation tasks. Dryad considers computation tasks as DAGs, where the vertices represent computation tasks and the edges act as communication channels over which the data flows from one vertex to another.

The advantage of Dryad over MPI and other interfaces is that its framework is optimized for data locality rather than CPU utilization to support jobs that are primarily bound on disk I/O.

DryadLINQ compiles LINQ programs to Dryad jobs. It is actually a language extension that supports high-level language to write data-parallel code. Languages supported by DryadLINQ are LINQ, C#, VB, F#, and so on. Here is a screenshot of the Dryad execution framework:

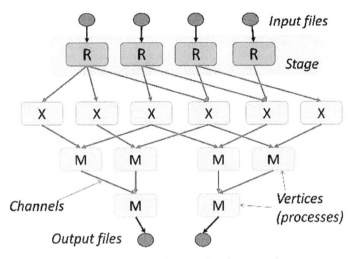

Figure 8.3: Dryad execution framework

Eucalyptus cloud platform

Eucalyptus is an open source, Amazon Web Services-compatible, private and hybrid cloud computing environment. It is an acronym for **Elastic Utility Computing Architecture for Linking Your Programs To Useful Systems**. As the name suggests, it is an elastic computing structure that can be utilized to attach the users' programs to the helpful systems. The goal of Eucalyptus is to allow sites with existing clusters and server infrastructure to host a cloud that is interface-compatible with Amazon's AWS and the Sun Cloud open API. In 2014, it was acquired by HP (Hewlett-Packard), which has its own cloud offerings under the HPE Helion banner. Now, Eucalyptus is a part of the HPE portfolio and is called **HPE Helion Eucalyptus**.

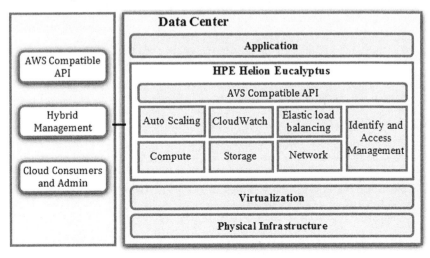

Figure 8.4: Eucalyptus cloud platform

Components of Eucalyptus

The components are as follows:

- **Cloud Controller**: It is the main controller, also called as **CLC**, which manages the entire cloud platform. It provides a web and EC2 compatible interface. All the incoming requests come through the CLC. It performs scheduling, resource allocation and accounting.

- **Walrus**: It is similar to **AWS S3 (Simple Storage Service)**. It provides persistent storage to all the instances.

- **Cluster Controller (CC)**: It manages the VM (instance) execution and service level agreements. It communicates with the storage and network controller.

- **Storage Controller (SC)**: It is similar to **AWS EBS (Elastic Block Storage)**. It provides block level storage to instances and snapshots within a cluster.

- **Node Controller**: It hosts all the instances and manages their end points.

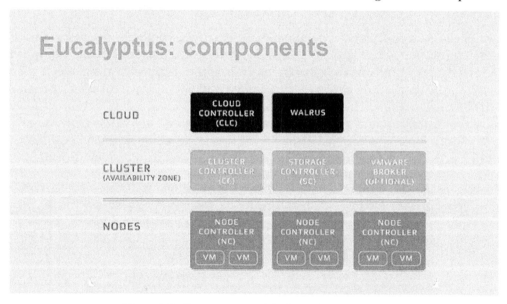

Figure 8.5: Component model of Eucalyptus Cloud

There are many other tools like Euca2ool, s3curl, s3fs, CloudBerry s3 explorer which can be used as an extension for management and development. Eucalyptus can be used with DevOps tools such as Puppet and Chef. Also, SDKs like AWS SDKs for Java and Ruby and Fog work smoothly with Eucalyptus.

OpenNebula cloud platform

OpenNebula is an open source cloud service framework used to manage heterogeneous distributed data center infrastructures. It is a complete solution to build private clouds and manage data center virtualization.

OpenNebula is a standard-based open source management toolkit that enables virtualized data centers to facilitate cloud deployment at various levels.

The following diagram shows the basic architecture of OpenNebula:

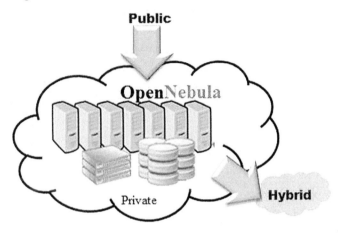

Figure 8.6: Cloud computing architecture with OpenNebula

Why should we use OpenNebula?

- Easy to download, install and update through packages
- Fully open-sourced and distributed under an Apache license
- Enables easier running of virtualized data centers for both private and hybrid clouds
- Supports any platform, storage and networking resource
- Open and extensible architecture with the possibility to build customized cloud services

OpenNebula features are as follows:

- **Adaptable**: Assimilation abilities to integrate into any infrastructure
- **Enterprise-ready**: Upgrade process and commercial support
- **No lock-in**: Expansive infrastructure and platform independent
- **Light**: Efficient and intuitive

- **Proven**: Thoroughly tested, established and commonly used
- **Powerful**: Advanced features for virtualization
- **Scalable**: Single instance and multi-tier architectures
- **Be interoperable**: Extensive set of APIs and interfaces
- **Open source**: Apache License v2

Layers of OpenNebula

OpenNebula operates at two main layers, which are as follows:

- **Data center virtualization management**: This layer is used to manage data center virtualization, consolidate servers, and integrate existing IT assets for computing, storing and networking. In this deployment model, OpenNebula directly integrates with hypervisors (like KVM) and has complete control over virtual and physical resources, providing advanced features for capacity management, resource optimization, high availability and business continuity.

- **Cloud management**: This layer is used to provide a multi-tenant, cloud-like provisioning layer on top of an existing infrastructure management solution.

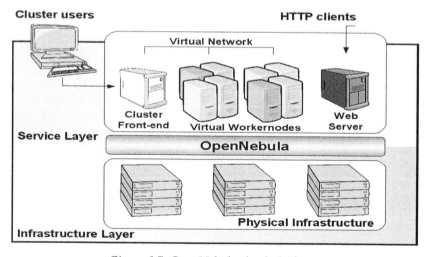

Figure 8.7: OpenNebula cloud platform

Features of OpenNebula

OpenNebula brings a rich and flexible management model and the latest innovations in data center virtualization for the deployment of enterprise clouds in your existing infrastructure:

- **Cloud bursting**: Extension of the local private infrastructure with resources from remote clouds.

- **On-demand provision of virtual data centers**: A **Virtual Data Centers (VDC)** is a fully-isolated virtual infrastructure environment where a group of users under the control of the VDC administrator can create and manage computing, storing and networking capacity.

- **Multiple zones**: Centralized management of multiple instances of OpenNebula (zones) for scalability, isolation or multiple-site support.

- **Multi-VM application management**: Automatic execution of multi-tiered applications with auto-scaling.

OpenStack cloud platform

OpenStack is a free and open-source software platform for IaaS cloud. It provides a modular cloud infrastructure that allows you to deploy the tools of your choice, when you need them, using a single dashboard based on the OpenStack API.

Basically, it acts like a cloud operating system of a private or public cloud that controls a large pool of computing, storing and networking resources.

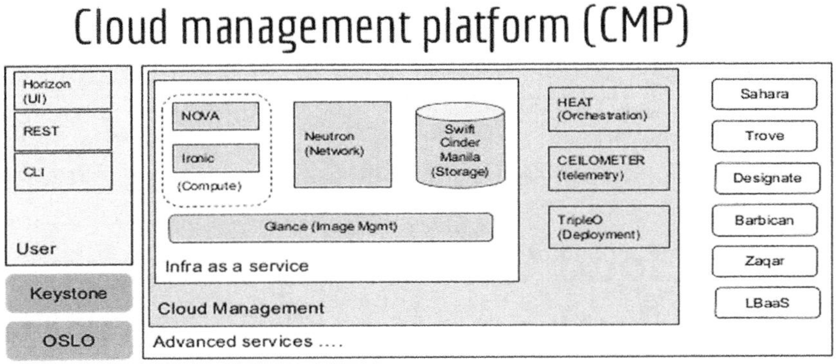

Figure 8.8: OpenStack cloud platform

OpenStack components

The OpenStack cloud platform is integration of different software modules developed by the open source community. A few major components are discussed as follows:

- **Nova**: It is responsible to implement services and associated libraries to provide massively scalable, on-demand, self-service access to compute resources, including bare metal, virtual machines and containers.

- **Glance**: It is a service that discovers, registers and retrieves **virtual machine (VM)** images.

- **Zun**: It provides an API to launch and manage containers.

- **Keystone**: It is the authentication and authorization component built into each OpenStack cloud.

- **Neutron**: It is responsible for creating the virtual networks within an OpenStack cloud; this means creating virtual networks, routers, subnets, firewalls, load balancers, and so on.

- **Cinder**: It provides virtualized block storage as a service to an OpenStack cloud.

Benefits of Open Stack

- **Private clouds**: Ease of installation and service management made OpenStack a significant, more valuable and better choice for private cloud distributions.

- **Public clouds**: OpenStack is the leading open source option for building public cloud environments.

- **Network virtualization**: OpenStack supports **Network Function Virtualization (NFV)** which involves separating a network's key functions so they can be distributed among environments.

- **Containers**: OpenStack containers speed up application delivery while simplifying application deployment and management.

Nimbus Cloud Computing Platform

Formerly known as **Virtual Workspace Service (VWS)**, Nimbus is an **Infrastructure-as-a-Service (IaaS)** cloud which deploy and configure VMs on remote resources. In simpler words, it can be stated that Nimbus allows the client to lease remote resources which can be accessed using multiple credential protocols. It is an open source cloud platform which is programmed in Python and Java under Apache license.

There are two basic products of Nimbus:

- **Nimbus Platform**: It is a versatile integrated set of tools that provides infrastructure services like deployment, scaling cloud resource management, and so on. The power of Nimbus is that it allows us to combine itself with other cloud platforms like OpenStack, Amazon, and so on.

- **Nimbus Infrastructure**: It is an open source EC2/S3-compatible IaaS solution with features like support for auto-configuring clusters, proxy credentials, batch schedulers, best-effort allocations, store VMs with no private credentials, and so on.

Features of Nimbus

- Open Source Infrastructure as a Service Solution
- Remote deployment and lifecycle management of VMs
- Compatibility with Amazons Network Protocols
- Multiple credential protocols support
- Local resource management, XEN & KVM plugins

The Apache Hadoop ecosystem

Hadoop is an Apache-based distributed computing ecosystem used for analyzing, storing and processing of voluminous unstructured data. The framework is open source and programmable with Java language. Hadoop is able to handle terabytes of data and due to its distributed nature, applications can run on thousands of hardware nodes. The distributed file system results in faster transfer of data between these nodes. Some best known tools of the Hadoop ecosystem are Spark, Hive, HBase, YARN, MapReduce, Pig, Zookeeper, HDFS, and so on:

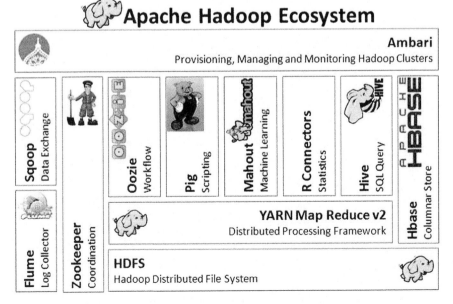

Figure 8.9: Apache Hadoop ecosystem

Architecture of Hadoop

The architecture of Hadoop comprises of various Hadoop components through which complex data problems are solved. The architecture is based on the traditional master-slave style. Data files are stored on multiple servers which are called nodes. Each node has a computational power. The master node is called **NameNode** and it controls the operation of data whereas the slave nodes are called **DataNodes** which write the data to the local storage:

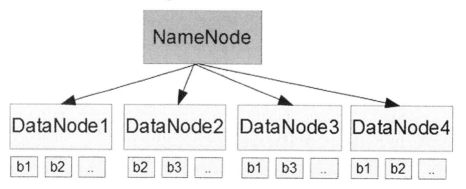

Figure 8.10: Hadoop client server architecture

Major components of Hadoop

The key components of the Hadoop ecosystem are discussed as follows:

- **HDFS (Hadoop Distributed File System)**: It is the core component of Hadoop which provides reliable and distributed storage for huge amount of structured, unstructured and semi-structured data. **NameNode** and **Datanode** are two key components of HDFS:

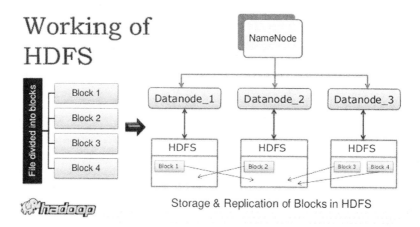

Figure 8.11: HDFS architecture

- **YARN (Yet Another Resource Negotiator)**: It is the brain of Hadoop and responsible for providing computational resources, managing workloads and job scheduling needed for application executions:

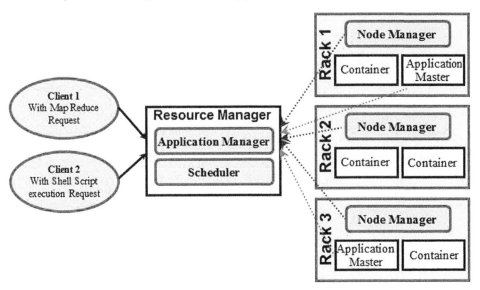

Figure 8.12: YARN architecture

The two major components of YARN are as follows:

- **Resource Manager**: It is the master node and there is one per cluster. It is responsible for passing the part of requests to the appropriate node manager. Resource scheduling, monitoring and event handling are the major tasks of the YARN resource manager node.

- **Node Manager**: It is a slave node and has a many-to-one relationship with the resource manager. Each **Node Manager** is divided into a number of containers that offers some resources to the cluster.

- **MapReduce**: It is a data processing layer for parallel processing of large datasets either structured or unstructured. It is a combination of two operations, namely, Map and Reduce. The concept is to break a job into multiple independent sub jobs and process them one by one:

- Map is where all logical and complex codes are defined. It is responsible for grouping, sorting and filtering operations.

- Reduce is where the jobs are broken down into sub jobs and processed individually. It is responsible for summarizing and aggregating of results produced by map operations.

The basic concept is that the Map operation sends a query to various DataNodes for processing and the Reduce operation obtains the result of these queries and will output a single value. Job Tracker and Task Tracker are two daemons which track the live status of jobs and tasks.

- **Hive**: It is an open source data query system used to query or analyze large unstructured and semi-structured datasets stored within the Hadoop ecosystem. Hive is integrated with HDFS components and is based on the HQL language (similar to SQL) which automatically translates queries into MapReduce jobs.

- **Apache Pig**: It is a high-level procedural language used for parallel processing of large datasets in the Hadoop ecosystem. The objective of Pig is data loading, performing the necessary operations and arranging the final output in the required format. There are two major components, which are as follows:

- Pig Latin has very less coding components and contains SQL-like commands.

- Pig run time is just like JVM.

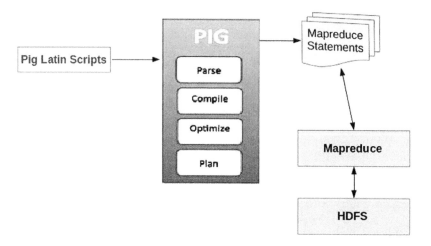

Figure 8.13 Apache Pig

At the back-end of Pig Latin, the MapReduce job executes. The compiler converts the Latin into MapReduce and produces sequential job sets, which is called an abstraction.

- **HBase**: It is an open source and non-relational or NoSQL database runs on the top of Hadoop. It supports all data types and can store voluminous structured data in the form of relational tables. It also provides real-time access to read and write operations in HDFS. HBase is designed to solve the problems, where a small amount of data or information can be searched in a huge amount of data or database.

- **Apache Mahout and Spark MLlib**: Apache Mahout and Apache MLlib are both open source frameworks used for creating scalable machine learning algorithm and data mining library over the Hadoop ecosystem.

  Both Mahout and MLlib (fits into Spark's APIs) includes algorithms like classification, regression, decision tree, clustering, etc. and interoperates with NumPy in Python and R libraries. Any Hadoop data source (for example, HDFS, HBase, or local files) can be used which makes it easy to plug into Hadoop workflows.

- **Apache Zookeeper**: It is a centralized service used for maintaining configuration information, naming, providing distributed synchronization, and providing group services in Hadoop. Many big brands like eBay, Yahoo and Rackspace are using Zookeeper for many of their use-cases.

Hadoop and cloud

As we are now aware that cloud computing is a prevailing source of computation power, integration of the Hadoop framework together will assuredly ease the overheads of parallel processing in big data applications. Beyond assimilation, high-end capabilities of Hadoop like distributed computing, data mining, and data analytics will be provided along with the cloud infrastructure.

Cloud-Hadoop alliance is very trendy nowadays. From the following points, we can analyze that integration of both the frameworks will result in wonders for big data analytics and processing:

- **Cost effectiveness**: Cost of computational power, infrastructure and other extra investments will be lowered down instantly.

- **Resource procurement**: For small-scale companies, procurement of resources is not always beneficial or sometimes possible. The best solution is to run Hadoop on the cloud where heavy or expensive resources can be procured automatically whenever needed and released once the objective is complete.

- **Workload management**: The main objective of the Hadoop framework is job scheduling and processing of data. Data collected from heterogeneous sources should be properly analyzed to derive meaningful insights. Cloud helps to analyze user patterns effectively and even clusters can be divided into suitable sizes at the right time when needed.

- **Job management**: Jobs in Hadoop requires variable computational resources, that is, a few demands more computational power while others require the job completion within deadlines. Hadoop running on cloud provides more adaptable solutions by suggesting proper scheduling algorithms and availing necessary computing resources.

- **Data privacy and isolation**: Loads of MapReduce jobs execute in a shared cluster. Therefore, multi-tenancy issues like interference of jobs and implementing security constraints is the need of the hour. The multi-tenancy architecture of cloud helps the users to configure clusters with varied characteristics and features.

Summary

- Cloud computing tools for HPC are Hadoop, Dryad and MapReduce.
- CGL-MapReduce is an extension of the MapReduce programming model.
- Eucalyptus, Nimbus and OpenNebula are examples of the cloud computing platform.
- Eucalyptus is an open source, Amazon Web Services-compatible, private and hybrid cloud computing environment.
- Hadoop is an Apache-based distributed computing ecosystem for analyzing, storing and processing of voluminous unstructured data.
- HDFS, YARN, MapReduce, Hive, Pig, HBase, Mahout/Spark are some major components of Apache Hadoop.
- HDFS is a reliable and distributed storage for huge amount data.
- YARN provides computational resources, manage workloads and job scheduling functionality.
- Map-Reduce is the data processing layer of Hadoop.
- Hive is an open source data query system.
- Apache Pig is a high-level procedural and scripting language.
- Cloud-Hadoop alliance is very trendy nowadays.

Exercise

Tick the correct option

1. YARN is an acronym for?

    a. Yet Another Resource Negotiator

    b. Yet Another Resource Navigator

    c. Yes Another Resource Negotiator

    d. Yet Again Resource Navigator

2. Which of the following is not a component of the OpenStack cloud platform?

    a. Nova

    b. Keystone

    c. Neutron

    d. Walrus

3. Which is an open source data query system?

    a. Walrus

    b. Hive

    c. Pig

    d. Glance

4. Which Hadoop tool also provides support for a columnar database?

    a. HDFS

    b. Pig

    c. Hive

    d. HBase

5. Which component is responsible for providing simple storage service in Eucalyptus cloud platform?

    a. Cluster Controller

    b. CLC

    c. Walrus

    d. Node Controller

6. Which of the following is an open source cloud platform?

    a. Eucalyptus

    b. Amazon EC2

    c. Google App Engine

    d. Azure

7. MPI stands for?

    a. Massively Parallel Interconnect

    b. Message Passing Interface

    c. Message Passing Interconnect

    d. Mostly Parallel Interface

8. Map Reduce is a linear programming model.

    a. True

    b. False

9. Which component of Eucalyptus is similar to AWS EBS (Elastic Block Storage)?

    a. Node Controller

    b. Cloud Controller

    c. Storage Controller

    d. Walrus

10. Which component of the OpenStack cloud is responsible for creating the virtual networks?

    a. Nova

    b. Glance

    c. Keystone

    a. Neutron

Answers:

1. a. Yet Another Resource Negotiator
2. d. Walrus
3. b. Hive
4. d. HBase
5. c. Walrus
6. a. Eucalyptus
7. b. Message Passing Interface
8. a. True
9. c Storage Controller
10. d. Neutron

Fill in the blanks

1. The master node is called _____ and it controls the operation of data whereas the slave nodes are called _____.
2. Dryad considers computation tasks as_____.
3. DryadLINQ compiles_____ to Dryad jobs.
4. _____is a service of OpenStack that discovers, registers and retrieves virtual machine images.
5. _____ and _____are both open source frameworks for creating scalable machine learning algorithm and data mining library in Hadoop.

Answers:

1. NameNode and DataNode
2. Direct Acyclic Graphs
3. LINQ programs
4. Glance
5. Apache Mahout and Apache MLib

Descriptive questions

1. What are the cloud architecture design principles? Explain them in detail.

2. What is high-performance computing (HPC)?

3. How high-performance parallel computing can be integrated with cloud computing?

4. What is the MapReduce model? How is it efficient in the Hadoop architecture?

5. What is Apache Hadoop? Explain the various components in the Hadoop Architecture with a suitable diagram.

6. With a suitable diagram, explain the structure of the Apache Pig scripting language.

7. How is the integration of Hadoop with the cloud framework beneficial to the programming community? Give reasons to support you answer.

8. Differentiate HDFS from distributed databases.

9. Compare OpenStack and OpenNebula cloud platforms.

10. With a suitable architectural diagram, discuss the role of the various components of the Eucalyptus cloud platform.

CHAPTER 9

Adoption of Cloud Computing

"Cloud computing is the third wave of the digital revolution."

~ Lowell McAdam, CEO of Verizon

Objectives

- To learn about the basic concepts of cloud computing adoption
- To know the adoption strategies and different factors of cloud computing adoption
- To discuss the various areas of application of cloud computing
- To explore the cloud computing adoption in Sub-Saharan Africa and India
- To know about the various cloud computing international certifications

Technology is making significant developments in the modern world. One of the most essential driving forces behind this advancement is undoubtedly a greater computing capacity. Cloud computing is serving as a major element to this hi-tech progression. This chapter lays emphasis on the issues affecting the adoption of cloud computing with strategies for its adoption. Additionally, we will briefly explore existing applications in key socio-economic areas along with case studies.

In this chapter, we will cover the following topics:

- Introduction to adoption of cloud computing
- Adoption of cloud computing in the current era

- Strategies and factors affecting cloud computing adoption
- Cloud computing existing areas of application
- Cloud computing adoption in Sub-Saharan Africa
- Cloud computing adoption in India
- Cloud computing certifications

Over the last two decades, **Artificial intelligence (AI)**, autonomous vehicles, 3D printing, robots and drones, **Internet of Things (IoT)**, big data analytics, and social media are increasing rapidly while completely redefining human civilization and its modernization. Organizations are in the process of digital transformation as they want to modernize traditional operations and services both for their survival and subsequent growth. These radical changes have led to successive innovations commonly referred to as a *digital revolution*. With the adoption and proliferation of computers and immense record keeping, this fusion of technologies is blurring the lines between the physical and digital realms.

Adoption of cloud computing in the current era
Cloud computing in the IT industry

According to the **Internet Data Center (IDC)** in South Korea, IT spending has been growing at a rate of 4.5 times since 2009, and it is rapidly growing, boosting total spending on public cloud computing from $67 billion in 2015 to $162 billion by 2020. From these anticipated changes, companies have realized the importance of cloud computing adoption. Adopting cloud computing is considered a prerequisite for any attempt at digital transformation. Consequently, firms need to make a proper decision on cloud computing adoption in order to reflect organizational and technological changes. In this virtual environment, cloud service providers like Amazon and Google are leading the industry.

Cloud computing continues to revolutionize the way organizations provide services. For this reason, the migration to the cloud requires considerable awareness among industry stakeholders to adopt it and tap into a well-established global data pool. In the near future, the cloud computing infrastructure will become an inherent part of society. Consequently, when organizations migrate to a cloud computing platform, they will be better equipped in this dynamically connected digital world.

Factors affecting cloud computing adoption

Adoption and influence factors

Cloud computing is changing our lives in many ways and can bring benefits to both organizations and countries. There are some technological, organizational and environmental factors that could hinder the adoption of these technologies in developing countries. Accordingly, the decision-making framework to adopt cloud computing was developed based on the **technology-organization-environment (TOE)** framework mentioned earlier. All the identified factors from prior research regarding cloud computing adoption were considered as options for the factors and attributes in the research model. These factors were placed accordingly by nature into factors and attributes in the framework:

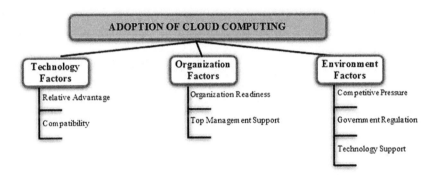

Figure 9.1: Different factors for cloud computing adoption

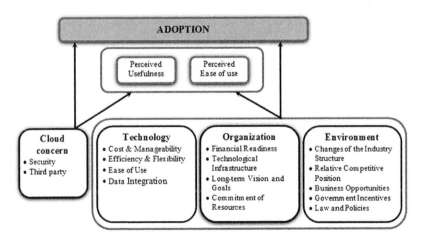

Figure 9.2: Cloud adoption factors and sub-factors for adoption

Technological factors

There are primarily two technological concerns when adopting a cloud computing system. They are the relative advantage and compatibility issues, each with its own technical variables. When adopting or migrating to a new technology, especially the one as dynamic as the cloud, companies must weigh its pros and cons carefully.

Relative advantage

Firms must consider whether the innovation that is being adopted is better than the idea it supersedes. Cloud computing has more advantages than other technologies because it is more flexible, mobile, and it has an infinite range of scalability.

Cost and manageability

When comparing IT costs, it is better to adopt a cloud computing system. Investment costs are one of the most important decision-making factors. Consider an initial outlay a company would need for acquiring the IT hardware infrastructure like servers, cables, routers, firewalls, **uninterruptible power supplies (UBS)**, **heating, ventilation, and cooling (HVAC)**, units, as well as the physical space to store these equipments. Moreover, consider the costs associated with setting up, troubleshooting, and maintaining all these components. Finally, consider the costs of licensing software for each user in the organization. The resulting reduction in direct IT spending would be extremely beneficial to start-ups or small businesses.

Efficiency and flexibility

With cloud computing, not only is the physical infrastructure provided by the cloud service provider on a subscription basis, but also all the needed software applications are readily available. This eliminates the headache associated with procuring, installing, and maintaining IT equipments and software. As a result, your business can use its overall human and financial resources more efficiently. Managers can then focus their efforts somewhere else knowing that the cloud services are more than flexible to meet its growth, and because of its continuity, the cloud platform is more reliable.

Compatibility

Because the Internet has become the predominant form of information sharing and communication globally, cloud computing platforms, which are in alignment with the Internet platform, will allow companies to conveniently import and export applications and customize their services in a seamless way.

Ease of use and data integration

Cloud-based services should be compatible with all existing file formats, user interfaces, and other structured data in an attempt to increase interoperability among the users of technology. Additionally, the time taken to perform tasks, transfer data, and integrate computer data into existing work would be much less. As a result, computer systems would be less complex to understand with higher functionality across various platforms.

Organizational factors

From an organizational standpoint, strategic objectives must be established in order to outline expected outcomes and guide employees' efforts in achieving these objectives. As a result, a firm's top management must support all efforts to ready the organization to meet these objectives and overall goals. Again, when adopting or migrating to the cloud, managers must weigh its pros and cons carefully.

Organizational readiness

If a firm claims that it is ready to adopt or migrate to a new platform of technology, it must have both the financial resources and the technical infrastructure to support such an adoption. Many of the toughest challenges related to cloud are not with the technology, but with how to operate it in this dynamic world to realize its full benefits.

Financial readiness

Financial resources are key drivers of technology adoption. They are also one of its main constraints, especially in developing countries. From a monetary perspective, it is essential that managers consider the financial readiness and likelihood of migrating to the cloud. Scarce financial resources restrain IT capabilities that could improve an organization's effectiveness, so cloud computing attempts to address these economic limitations with useful, user-friendly, and less costly solutions for the organization.

Technological infrastructure

The IT infrastructure refers to the composite of physical components like computer and networking hardware and facilities as well as various software and network components required for the existence, operation and management of an IT environment. Successful firms should have some effective technology infrastructures with expert professionals managing them. When companies plan to operate in a cloud computing environment, their cloud IT infrastructure will allow them to become more agile, efficient, and innovative to meet the growing demands of their users. They will be more responsive to the meet the needs of their customers while providing increasingly better quality of services.

Top management support

Top management support is considered one of the main factors in project management. Therefore, effective administrative involvement can considerably improve the success of the project. Sometimes, when resources are limited, strategies such as shifting resources from low-value adding activities to high-priority activities can help. It ensures long term vision, commitment of resources, and optimal management of resources in the establishment and realization of the company's goals. Studies show that when companies fail to get sufficient top management support for IT projects, these projects have little chance of succeeding in this situation or they fail altogether.

Long-term vision and establishment of goals

A vision is a long-term goal that expresses what an organization wants to become, be known as, or be known for. In this information age, organizations are accumulating vast amount of digital data. As the business landscape evolves into a more technological one, countless firms in various industries are incorporating cloud computing strategies into their long-term IT plans because managers believe that cloud systems can easily scale to meet their companies' expectations without the need for new capital expenditures on hardware and software purchases, IT equipment security and maintenance, as well as other associated costs.

Commitment of resources

For a firm to effectively and efficiently achieve its goals, it must be ready and willing to commit its resources. Information needs are increasing and in order for firms to stay competitive in the global market, they need to adopt some information systems to accommodate the growing demands of information. Management must commit financial resources to acquire a suitable IT infrastructure such as a cloud-based system to handle all its information needs. Moreover, they need to train and educate human resources about the use of cloud computing so that they can operate freely in this new technological environment.

Environmental factors

Cloud computing can bring many benefits to organizations and countries around the world. However, pressure from global competitors, government regulations, and comprehensive product support in new technology systems are important factors to be considered during an organization's data digitization. These factors may vary depending on the economic, social, and political environments of the countries in which companies operate, but as the internet continues to make transfer of information more accessible across international borders, these factors can become relatively uniform.

Competitive pressure

As competition usually compels providers of products to increase quality standards, it is strategically necessary to adopt new technologies to compete in the market. Adopting information systems is useful for a firm to change its industry structure in efforts to increase its relative competitive position.

Changes of the industry structure

Cloud computing is maturing in the IT industry as many companies are adopting it into their existing infrastructure as well as in their business processes. As more powerful computer hardware and software become available, this industry will continue to grow exponentially. The only hindrance to the cloud's continued growth is the availability of skilled IT professionals.

Increase in the relative competitive position

Competitive advantage is the leverage that a firm has over its competitors. It refers to the ability gained through strategies and resources to perform at a higher level than others in the same industry or market. When businesses adopt a cloud computing system, their data resources increase significantly, and thereby facilitating better information provision that adds value to its products. As businesses create more value for their clients by differentiating their product offerings from others in the competitive landscape either through lower costs or better quality, their relative competitive position increases, and the target markets recognize these unique products or services, resulting in brand loyalty.

Generation of new business opportunities

There are countless reasons why cloud computing (https://www.theguardian.com/media-network/cloud) will benefit organizations, but perhaps the primary benefit rests in its ability to allow small and medium businesses to compete with their larger rivals, and even surpass them in some instances. Additionally, the cloud environment enhances an organization's working efficiency, offering seamless collaboration and communication among employees while extending its reach to discover new business channels. Because the cloud enables businesses to utilize computing resources over the Internet without having to invest in the underlying software and hardware infrastructure, the cloud serves as an ideal foundation on which managers can build a digital enterprise.

Government regulations

One of the key tasks of an organization is to keep data private and secure. Security and legal issues regarding data jurisdictions, security risks and data confidentiality must be considered when attempting to upload data into the cloud. In fact, with recent breaches (https://www.cloudwards.net/prism-snowden-and-government-surveillance/) of privacy laws such as the Facebook scandal (https://www.cloudwards.net/state-of-the-cloud-may-2018/) in the United States and the Google scandal in China, these concerns are more significant than before. Many times, businesses focus so much on the technological aspect of incorporating a cloud platform into their business management strategy that government regulatory compliance gets overshadowed.

Government incentives

In many developing countries, governments have strived to keep up with the current pace of IT innovation. In 2010, the United States Federal Government created the first cloud strategy called **Cloud First**, which provided government agencies broad authority to adopt cloud-based solutions for IT modernization. In line with this, the federal government had stated it would allocate around $20 billion of its information technology resources to hybrid, public or private computer clouds throughout the upcoming four years.

Law and policies

Regulatory compliance is when a company obeys the laws, guidelines, and specifications that pertain to its business. In a global economy, it is necessary to be aware of the laws that are enforced not just pertaining to your industry but also in the countries where your customers live.

Technology support

The shortage of tech professionals has been a major constraint in the business community for many years since the advent of IT. Since almost every organization is dependent on some form of technology, hiring and retaining top tech professionals may be arguably the main obstruction to its growth. As companies continue to migrate their internal systems to the cloud, it drastically lowers the demand for IT professionals within an organization because adequate user and technical support services will be delivered by cloud providers.

Cloud computing existing areas of application

Cloud computing is highly utilized in numerous segments of the global economy. Across the world, scholastic, industrial, commercial, governmental, healthcare, and social welfare organizations are all presently in the process of digital transformation as they reform conventional methods of operations both for their survival and progression. Accordingly, cloud computing provides both effective and efficient means for participants in these sectors to not only solve various existing problems but also to deliver standardized services in a timely and cost-effective manner. Conversely, cloud adoption in these key areas is subject to some intrinsic threats such as data security; yet as the benefits far outweigh the rewards, migration to the cloud remains the logical solution.

Cloud computing in education

Education is a crucial aspect fostering a country's economic growth, especially for underdeveloped ones. Today, students have become more technologically savvy as teaching and learning utilizes more innovative technology on a daily basis. Many educational institutions throughout the world have become exceedingly dependent on **Information Communications Technology (ICT)** to service their academic and commercial requirements. As such, cloud computing has begun to play a pivotal role in servicing these demands to be the primary provider of information services in the generations to come.

Access to on-demand information and computing resources increases the output of students and academic professionals alike. As an alternative to contemporary academic mediums (textbooks, paper worksheets, and so on), the use of internet technologies in primary, secondary, and tertiary scholastic institutions by the faculty and students has become the standard of data research, productivity, and information sharing. Presently, schools, libraries, and other academic establishments are taking advantage of cloud-based applications provided by various cloud service providers to allow their faculty and students to accomplish many academic tasks based on their individual requirements.

The use of cloud computing in the academia is one of the world's fastest-emerging trends. As the world modernizes, the demand for education will always increase. Cloud computing in education unlocks opportunities for improved research, intellectual discourse as well as collaborative and cooperative learning. By providing a software-centered environment, cloud computing reduces the dependency on expensive hardware whose costs can otherwise be diverted to more education-related resources. Cloud computing also allows courses to be offered and run from remote locations, as evidenced by distant learning and **Massive Open Online Courses (MOOCs)** offered by many renowned universities. Scholastic establishments are now better equipped to manage data more efficiently and less expensively than they could if they relied on their own IT infrastructure. However, since these entities no longer have total control over their private data, they need to rely heavily on the cloud computing service provider(s) to make sure security systems are in place to guarantee that their data is preserved and utilized appropriately.

The following diagram illustrates the recipients of cloud services in the educational sector:

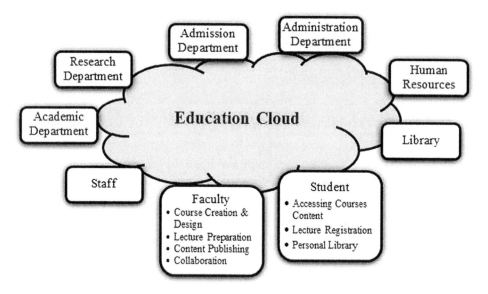

Figure 9.3: Cloud computing beneficiaries in education sector

Cloud computing services can be utilized by academia through the following service models.

- **Software-as-a-Service (SaaS)**: This service model allows scholastic organizations to use application software through a cloud platform via the internet. These subscription-based resources are readily available in a variety of options, facilitating e-learning for both novice and advanced users. For example, YouTube is an extremely popular video resource SaaS that many students and teachers worldwide use to watch and even download videos related to their various subjects. Students can watch subject-related videos to understand what is taught in class and teachers can also watch the videos to get presentation ideas to drive home the concept of the lesson that seem difficult to teach/present to students. Some prominent education SaaS platforms include Canvas, CampusAnyware, College Office, and CloudEMS.

- **Platform-as-a-Service (PaaS)**: This service model supports teachers in their development or acquisition of applications via programming languages, services, and tools that the cloud platform providers offer. For example, an educator can design a customized virtual lab for the students using a PaaS. And for this, they will have to possess technical know-how or hire an IT team for application development. Google App Engine, Windows Azure, and Force.com are a few of the industry leaders in PaaS service provision to schools. Two of the industry's leading education PaaS are **Amazon Web Services (AWS)** and **Google App Engine (GAE)**.

- **Infrastructure-as-a-Service (IaaS)**: This service model provides educators with the virtual infrastructure to deploy and run software, including applications and operating systems. Especially in IT education, students need to develop their problem-solving skills through hands-on practice. For practicality, computer labs are the key elements in the teaching and learning of information technology. Moreover, IT education comprises a host of dynamic subjects which involve diverse technologies. Every so often, the computer lab designed for one IT course may not be suitable for others. For example, the computer lab configured for teaching networking is not appropriate for teaching programming. By adopting the cloud computing IaaS, it is not necessary for the two departments to develop their own IT infrastructure to cater to their students. Consequently, the instructors of the networking courses may alter the IaaS set up so that the others may access the programming courses server. Some notable education IaaS include AWS) Cisco Metapod, **Google Compute Engine (GCE)**, and Microsoft Azure.

Benefits of cloud computing in higher education sector

The benefits are as follows:

- **Enhanced productivity and more efficient educational practices**: One of the primary usages of the cloud is to integrate face-to-face/classroom training and online education with courses offered over the Internet or on other digital formats. The Internet plays host to a warehouse of online manuscripts and other scholastic media materials.

- **Reduced expenditures**: IT investment and operation costs have reduced significantly with institutions only spending on services they actually utilize. Rather than purchasing individual or institutional software licenses for a few computers, many higher education institutions generally pay for specific software packages to be used online from varied locations. This instant access to vast stores of information reduces the cost of maintaining and leveraging physical resources such as textbooks.

- **Increase in collaborative work**: Students and faculty can retrieve information from their individual computers without the need of specific software or hardware resources. This typically allows you more flexibility in facilitating interdepartmental cooperative work. Documents can be created and modified by different users simultaneously from any computer. This synchronizing of cloud services enables an efficient distribution of tasks, thereby improving the quality of the information.

- **Backup of information**: Cloud providers customarily store multiple copies of the same piece of information in numerous servers around the world. This redundancy ensures immediate access to files with back up safeguards in case of any physical or virtual problem in which the institution's critical information may be lost.

- **Support in financial and HR management**: According to **Times Higher Education (THE)**, 76% of UK institutions use the cloud for payment and administration. In some institutions, faculty members can manage their income information online. Cloud services enhance the timely administration of employee-related information to relevant parties, thereby improving the institution's effectiveness and management efficiency when dealing with employee-employer relationship around academic issues.

- **Fostering of university accreditation**: Higher education institutions must provide evidence and indicators that endorse their academic standard of quality to external parties. Moreover, confidential evaluations such as entrance and placement examinations, student grades, and instructor academic performance surveys need to be communicated instantaneously to authorized users. The cloud's elasticity can help manage periods of high demand for undergraduate or postgraduate applications.

- **Promoting instructor flexibility**: Cloud computing offers instructors the freedom to work outside the classroom. When presented with the opportunity to review curriculums, prescribe reading materials, administer coursework, and submit grades online, instructors can be more productive in completing the tasks at a time most convenient to them.

Challenges of cloud computing in education

As with all other forms of technology adoption, cloud computing has its own constraints. Some of these challenges include security, data privacy as well as insufficient network. Data handling issues and privacy laws are matters of concern for any organization. A lot of academic institutions may be skeptical about sharing the hosting of sensitive data and services outside the institution. Some key issues considered by educational establishments when migrating to the cloud include the following:

- **Security and privacy**: Cloud computing requires the approval of a third-party data management service provider that receives and provides sensitive data over the Internet. Hence, the risks of hacking and intrusion are significantly increased.

- **Real benefits**: Many higher education institutions are still apprehensive about adopting cloud computing because they are still not convinced about its benefits. As a result, these institutions are more concerned about acquiring and maintaining their own traditional IT infrastructure.

- **Lack of adequate network responsiveness**: Many learning institutions, especially in underdeveloped countries, lack satisfactory Internet infrastructure that leads to low bandwidth. While there are usually ways to reduce the latencies and improve the response time, the network speed of the **Internet Service Providers (ISPs)** within a certain geographical location represents a fixed performance of the cloud service which cannot be altered.

- **Data security**: This is arguably the biggest challenge faced when adopting cloud computing. Institutions are more comfortable when their data is hosted within the institution because whether at rest or in transit, the possibility of loss or leakage is still high when the data is stored remotely with no physical control over it. Furthermore, if there is a breach of confidential data such as those in environments such as a public cloud, affected parties may take legal action against the institution to bring all types of unfavorable publicity and unnecessary legal costs.

- **Unsolicited advertising**: Since cloud service providers have access to an institution's data, the data collected by the cloud providers may be sold to commercial entities that may use this contact information to send unsolicited advertisements or promotional emails to users who may be unaware that their personal information is now in the possession of a third-party. In some parts of the world, unsolicited advertising is illegal.

- **Lock-in**: When preparing to migrate an institution's data to the cloud, clients must make sure that they choose a reputable cloud service provider that will cater to every need that may arise, especially in the future because the vendor lock-in problem is common as clients are dependent on a single cloud provider and its accompanying technology. The problem arises when the client decides to switch between cloud providers for whatever reasons and find it extremely difficult to integrate into or migrate to, or terminate the services of one cloud vendor and migrate to the next without losing data due to technical software incompatibilities, paying high switching costs, or dealing with some other legal constraints. This can be overcome by doing due diligence and selecting the right cloud service provider.

Cloud computing in healthcare

Cloud services are progressively altering the manner in which health practitioners and healthcare organizations deliver quality, cost-effective services to their patients. Just as the global trend in technology shows many institutions moving to the e-platform, the demand for cloud technologies in the healthcare sector is also steadily increasing. This is because doctors, research clinics as well as private and public healthcare facilities are considering alternatives to traditional patient care and documentation in order to expand the services provided to their patients, improve facilities' capacities, disseminate relevant information easily and timely, and to reduce operational costs.

The following diagram illustrates the cloud services data flow in the healthcare sector:

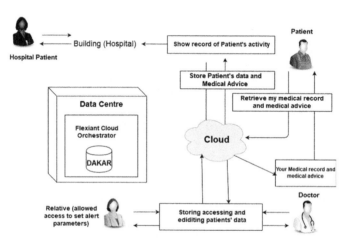

Figure 9.4: Cloud computing healthcare system flow of information

The benefits of cloud computing in healthcare are as follows:

- **Mobility of records**: Many physicians believe that it is easier to collaborate and offer patient care as a team. Occasionally, a patient's medical information is needed by two or more healthcare facilities. Similarly, scientists at research laboratories may need to compare findings and other research data with each other from remote locations. Medical organizations can combine these technologies and easily share industry data to create even more comprehensive big data pools for industry stakeholders to learn from larger and more complex systems. The cloud platform's streamlined synchronization of data among users facilitates information sharing and collaboration.

- **Speed**: Cloud-based services facilitate faster access to all the vital information regarding an institution's medical services. Using cloud services to manage patient data in real-time allows healthcare providers to fully utilize the speed of the cloud platform for medical research, referral generation, trend-spotting, and more personalized healthcare. Furthermore, in the same manner that cloud computing makes it possible for doctors to treat their patients in a better way and more quickly, the cloud makes it possible via storing and sharing data to speed-up the research process.

- **Security and privacy**: In the healthcare sector, cloud computing services mainly comprise the storage of medical records online. Accordingly, data encryption and secure backup of this highly sensitive, personalized data is a key focus of the cloud service providers.

- **Reduction of costs**: The need to minimize costs in the healthcare industry is a significant driver for the adoption of cloud computing. When medical practitioners migrate to a cloud-based system, there is no need for them to invest in costly hardware infrastructure and recurring maintenance because these issues are already taken care of by the cloud computing providers. The cloud makes it possible to not only hold more information but also to do it at a lower cost.

The challenges of cloud computing in healthcare are as follows:

Before healthcare practitioners and medical practitioners can realize the benefits of cloud computing, the following issues must be addressed:

- **Security**: Considering all the sensitive data held by healthcare organizations, cloud computing security concerns are genuine. Despite the potential benefits of cloud computing in e-health services, security problems have become more complex in the cloud models and require additional investments to implement data management policies.

- **Vendor stability and compatibility**: Another big concern is whether particular technologies and cloud service providers will still be around in the future. If a cloud provider becomes insolvent down the road, critical data may be lost leading to catastrophe. Cloud clients must make sure cloud services are compatible with their organization's existing IT infrastructure and assess a particular vendor's cloud platform to see if the data can be easily migrated to another cloud provider if circumstances call for it.

- **IT skills**: As more organizations migrate to the cloud, there is a high demand for IT professionals with cloud computing skills. Accordingly, the costs of hiring and maintaining cloud system experts may prove to be costly even though it may be less exorbitant than contracting outside help.

Cloud computing in politics

Cloud computing has many practical applications in finance and commerce, academia, multimedia, healthcare, agriculture, and other industries. Likewise, cloud applications are becoming prevalent in governance and the political arena as evidenced by applications such as Election Mall Campaign Cloud, Google Moderator, Synteractive Social Rally. In the political domain, cloud applications provide political figures with low election forecast costs, while using vast repositories of hosted voter data that can be processed for many reasons. In fact, Barack Obama's 2012 presidential campaign ran on the AWS *Elections as a service* cloud platform which was specifically designed to provide elections management support for his political activities while he and his associates focused on politics without worrying about the underlying technology. Along with other key mechanisms that his team put in place, the cloud services played an integral role that ultimately lead to his subsequent victory.

Following Obama's success, the AWS *Elections as a service* has been effectively used by other political actors. This cloud computing platform's strategic advantage ensures that regardless of the geographical or demographical scope of a political activity, an ideal solution can be realized for the following key areas:

- **Capital expenditure**: Political planners no longer require large investments for the IT infrastructure to run their websites and applications. Instead, they can scale on a pay-per-use basis to reduce costs of running civil applications and websites efficiently.

- **Political periods**: The fluctuation in the political activity would leave the IT infrastructure idle during non-political periods. Conversely, with the cloud's pay-per-use model, elasticity of service ensures that funds are not wasted during the troughs in political seasons.

- **Diverse levels of access**: With cloud computing, politicians do not need to worry about whether their audiences are using personal computers or mobile devices. Voters vary at different levels of technological access, so cloud providers support multiple types of platforms with the apps automatically conforming to be viewed optimally on any computing device, thereby reaching a larger number of voters anywhere in the world.

Cloud computing in business

One of the most widely used applications of cloud technology is business. Cloud computing provides businesses the access they need to comprehensively store and manage their information remotely within a virtual environment to satisfy customer demands. With the abundance of web-enabled devices used in today's business environment, access to commercial data is boundless.

The benefits of cloud computing in business are as follows:

- **Reduced IT costs**: Migrating to the cloud significantly reduces the IT infrastructure costs resulting from expensive IT hardware acquisition, maintenance and system upgrades, IT support staff, and electrical energy consumption.

- **Scalability**: Firms can scale their applications and storage services up or down to reflect their operational conditions.

- **Business continuity**: Regardless of physical or digital catastrophes, having data stored in the cloud guarantees that it is backed up and safeguarded in a secure location.

- **Collaboration efficiency**: The cloud environment's shared pool of resources ensures that personnel, freelancers, and external parties have access to the same files.

- **Flexibility of work practices**: Cloud computing gives the company staff more flexibility in the performance of their duties from remote locations through virtual offices.

The following diagram outlines the benefits of business entities adopting the cloud computing service model:

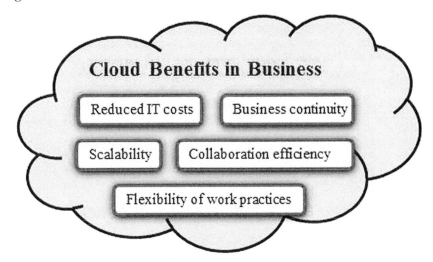

Figure 9.5: Benefits of cloud computing in business

Cloud computing in agriculture

In the present age, cloud computing is proving to be an indispensable asset in consolidating agriculture-related information such as weather conditions, soil and crop test data, cultivation and production equipment, farming and breeding practices, consumer databases, supply chains, billing systems, and so on. This plethora of information can be uploaded to the cloud, which provides enough storage, speed, and computing power to analyze the collected data and package it in a form useful to farmers. 'Timely processing of data allows producers to take action within a growing season and rectify problems before they become detrimental to yield.' The adoption of cloud computing is emerging slower in agriculture than in other industries. However, countries like Japan, China, and USA are leading in this industry. Even parts of East Africa have been able to tap into this ubiquitous technology, though the practice is still in an infant stage.

The following diagram illustrates the practical applications of cloud computing in the agriculture sector:

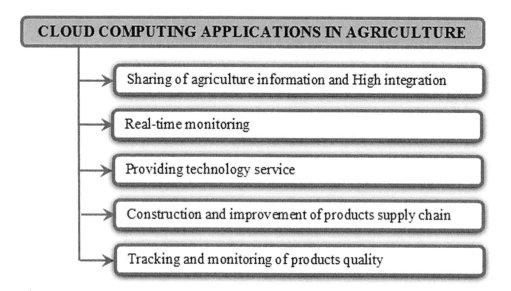

Figure 9.6: Use of cloud computing applications in agriculture

The benefits of cloud computing in agriculture are as follows:

- **Reduced cost**: Initial and recurring costs are considerably lower than traditional computing.

- **Increased storage**: The boundless information storage in the cloud infrastructure gives farmers more data to make better decisions.

- **Minimize infrastructure risk**: Cloud security controls can lower the probability that an infrastructure's vulnerabilities can be exploited.

The challenges of cloud computing in agriculture are as follows:

- **Speedy Accessibility**: Cloud resources can be accessed quickly in developed countries with abundant Internet bandwidth. However, this is not the case in developing countries where there are serious problems with high-speed internet access and lack of stable electricity.

- **Protection**: The fear of losing highly sensitive data to competition is one of the biggest concerns of any company. Accordingly, many small-scale farmers are wary of uploading their confidential information to the cloud because they are afraid that big companies may have access to it.

- **Data recovery and availability**: But utilizing the cloud for the agricultural sector is not without its issues. Cloud solutions offered by large companies usually come at a high cost, which small-scale farmers can't always afford. Additionally, these cloud solutions are often developed for large farms equipped with fast internet speed. Most rural farms have slow internet speed and those in remote areas have no connectivity at all.

Case studies

Many organizations are adopting cloud computing technologies into their existing infrastructure and service models. A study carried out by the **International Data Corporation (IDC)**, an information technology market research, analysis, and advisory firm, concluded that the cloud computing industry is expected to develop from a multi-million to a multi-billion dollar industry in the near future.

Cloud computing adoption in Sub-Saharan Africa

In our dynamically competitive world of information usage and global communication, technologies are constantly changing at a rapid speed. As the developed countries set the standard of information exchange through technology, organizations in underdeveloped countries, especially those in Sub-Saharan Africa need to keep up with trends in technology if they are relevant during this high-tech transformation. Presently, cloud computing is the information exchange standard that is being incorporated into existing IT infrastructures in numerous institutions across the globe.

A lot of organizations in Sub-Saharan countries have realized the importance of migrating to the cloud regardless of the challenges that it entails. Adoption costs, lack of trained or experienced specialists, inconsistent Internet connectivity and electricity are just a few of the constraints that are compounded to their traditional operational limitations. Nonetheless, the general acceptance of cloud computing technologies in these nations is still transforming their education, healthcare, governance, commerce, agriculture, and social paradigms.

Cloud computing is a fairly untapped platform in emerging markets across Africa, and leading the way are organizations in five countries (Kenya and Ethiopia are in East Africa and Ghana, Nigeria, and Liberia in West Africa).

Cloud computing in Kenya and Ethiopia

Several companies, government agencies, and scholastic institutions in Kenya have outsourced their information/data needs to cloud computing providers in efforts to integrate and automate their operations. Cloud computing is useful in terms of 'disaster recovery, business continuity, data consolidation, availability, and confidentiality and data integrity.'

Cloud computing in Ghana, Nigeria, and Liberia

Despite many advantages of migrating to the cloud, its adoption is very slow in Ghana and Nigeria. In Liberia, the significant scarcity of qualified ICT professionals, unsatisfactory technological and electrical infrastructure, insufficient funding, and matters relating to intellectual property rights pose serious threats to adopting cloud computing. These nations must each adopt a national policy framework that is keen on making ICT the focus of its long-term national development. The primary issue that needs to be addressed is cloud technology capacity building. Consequently, in 2019, BlueCrest University College, Liberia, a leading IT higher education institution in the country, has resolved to offer academic courses in various aspects of cloud computing as well as certification training from prominent cloud providers such as Google and Apple.

Cloud computing adoption in India

Presently, India possesses a dominant presence in terms of science and technology. The country has risen to the top five investment hubs for technology dealings. With over 20% of the country's population having access to the internet, India is now the second most connected country in the world, after China. The continued growth of the cloud services market will result from the adoption of cloud services for higher education, scientific research and technological development, advancement of agricultural systems, development of both space and medical science technology, information and communication technology infrastructure, and various fields of engineering (including software, chemical, mechanical, civil, electrical, electronic, and so on). The article in TechTarget E-Guide regarding e-governance in India outlines how India's Department of Electronics and Information Technology proposed IT solution policies to foster the national migration to the cloud.

Companies are doing marketing or branding of their products and services using digital media. Life is becoming so smooth and transparent by sharing of information through the digital mediums. Whether it is a small or a big company, everybody is running for competition because they want to lock their customers. In this paper current market scenario is included with respect to Government data which is publicly accessible should have some policies. Cloud computing is likely to be one of the key pillars on which various e-Governance services would ride. Digital India is a program to prepare India for knowledge and digitized future. Digital India should have a policy wherein the government will provide information and services to internal and external stakeholders. Cloud computing has become the most stimulating development and delivery alternative in the new millennium. A lot of departments are showing interest to adopt cloud technology, but awareness on cloud security needs to be increased. The adoption of cloud is helping organizations innovate, do things faster, become more agile and enhance their revenue stream.

In a similar article, Anuj Sharma stated how cloud computing will transform the Indian IT industry with many of the major telecommunications service providers committing their present IT infrastructure to deploy public cloud services. According to Sharma, cloud computing has a profound effect within the Indian IT industry in the following areas:

- **Surge in demand for cross-domain skilled resources**: With the increase in migration to the cloud, the demand for skilled IT professionals with cloud knowledge and experience will increase.

- **Companies' reliance on SaaS**: With providers such as Amazon, Google, and Microsoft, more companies are deliberating using SaaS to escape the stress of dealing with difficult IT applications while significantly cutting down software costs.

- **The software industry utilizing PaaS**: With many small Indian startups creating software for companies worldwide, PaaS provides developers diverse platforms.

- **More IaaS public cloud offerings**: The upsurge in IT firms and Internet service providers providing IaaS will promote SMEs growth and development.

These technological activities will foster economic growth, create employment opportunities, increase access to computing resources across the spectrums of India's industrial and social environments. However, this progress will be delayed if the internet bandwidth and network costs remain high, as is the case in India. Additionally, internal resistance from corporate managers apprehensive about outsourcing IT infrastructure could lead to security and privacy issues also called cloud adoption barriers. Nonetheless, India has overcome multiple obstacles to cloud computing technology adoption. With the proliferation of more platforms for its people to learn, grow and become more productive than ever before, India seems to be the new Silicon Valley of Asia.

Nowadays everybody wants to get connected with the world. People are getting notifications or messages in their mobile phones from various companies. These companies are doing marketing of their products and services using digital media. It is very easy to share the information through the digital medium. For a small, medium or big company, competition is everywhere because they want to lock their customers. Customers are looking for organizations or companies from where they can gain more and more profits. Market is also growing fast with the usage of the latest technology. To enable Digital India, it is necessary to evaluate the type of services that will be provided to citizens. Government services will be real time for both online and mobile platforms by integrating with government laws and jurisdictions. One of the simplest technologies is cloud computing. Some of the uses of cloud computing in industry sectors are banking, education, government, healthcare, media, manufacturing, and so on. With the help of cloud computing, we can maximize the effectiveness of the shared resources. The cloud has changed the nature of computing and it will continue to do so through 2020. One of the key features of cloud is that it is provisioned by the user. Cloud is elastic, and it can be metered so that you can charge on the basis of usage. The information and services from the government bodies can use public cloud vendors such as AWS or Microsoft Azure of Google Cloud. This might not be totally secure, and it requires having a strong architecture principle and policy to host data and services to relevant cloud computing.

The speed of implementation of cloud computing in the government sector is slow compared to private organizations. Public sector institutions are now increasingly discovering the benefit of information systems which is hosted on third-party data centers by the SaaS, PaaS or IaaS. The government of India already knows about the benefits that cloud computing can bring and how it can be an excellent platform for fast and affordable service deployment and delivery. Cloud computing leads to flexible resource allocation since it allows information technology to respond to changing demands of system administrators. Administrators can manage the resources as the demand occurs. Not all IT services and applications are suited for the cloud. The vision of Cloud Digital India initiative, which we are trying to absorb, is going to be on the cloud as the Cloud First Policy. We will see new architectures propagating and applications getting restored to ensure the benefits that the cloud can give, and it would be made available in the various projects that are going to come up in the near future. Clearly, the move to cloud is about business-aligned IT where the cloud drives business innovation and helps meet business goals. High-speed internet shall be made available in all villages. With the help of mobile banking and net banking in villages, participation in digital and financial space at individual level will be increased. All digital resources are universally accessible such as government documents available on the cloud. Also, the collaborative digital platforms for participative governance provide portability of all entitlements for individuals through the cloud. On the occasion of the launch of Digital India week, Satya Nadella

CEO of Microsoft said technology can support the government's initiatives in key areas of the program, including rural internet connectivity, digital cloud services for all, and communications and productivity services for the government. He also said that we are bringing our marquee cloud services—Microsoft Azure, Dynamics and Office 365—to local data centers in India to accelerate cloud innovation, connect every Indian and every Indian business to the world through our global hyper-scale cloud. In India, broadband network initiatives will eventually stimulate greater acceptance and convenience of cloud services. Cloud computing allows common platforms across multiple agencies, reduce ownership of infrastructure, and improve citizen access to service and information. The government can make things more transparent and help bridge the digital divide by simplifying access using cloud computing. What the government of India can do with cloud? A government organization should start with non-critical applications and non- sensitive data when getting on to the cloud. The government may adopt only private cloud to be built and managed within an enterprise. The main concept is to utilize the maximum resources in a more flexible, scalable and lower-cost manner. In case of private cloud, data can be more secure. Many people have anxiety that their data will not be in their control. But a clear understanding of setting up cloud should be there. Another problem is that various departments do not have the technical resources and strengths. Many Indian projects like Indian Railway and Aadhaar would benefit enormously from cloud computing. Also, creating more and more servers for information sharing will be helpful for the government and citizens of India. The Digital India project demands very strong network security at all levels of operation. We should ensure that data will be managed and controlled by each data center using security policies. Some of the barriers to adoption of cloud in the government can be attributed to diverse service level agreements, data privacy, open standards, business stability, and vendor lock-in. Mr. Anil Ambani said, "The availability of unlimited cloud computing power and data centers are crucial pre-condition for the success of Digital India." He also said, "We have committed to invest nearly Rs 10,000 crore over the next few years to fund these transformational initiatives across the digital, cloud and telecom space." Cloud will be the pillar in facilitating in the delivery of various e-governance services. The Government of India has embarked upon a very striving and important initiative. It is going to be an extremely important component that can bring a standard shift in the way government secures and deploys IT tools and implements e-Governance applications in the country. Many applications of e-governance were written using the client server paradigm. So, there is a very tight coupling trying to split up the applications to make it multi-talented so that the same application can be used by multiple departments across multiple states, which would not be an easy task. There is a cloud server which is managed by the government but hosted by a cloud service provider as a private cloud. This type of model can be cost-effective and secure in terms of capital investments and infrastructures. The public cloud is cost optimizer, controllable, responsive, secure, scalable, and citizen service-oriented. The tools required to create multitalented, user-provisioned, highly secure applications that can scale across hundreds of thousands of servers is still not being used in our country. The government has a policy to release its open data policy to provide access to the data. To achieve a secure cloud environment, we require a combined effort between cloud service vendors and users. Building trust with public cloud service providers while maintaining control of security policies internally are the foundation of building security in the cloud. Gartner said that just 7 percent of consumer content was stored in the cloud in 2011, but this will grow to 36 percent in 2016.

Currently, it is in an early stage but will continue to move to normal adoption with its economic, green and scalable development, and delivery mechanism. A look at the present government's manifesto is good enough to suggest that it intends to leverage IT in each and every segment, without an exception. Multiple levels of security for networks, software and applications are required. If there are thousands of servers in a data center, a lot of care needs to be taken to design and build it because the current generation of data centers has efficiency that is two to four times better than what we are seeing currently in India. More industries are turning to cloud technology as an efficient way to improve quality services due to its capabilities to reduce overhead costs, downtime, and automate infrastructure deployment. The DIT, Government of India, is in discussion with industry representatives on faster adoption and selection of the right paths for sharing of resources.

Cloud computing certifications

Depending on the users, the term *cloud computing* has many different interpretations. Furthermore, to legitimize its tenancy in the technology sector, certification providers and companies that offer cloud-related products such as Google, IBM, Microsoft and **Amazon Web Services** (**AWS**), and VMware are accrediting technology professionals.

Google Cloud Certifications

Google Cloud Certified IT professionals are proficient in designing, developing, managing and administering the application, platform, and infrastructure data solutions using the Google Cloud technology. The Google Cloud Certification indicates that the technician has proven that he/she has acquired the required knowledge and skills to leverage the Google Cloud technology in a manner that revolutionizes businesses and positively affects the customers they cater to. To earn any of these certifications, one must pass the corresponding exam.

Benefits of certifications

The benefits are as follows:

- Respect and recognition by industry authorities
- Validation of technical capabilities
- Extension of IT career opportunities

Google provides the following internationally recognized certifications:

- Associate Cloud Engineer
- Professional Cloud Architect
- Professional Data Engineer
- Professional Cloud Developer

Associate Cloud Engineer: This certified cloud specialist deploys applications, monitors operations, and manages enterprise solutions. This individual is able to use Google Cloud Console and the command-line interface to perform common platform-based tasks to maintain one or more deployed solutions that leverage Google-managed or self-managed services on Google Cloud.

The Associate Cloud Engineer exam evaluates a person's ability to:

- Set up a cloud solution environment
- Plan and configure a cloud solution
- Deploy and implement a cloud solution
- Ensure successful operation of a cloud solution
- Configure access and security

Professional Cloud Architect: This certified cloud specialist designs, develops, and manages robust, secure, scalable, highly available, and dynamic solutions to accomplish business objectives. Professional cloud architects must possess a thorough understanding of the cloud architecture and the Google Cloud Platform.

The Professional Cloud Architect exam assesses a person's ability to:

- Design and plan a cloud solution architecture
- Manage and deliver the cloud solution infrastructure
- Design for security and compliance

- Analyze and optimize technical and business processes
- Manage implementation of the cloud architecture
- Ensure reliable solutions and operations

Professional Data Engineer: This certified cloud specialist designs, builds, maintains, and troubleshoots data processing systems with particular emphasis on the security, reliability, fault-tolerance, scalability, fidelity, and efficiency of such systems.

The Professional Data Engineer exam assesses a person's ability to:

- Build and maintain data structures and databases
- Design data processing systems
- Analyze data and enable machine learning
- Model business processes for analysis and optimization
- Design for reliability
- Visualize data and advocate policies
- Design for security and compliance

Professional Cloud Developer: This certified cloud specialist builds scalable and highly available applications using Google recommended practices and tools that leverage fully managed services. This individual has experience with the next generation databases, runtime environments and developer tools and he/she is familiar with at least one general purpose programming language and is skilled in using StackDriver to produce meaningful metrics and logs to debug and trace code.

The Professional Cloud Developer exam assesses your ability to:

- Design highly scalable, available, and reliable cloud-native applications
- Build and test applications
- Deploy applications
- Integrate Google Cloud Platform services
- Manage application performance monitoring

Figure 9.7: Sample of Google Cloud Architect Certificate

IBM Cloud Certifications

The IBM Professional Certification Program offers industry-recognized credentials based on IBM technology. IBM Cloud Certification covers a variety of technical areas, including Cloud, Watson, IoT, Security, and so on. To earn any of these certifications; one must pass the corresponding exam.

IBM provides the following internationally recognized certifications:

- **Solution Advisor**: Cloud reference architecture V5
- **Solution Architect**: Cloud platform solution V2
- **Solution Advisor**: DevOps V1
- **Application Developer**: Watson V3
- **Advanced Application Developer**: Cloud platform V1

IBM Certified Solution Advisor - Cloud reference architecture V5: This certified cloud specialist can openly describe the advantages and fundamental ideas of cloud computing.

IBM Certified Solution Architect - Cloud platform solution V2: This certified cloud specialist can design and construct a cloud infrastructure.

IBM Certified Solution Advisor - DevOps V1: This certified cloud specialist can convey the advantages and core concepts of DevOps.

Certified Application Developer - Watson V3: This certified cloud specialist understands the concepts crucial for building applications using IBM Watson services on Bluemix.

Certified Advanced Application Developer - Cloud platform V1: This certified cloud specialist understands the advanced concepts critical to the development of applications that span multiple cloud and on-premise environments.

On completion of the certification exam, successful candidates are issued each of these certifications along with a badge in the IBM Open Badge program confirming that they have acquired the necessary skills to perform the associated tasks. Here is a screenshot of the IBM Certified Solution Advisor Badge:

Figure 9.8: IBM Certified Solution Advisor Badge - Cloud reference architecture V5

Amazon Web Services (AWS) Cloud Certifications

Organizations demand professionals with cloud dexterity to help transform their business. As the global leader in cloud services, AWS provides its own training and certification program. To earn any of these certifications, one must pass the corresponding exam.

AWS provides the following internationally recognized certifications:

- AWS Certified Cloud Practitioner
- AWS Certified Solutions Associate Architect
- AWS Certified Solutions Associate Developer
- AWS Certified Solutions Professional Architect

AWS Certified Cloud Practitioner: This certified cloud specialist possesses the knowledge and skills required to effectively demonstrate a general understanding of the AWS Cloud.

AWS Certified Solutions Associate Architect: This certified cloud specialist exhibits the skills of how to develop and deploy secure and powerful AWS-based applications.

AWS Certified Associate Developer: This certified cloud specialist has years of practical experience constructing and maintaining AWS-based applications.

AWS Certified Solutions Professional Architect: This certified cloud specialist possesses advanced technical skills and experience in designing distributed AWS-based applications.

Summary

- Cloud computing has become the most stimulating development and delivery alternative in the new millennium.

- The adoption of cloud is helping organizations innovate, do things faster, become more agile and enhance their revenue stream.

- Adoption of cloud computing can bring many benefits in the developing and developed countries. There are technological, organizational, and environmental factors that could hinder the adoption of cloud technologies in the world.

- Technology factors are relative advantages and compatibility.

- Organizational factors are organizational readiness and top management support.

- Environmental factors are competitive pressure, government regulation and technology support.

- Cloud computing provides both effective and efficient means for its actors in various sectors, which include education, healthcare, politics, business, and agriculture, to not only solve various existing problems but also to deliver standardized services in a timely and cost-effective manner.

- Many organizations are adopting cloud computing technologies into their existing infrastructure and service models.

- A lot of organizations in Sub-Saharan countries have realized the importance of migrating to the cloud regardless of the challenges that it entails.

- The government of India already knows about the benefits that cloud computing can bring and how it can be an excellent platform for fast and affordable service deployment and delivery.

- The main concept behind the Digital India Program is to utilize the maximum resources in a more flexible, scalable, lower-cost, effective and efficient manner.

- Many multinational companies are providing the internationally recognized certifications to brush up the technical and practical knowledge in the cloud technology.

- Google provides the following internationally recognized certifications: Associate Cloud Engineer, Professional Cloud Architect, Professional Data Engineer, and Professional Cloud Developer.

- **International Business Machines (IBM)** Professional Certification Program provides the following internationally recognized certifications: Solution Advisor - Cloud reference architecture V5, Solution Architect - Cloud platform solution V2, Solution Advisor - DevOps V1, Application Developer - Watson V3, and Advanced Application Developer - Cloud platform V1.

- Amazon Web Services (AWS) provides the following internationally recognized certifications: AWS Certified Cloud Practitioner, AWS Certified Solutions Associate Architect, AWS Certified Solutions Associate Developer, and AWS Certified Solutions Professional Architect.

Exercise

Tick the correct option

1. What are the three main factors of the cloud computing adoption?

    a. Technological, governmental and environmental

    b. Technological, organizational and environmental

    c. Technological, organizational and cultural

    d. Technological, cultural and industrial

2. Google provides the following internationally recognized certifications:

    a. Associate Cloud Engineer

    b. Professional Cloud Architect

    c. Professional Data Engineer

    d. Professional Cloud Developer

e. All of the above

3. The term MOOCs refers to _____.

    a. Massive Open Online Courses

    b. Massive Open Online Curriculum

    c. Massive Open Source Online Courses

    d. None of the above

4. Which of the following benefit is related to create resources that are pooled together in a system that supports multi-tenant usage?

    a. On-demand self-service

    b. Broad network access

    c. Resource pooling

    d. All of the above

5. Which of the following allows you to create instances of the MySQL database to support your web sites?

    a. Amazon Elastic Compute Cloud

    a. Amazon Simple Queue Service

    b. Amazon Relational Database Service

    c. Amazon Simple Storage System

Answers:

1. b. Technological, organizational and environmental

2. e. All of the above

3. a. Massive Open Online Courses

4. a. On-demand self-service

5. c. Amazon Relational Database Service

Fill in the blanks

1. Top management support is considered one of the main success _____ in project management.

2. Security and legal issues regarding data jurisdictions, security risks and _____ must be considered when attempting to upload data into the cloud.

3. Two of the industry's leading education PaaS are _____ and Google App Engine (GAE).

4. In the healthcare sector, cloud computing services mainly comprise the _____ of medical records online.

5. The AWS _____ has been effectively used during Obama's political campaign in the US.

Answers:

1. factors

2. data confidentiality

3. Amazon Web Services (AWS)

4. storage

5. Elections-as-a-service

Descriptive questions

1. What are the factors influencing the adoption of cloud computing?

2. Explain the technology factors in detail.

3. Explain the organizational factors in detail.

4. Explain the environmental factors in detail.

5. What are the benefits and challenges of cloud computing adoption in the education sector?

6. Explain in detail the Google Cloud Certification.

7. How can government regulations play an important role in the adoption of cloud computing? Explain in detail.

8. Which area of application of cloud computing is popular and why? Explain with examples.

9. What are the benefits and challenges of cloud computing adoption in the healthcare sector?

10. Write a short note on the following:

    a. Cloud computing adoption in Sub-Saharan Africa

    b. Cloud computing adoption in India

    c. IBM cloud certifications

    d. AWS cloud certifications

Model Paper 1

Multiple Choice

1. Which of these is NOT a technical characteristic of the cloud?
    a. High scalability
    b. Resource pooling
    c. Resource scheduling
    d. Multitenancy

2. Which of the following is associated with cluster computing?
    a. Loose coupling
    b. Tight coupling
    c. Distributed job management
    d. Diversity

3. Public cloud is defined by
    a. Portability
    b. Ownership
    c. Storage size
    d. Accessibility

4. One of the following is not a characteristic of the public cloud

    a. Homogenous resources

    b. Multi-tenancy

    c. Economies of scale

    d. Heterogeneous resources

5. Which of these techniques is vital for creating cloud computing centers?

    a. Virtualization

    b. Transubstantiation

    c. Cannibalization

    d. Insubordination

6. Which of the following cloud concept is related to pooling and sharing of resources?

    a. Polymorphism

    b. Abstraction

    c. Virtualization

    d. None of the mentioned

7. Which standard describes the interface of web services?

    a. SOAP

    b. ESB

    c. BPEL

    a. XML

8. What are the core components of a Web Service?

    a. XML & XML Schema

    b. SOAP & HTTP

    c. WSDL & XML

    d. ESB & WS-Policy

9. Potential defense mechanism to repudiation include all of the following except?

    a. Digital signatures

    b. Time-stamps

    c.   Audit trails

    d.   Filtering

10. Authentication, authorization, throttling and filtering are potential defense mechanism for

    a.   Data tampering

    b.   Repudiation

    c.   Information Disclosure

    d.   Denial of Service

11. Which of these companies is not a leader in cloud computing?

    a.   Google

    b.   Amazon

    c.   Intel

    d.   Microsoft

12. Which is not a major cloud computing platform?

    a.   Apple iCloud

    b.   IBM Deep Blue

    c.   Microsoft Azure

    d.   Amazon EC2

13. YARN is an acronym for?

    a.   Yet Another Resource Negotiator

    b.   Yet Another Resource Navigator

    c.   Yes Another Resource Negotiator

    d.   Yet Again Resource Navigator

14. What are the three main factors of the cloud computing adoption?

    a.   Technological, Governmental and Environmental

    b.   Technological, Organizational and Environmental

    c.   Technological, Organizational and Cultural

    d.   Technological, Cultural and Industrial

15. Google provides the following internationally recognized certifications:

    a. Associate Cloud Engineer

    b. Professional Cloud Architect

    c. Professional Data Engineer

    d. Professional Cloud Developer

    e. All of the above

Fill in the Blanks

1. Data protection is often managed using _____with defined roles and privileges on data encryption keys management.

2. _____are the basic foundational building blocks of the cloud computing environments.

3. The _____mechanism is an autonomous and lightweight software application that is responsible for harvesting and processing the usage data of compute IT resource.

4. The intermediary that provides connectivity and transference of cloud services between Cloud Providers and Cloud Consumers is called_____.

5. A commitment between a cloud service provider and a client is known as _____.

6. In SOA, _____are developed, maintained and owned by multiple stakeholders

7. _____is a component of the virtual machine that enables host isolation and resource sharing.

8. _____allows credentials to be issued following standards like Security Assertion Markup language (SAML) and Simple Public Key Infrastructure (SPKI)

9. _____measures the quality of the efficiency of the connection and data transfer between internal service instances, different cloud services, or between external consumer and the cloud.

10. GAE is software that facilitates users in running web applications on _____infrastructure.

Short answer questions

1. Differentiate between Cloud Datastore and Relational Database.

2. What is high performance computing (HPC)?

3. What is MapReduce Model?

4. What are the four major design goals of cloud computing?

5. What is VMM?

Descriptive Questions

1. With suitable architectural diagram, discuss the role of various components of Eucalyptus Cloud Platform.

2. What are the benefits and challenges of cloud computing adoption in education sector?

3. Differentiate between Cluster, Grid and Cloud computing.

4. What are the drivers of cloud computing adoption.

5. What is Google Cloud Datastore? List the features of the Google Datastore.

6. Write short note on the followings:

    a. BLOB

    b. AWS

    c. Amazon Simple Storage Service (S3)

7. Differentiate between various cloud computing platforms - Dropbox, Google Drive, Amazon Cloud Drive and Apple iCloud.

8. Differentiate between Amazon EC2 and Windows Azure based on their main features.

9. Discuss what you understand by "Cloud Service Level Agreements", its components and types.

10. What do you understand by the Cloud CIA Security Model?

Model Paper 2

Multiple choice

1. Intergalactic computer network was proposed by who?
    a. IBM
    b. Oracle
    c. JCR Licklider
    d. Salesforce

2. One of the following can be used to enhance the deployment of successful private cloud architecture:
    a. HP Cloud Service Automation
    b. HP CloudAutumn Matrix server
    c. HP Aggregation Platform for SaaS
    d. HP BladeSystem Matrix server

3. Remote use of applications via network-based subscriptions is known as:
    a. Cloud service
    b. Infrastructure-as-a-Service
    c. On-demand service
    d. Software-as-a-Service

4. What is a common design element often found in cloud architectures?
   a. Single tiered
   b. Terminal emulators
   c. Synchronous web services
   d. Asynchronous web services

5. Identify the odd out of the following
   a. Cloud storage driver
   b. Resource replication
   c. Resource aggregation
   d. Cloud usage monitor

6. Power Usage Efficiency is associated with which of the cloud QoS measures:
   a. Sustainability
   b. Modifiability
   c. Reliability
   d. Reusability

7. Which of the following cloud-enabled migrations is also known as "cloudify"?
   a. Type I
   b. Type II
   c. Type III
   d. Type IV

8. IGT Cloud is an example of?
   a. Public cloud
   b. Private cloud
   c. Hybrid cloud
   d. Community cloud

9. How services communicate with each other in SOA?
   a. Using XML messages
   b. Using common data & communication model

    c. Using ESB (Enterprise Service Bus) layer

    d. Integration of business logic between services

10. Origin, in browser security means

    a. Different browser

    b. Same application

    c. Source browser

    d. Origin application

11. BladeSystem Matrix servers are products of which cloud vendor?

    a. IBM

    b. HP

    c. Salesforce

    d. RackSpace

12. One of this is not true about the on-premise private cloud?

    a. Highly standardized process

    b. Also referred to as internal cloud

    c. High scalability

    d. High level of security

13. Amazon EC2 provides virtual computing environments, known as:

    a. Chunks

    b. Instances

    c. Messages

    d. None of the mentioned

14. The component is responsible for providing Simple Storage Service in Eucalyptus Cloud Platform?

    a. Cluster Controller

    b. CLC

    c. Walrus

    d. Node Controller

15. Which of the following allows you to create instances of the MySQL database to support your Web sites?

    a. Amazon Elastic Compute Cloud

    b. Amazon Simple Queue Service

    c. Amazon Relational Database Service

    d. Amazon Simple Storage System

Fill in the blanks

1. _____uses IF-MAP standard to authorize users in real-time communication between the cloud provider and the consumer.

2. Amazon offers many different cloud services. The most central and well-known of these services are Amazon _____ (EC2) and Amazon Simple Storage Service (S3).

3. _____makes an expansion of cloud service provisioning business globally a reality in the cloud market.

4. Mobile cloud computing (MCC) is the incorporation of cloud computing into _____the applications.

5. _____reflects redundant provisioning of data storage and processing facilities to manage potential single point of failure events.

6. Cloud users may use _____to design, implement, test and deploy their own self-tailored applications and services within a cloud.

7. A _____is a processing program (module) that harvest usage data via event-driven communications with esoteric resource software.

8. _____refers to the ability share sensitive data among a number of users without violating the privileges granted by the data owner to each of the targeted user.

9. Top management support is considered one of the main success _____in project management.

10. Security and legal issues regarding data jurisdictions, security risks and _____must be considered when attempting to upload data into the cloud.

Short answer questions

1. What are web services? How they are important in SOA?

2. What are the characteristics of cloud computing?

3. What is Openstack?

4. What List and describe any five (5) cloud security threats with their associated potential defense mechanisms.

5. What are the factors influencing the adoption of Cloud computing?

Descriptive questions

1. Explain all the phases of the cloud computing life cycle (CCLC).

2. Differentiate between hypervisors and rogue hypervisors in a cloud computing environment?

3. Compare Open Stack and OpenNebula Cloud Platforms.

4. Google provides certain services in cloud environment. Discuss in terms of SaaS and PaaS.

5. (a) How AWS deals with Disaster recovery?
   (b) What is elastic load balancing and how it reduces the workload?

6. In which area of application cloud computing is popular and why? Explain with example.

7. What is the Purpose of Cloud Service Management? List any five Functional Requirements of Cloud Service Management.

8. What is the difference between IaaS, PaaS and SaaS?

9. Is Gmail SaaS or PaaS? Explain in detail.

10. What are the major actors of the NIST cloud computing reference?

Model Paper 3

Multiple choice

1. "Mean Time To Change" is associated with:
    a. Modifiability
    b. Usability
    c. Reusability
    d. Sustainability

2. Metered service to access and use computing resources is tagged
    a. Pay service
    b. Utility computing
    c. Metered access
    d. Pay-as-you-go

3. Techniques for provising quality of service to the cloud applications include all of the following except:
    a. Admission Control
    b. Scheduling
    c. Handoff
    d. Dynamic resource provisioning

4. Energy efficiency in cloud computing is termed?

    a. Energy-aware computing

    b. Energy Virtualization

    c. Green computing

    d. High performance computing

5. The user layer of the cloud security architecture consists of the following except

    a. Authentication

    b. Security-as-a-Service

    c. Infrastructure

    d. Browser Security

6. What are two traits of a cloud computing architecture? (Choose two.)

    a. Single tiered

    b. Not scalable

    c. On-demand access to resources

    d. Internet/intranet accessible server

    e. Client and server run in the same physical environment

7. HP Cloud Services Enablement for Infrastructure-as-a-Service is made up of all of the following except:

    a. HP Cloud Service Automation

    b. HP CloudAutumn Matrix server

    c. HP Aggregation Platform for SaaS

    d. HP BladeSystem Matrix server

8. A virtual server uses a combination of all of the following for identification except?

    a. Host name

    b. Password

    c. IP address

    d. Port number

9. Which of the following is not a component of Open Stack Cloud Platform?

    a. Nova

    b. Keystone

    c. Neutron

    a. Walrus

10. Which of the following costs is associated with the server costs?

    a. Network cost

    b. Storage cost

    c. Support cost

    d. Recovery cost

11. A cloud service level agreement is composed of all of the following except

    a. Service guarantee

    b. Service guarantee time period

    c. Service guarantee granularity

    d. Service guarantee inclusions

12. Customer Relationship Management is associated with one of the following cloud vendors

    a. IBM

    b. HP

    c. Salesforce

    d. RackSpace

13. Which of the architectural layer is used as front end in cloud computing?

    a. Cloud

    b. Soft

    c. Client

    d. All of the mentioned

14. Which of these is a key business driver of cloud computing?

    a. Costs reduction

    b. Scalability

    c. sharing

    d. Mobility

15. Difficulty in locating faults is common to?

    a. Mainframe Systems

    b. Cloud Computing

    c. Grid Computing

    d. Cluster Computing

Fill in the blanks

1. _____are entities that facilitate efficient and effective use of cloud services while ensuring peak performance and seamless delivery of such services.

2. _____can be referred to as a statistical concept associated with uncertain outcomes of business activities in the future

3. _____is the degree of quality of a cloud service provided to a cloud service consumer by a cloud service provider.

4. Service interoperability involves the ability of cloud users to access their unique set of data and provisioned services from multiple cloud providers via a _____.

5. A monitoring agent is a mediating, event-driven program that functions as a service agent and occupies existing communication paths to ensure a clear and apparent monitoring and analysis of _____.

6. The NIST cloud computing reference architecture defines five major actors: Cloud consumer, _____, Cloud carrier, Cloud auditor and Cloud broker.

7. SOA infrastructure comprises three levels: Core, Platform and_____.

8. Amazon Cloud Watch is a web service that provides monitoring for AWS cloud _____and applications.

9. In the healthcare sector, cloud computing services mainly comprise of the_____ of medical records online.

10. The AWS _____has been effectively used during Obama's political campaign in the US.

Short answer questions

1. Write a short note on trust in the context of cloud computing.

2. What are the major challenges faced in cloud?

3. In which area of application cloud computing is popular and why?

4. Give name of all the Google cloud certification.

5. What is Apache Hadoop?

Descriptive questions

1. With suitable diagram, represent the elements of a SOA message.

2. How integration of Hadoop with Cloud framework is beneficial to the programming community? Give reasons to support you answer.

3. With a block diagram, explain cloud computing reference models and service.

4. With a block diagram, explain AWS management console offered by Amazon.

5. How Government Regulation can play an important role for the adoption of cloud computing, explain in detail.

6. What are the factors influencing the adoption of Cloud computing?

7. Explain in detail about the Google cloud certification.

8. Write a short not on the followings:

   a. Cloud Computing adoption in Sub-Saharan Africa

   b. Cloud Computing adoption in India

   c. IBM cloud certifications

   d. AWS cloud certifications

9. What are the benefits and challenges of cloud computing adoption in education sector?

10. What are the cloud architecture design principles, explain them in detail?

Model Paper 4

Multiple choice

1. In which year was Oracle Cloud launched?

    a. 2014

    b. 2012

    c. Late 1990s

    d. Early 2000s

2. Which is an open source data query system?

    a. Walrus

    b. Hive

    c. Pig

    d. Glance

3. Cosine similarity is associated with none of the following trust management except?

    a. Reputation_based

    b. Prediction_based

    c. Recommendation_based

    d. Policy_based

4. Which Hadoop tool also provides support for Columnar database?

   a. HDFS

   b. Pig

   c. Hive

   a. HBase

5. Which of the following is a Cloud Platform by Amazon?

   a. Azure

   b. AWS

   c. Cloudera

   d. All of the mentioned

6. Cloud monitoring requirements are all of the following except?

   a. Migration,

   b. Scalability

   c. Portability

   d. Autonomy

7. What is true in case of SOA and BPM?

   a. Tasks can be rearranged with user interference

   b. Business rules can be dynamically changed

   c. New services can be created at runtime

   d. None of the above

8. Point out the correct statement:

   a. Cloud architecture can couple software running on virtualized hardware in multiple locations to provide an on-demand service

   b. Cloud computing relies on a set of protocols needed to manage inter-process communications

   c. Platforms are used to create more complex software

   d. All of the mentioned

9. Examples of ready-made environment pre-installed cloud resources are all of the following except

   a. Middleware

   b. Databases

    c. development tools

    d. Resource agents

10. The smallest unit of data and the lowest level of storage is called?

    a. Objects

    b. Dataset

    c. Block

    d. Files

11. The composite data together with its associated metadata which are grouped as web-based resources is called?

    a. File

    b. Object

    c. Block

    d. Dataset

12. Packet Loss Frequency is associated with which of the cloud QoS measures?

    a. Computation

    b. Communication

    c. Memory

    d. Transport

13. Cloud storage devices mechanisms provide standard logical classes of data storage known as?

    a. Cloud storage stages

    b. Cloud storage blocks

    c. Cloud Storage levels

    d. Cloud storage steps

14. The term MOOCs refers to _____.

    a. Massive Open Online Courses

    b. Massive Open Online Curriculum

    c. Massive Open Source Online Courses

    d. None of the above

15. Which of the following benefit is related to creates resources that are pooled together in a system that supports multi-tenant usage?

    a. On-demand self-service

    b. Broad network access

    c. Resource pooling

    d. All of the mentioned

Fill in the blanks

1. Google Drive provides _____ of Cloud storage space for free.

2. Windows Azure has five main parts: Compute, Storage, the _____, _____, the CDN, and Connect.

3. The speed of response to adjusted workload is known as _____

4. _____ is a document that contains the records of all service level management problems related to a group of certain users.

5. When a browser is incapable of generating cryptographically-valid XML tokens, such attack is known as _____.

6. _____ is a methodical set to advance a company's enterprise processes.

7. BPaaS stands for _____.

8. _____ is being used to isolate the network environment within the data center infrastructure.

9. _____ are mostly used to estimate message metrics and the network traffic.

10. The main stakeholders of the cloud ecosystem are the _____.

Short answer questions

1. What is Google Drive?

2. What is SOA?

3. Define Cloud, On Demand self-service.

4. Write short note on Google App Engine. (GAE)

5. Explain the details about the AWS cloud certification.

Descriptive questions

1. How high-performance computing be integrated with Cloud Computing?

2. What Compare Open Stack and OpenNebula Cloud Platforms.

3. Explain Amazon S3? Explain Amazon S3 API? What are the operations we can execute through API?

4. Explain SaaS with an example?

5. Explain in brief about the Future of cloud (FoC).

6. Explain about the Traditional and Cloud Computing Paradigms.

7. List and discuss any four (4) trust management techniques in the cloud.

8. What are the benefits and challenges of cloud computing adoption in healthcare sector?

9. State the use of Google App Engine and list Google App Engine Services.

10. Name and brief the main components provided by Windows Azure.

Index

Bibliography

1. Badger, L., Grance, T., Patt Corner, R., and Voas, J. (2011). Cloud Computing Synopsis and 2012 from http://reports.informationweek.com/abstract/24/7534/Storage-Server/research-cloudstorage.

2. Bayramusta, M., & Nasir, V. A. (2016). *A fad or future of IT? A comprehensive literature review on the cloud computing research*, International Journal of Information Management, 36(4), 635–644. http://dx.doi.org/10.1016/j.ijinfomgt.2016.04.006.

3. Bhaskar Prasad Rimal, Eunmi Choi, 2009, *A Taxonomy and Survey of Cloud Computing Systems*, Fifth International Joint Conference on INC, IMS and IDC, published by IEEE Computer Society.

4. Biddick, M. (2011). *Cloud storage: Changing dynamics beyond services*. Retrieved December

5. Buyya R., C. S. Yeo, and S. Venugopal, *Market-Oriented Cloud Computing: Vision, Hype, and Reality for Delivering IT Services as Computing Utilities*, in Proc. IEEE/ACM Grid Conf., 2008, pp. 50–57.

6. K. K. Hiran, R. Doshi, *The Proliferation of Smart Devices on Mobile Cloud Computing*, Germany: Lambert Academic Publishing, 2014.

7. KK Hiran, A Henten, MK Shrivas, R Doshi (2018), *Hybrid EduCloud Model in Higher Education: The case of Sub-Saharan Africa, Ethiopia*, 7th International Conference on Adaptive.

8. K. K. Hiran, R. Doshi, R. Rathi, *Security & Privacy Issues of Cloud & Grid Computing Networks*, International Journal on Computational Sciences & Applications, vol. 4, no. 1, pp. 83-91, February 2014.

9. Doshi R., *Adoption of the ICT application Moodle Cloud to enhance teaching-learning in large classes: Case of Sub-Sahara Africa*, Research Delight - An International Journal Vol. 1. Issue 1. November 2018.

10. Wireko K.J., Hiran, K. K. & Doshi, R. (April 2018), *Culturally based User Resistance to New Technologies in the Age of IoT in Developing Countries: Perspectives from Ethiopia*, International Journal of Emerging Technology and Advanced Engineering, 8(4), 96-105.

11. Peprah A. Nana, Hiran, K. K. & Doshi, R. (December 2018), *Politics in the Cloud: A Review of Cloud Technology Applications in the Domain of Politics*, Springer 3rd International Conference on Soft Computing: Theories and Applications (SoCTA 2018).

12. Doshi R., *An Institutional Adoption Framework of the Cloud Computing in Higher Education: Case of Sub-Saharan Africa*, International Journal of Research in Engineering, IT and Social Sciences, (June 2018), 8(6), 51-56

13. Garrison, G., Wakefield, R. L., & Kim, S. (2015). *The effects of IT capabilities and delivery model on cloud computing success and firm performance for cloud supported processes and operations.* International Journal of Information Management, 35(4), 377–393. http://dx.doi.org/10.1016/j.ijinfomgt.2015.03.001.

14. Gwendolyn, T., & Maxmillan, G. (2014). *Cloud Computing Adoption and Utilization amongst Zimbabwean NGOs: A Case of Gweru NGOs*, http://doi.org/10.1136/emj.2010.096966, Institute of Standards and Technology. Nist Special Publication, 145, 7.

15. John Harauz, Lorti M. Kaunan. Bruce Potter, *Data Security in the World of Cloud Computing*, IEEE Security & Privacy, Copublished by the IEEE Computer and Reliability Societies, July/August 2009.

16. Krishna Reddy, B. ThirumalRao, Dr. L.S.S. Reddy, P.SaiKiran, *Research Issues in Cloud Computing*, Global Journal of Computer Science and Technology, Volume 11, Issue 11, July 2011.

17. Mladen A. Vouk (2008). *Cloud Computing – Issues, Research and Implementations*, Journal of Computing and Information Technology - CIT 16, 2008, 4, 235–246.

18. Puja Dhar (2012*). Cloud computing and its applications in the world of Networking*, IJCSI International Journal of Computer Science Issues, Vol. 9, Issue 1, No 2, pp.430-433.

19. Spoorthy V., M. Mamatha, B. Santhosh Kumar, 2014. *A Survey on Data Storage and Security in Cloud Computing*, International Journal of Computer Science and Mobile Computing, Vol.3 Issue.6, June- 2014, pg. 306-313.

20. Vaquero L.M., L. Rodero-Merino, J. Caceres, and M. Lindner, *A Break in the Clouds: Towards a Cloud Definition*, Strategic Management Journal, vol. 22, 2009.

21. Amol, C. A., Vikram, D. S., Seema, H. P. & Gopakumaran, T. T., 2015. *Cloud Computing – A Market Perspective and Research Directions*. International Journal of Information Technology and Computer Science, 10(1), pp. 42-53.

22. Aniruddha, S. R. & Chaudhari, D. N., 2013. *Cloud Computing: Infrastructure as a Service*. International Journal of Inventive Engineering and Sciences, 1(3), pp. 1-7.

23. Astri, L. Y., 2015. *A Study Literature of Critical Success Factors of Cloud Computing in Organizations*. Procedia Computer Science, 59(1), pp. 188-194.

24. Bouyer, A., Jalali, M., Arasteh, B., & Moloudi, M. (2013). *The Effect of Cloud Computing Technology in Personalization and Education Improvements and its Challenges*. Procedia - Social and Behavioral Sciences, 83(0), 655-658.

25. Buyya R., C. S. Yeoa, S. Venugopala, J. Broberg, I. Brandic. (2008). *Cloud computing and emerging IT platforms: Vision, hype, and reality for delivering computing as the 5th utility.*

26. Buyya, R., Broberg, J., & Goscinski, A. (2011). *Cloud computing: principles and paradigms. cloud computing: principles and paradigms*. New Jersey: John Wiley & Sons, Inchttp://dx.doi.org/10.1002/9780470940105.

27. Grossman R. L, *The Case for Cloud Computing*, IT Professional, vol. 11(2), pp. 23-27, 2009, ISSN: 1520-9202.

28. Hsu, P. F., Ray, S., & Li-Hsieh, Y. Y. (2014). *Examining cloud computing adoption intention, pricing mechanism, and deployment model*. International Journal of Information Management, 34(4), 474–488. http://dx.doi.org/10.1016/j.ijinfomgt. 2014.04.006.

29. Kumar, M., 2014. *Software as a Service for Efficient Cloud Computing*. International Journal of Research in Engineering and Technology, 3(1), pp. 178-181.

30. Liang – Jie Zhang and Qun Zhou, 2009, New York, USA,CCOA: *Cloud Computing Open Architecture*, 978-0-7695-3709-2/09 $25.00 © 2009 IEEE DOI 10.1109/ICWS.2009.144

31. Nazir, A. & Jamshed, S., 2013. *Cloud Computing: Challenges and Concerns for its Adoption in Indian SMEs.* International Journal of Software and Web Sciences, 4(2), pp. 120-125.

32. Ratten, V. (2015). *Factors influencing consumer purchase intention of cloud computing in the United States and Turkey.* EuroMed Journal of Business, 10(1), 80–97. http://dx.doi.org/10.1108/emjb-02-2014-0007.

33. Rezaei, R., Chiew, T. K., Lee, S. P., & Shams Aliee, Z. (2014). *A semantic interoperability framework for software as a service systems in cloud computing environments.* Expert Systems with Applications, 41(13), 5751–5770. http://dx.doi.org/10.1016/j.eswa.

34. Sultan, N. (2010). *Cloud computing for education: A new dawn?* International Journal of Information Management, 30(2), 109-116.

35. Sumit, G., 2014. *Public vs Private vs Hybrid vs Community - Cloud Computing: A Critical Review.* International Journal of Computer Network and Information Security, 3(1), pp. 20-29.

36. "Alessandro Perilli" *Step-by-step virtualization adoption: ROI calculation,* September, 16

37. Irene Maida, 10 BENEFITS OF VIRTUALIZATION, September 2016

38. "Contel Bradford" *Virtualization Barriers: Top Five Challenges of Adoption*

39. "Sam's Solution" *Virtualization Techniques in Cloud computing,* August 2017

40. Jonathan Strickland, *How server Virtualization Works,* 2017

41. Marie Gassee, *What Is Virtualization and How Does It Work for Your Small Business?,* June 2010.

42. Mohammad Dosoukey, *How to Create Virtual Machines in Linux Using KVM (Kernel-based Virtual Machine) – Part 1,* February, 2015

43. Margaret Rouse, *Dig Deeper on VMware desktop software and desktop virtualization,* 2009

44. Borko Furht,Armando Escalante, *Handbook of Cloud Computing,* 2010

45. Nader Benmessaoud n CJ Williams n Uma Mahesh Mudigonda Mitch Tulloch, *Network Virtualization and Cloud Computing,* 2013

46. Martin Keen, Rafael Coutinho, Sylvi Lippmann, Salvatore Sollami, Sundaragopal Venkatraman, Steve Baber, Henry Cui, Craig Fleming, *Developing Web Services Applications*, 2012

47. Arpit Sud, *Service Oriented Architecture*, 2010.

48. White Paper on *"NETWORK VIRTUALIZATION.*

49. Malhotra L, Agarwal D and Jaiswal A, *Virtualization in Cloud Computing*, 2014

50. Andreas Rivera, *Virtualization vs. Cloud Computing: What's the Difference?* July, 2018

51. Adesh Kumar (2013). *Security architecture of cloud computing*, International Journal of Innovations in Engineering and Technology, 2(2), pp. 400-403.

52. Aleksandar Hudic, Shareeful Islam, Peter Kieseberg, Edgar R. Weippl, *Data Confidentiality using Fragmentation in Cloud Computing*, Int. J. Communication Networks and Distributed Systems, Vol. 1, No. 3/4, 2012.

53. Arshad, J, Townsend, P. and Xu, J. (2013). *A novel intrusion severity analysis approach for Clouds.*

54. Bowers K.D., A. Juels, and A. Oprea, *HAIL: A high-availability and integrity layer for cloud storage*, in proceedings of 16th ACM conference on Computer and communications security, 2009.

55. Casola, V., Cuomo, A., Rak, M. and Villano, U. (2013). *The CloudGrid approach: Security analysis and performance evaluation.* Future Generation Computer Systems, 29, 387–401. doi:10.1016/j.future.2011.08.008

56. Catteddu, D. and Hogben, G. (2009). *Cloud Computing: benefits, risks and recommendations for information security.* Communications in Computer and Information Science. 72(1, 17).

57. Farzad Sabahi, *Cloud Computing Security Threats and Responses*, IEEE 3rd international conference on May 2011, 245 – 249.

58. *Future Generation Computer Systems*, 29, 416–428. doi:10.1016/j.future.2011.08.009.

59. G.Praveen Kumar, S.Kavitha (2017). *A Survey on Security and Privacy Issues in Cloud Computing*, International Journal of Innovative Research in Computer and Communication Engineering, 5(7), pp. 13348-13352.

60. H. Saini and A. Saini, *Security Mechanisms at different Levels in Cloud Infrastructure*, Int. J. Comput. Appl., vol. 108, no. 2, 2014.

61. Haider Abbas & Olaf Maennel & Saïd Assar (2017). *Security and privacy issues in cloud computing*, Ann. Telecommunication, 72:233–235.

62. Hamisu, A. A., 2015. *Cloud Computing Security: An Investigation into the Security Issues and Challenges Associated with Cloud Computing, for both Data Storage and Virtual Applications*. International Research Journal of Electronics & Computer Engineering, 1(2), pp. 15-20.

63. Harshpreet Singh, Promila Manhas, Deep Maan and Nisha Sethi (2016). *Cloud Computing Security and Privacy Issues - A Systematic Review. International Journal of Control Theory and Applications*, 9(11) 2016, pp. 4979-4992.

64. Johndavid Kerr and Kwok Teng (2016). *Cloud computing: legal and privacy issues*, Journal of Legal Issues and Cases in Business. pp. 1-11.

65. Krishna Reddy V. and Reddy L.S.S. (2011). *Security Architecture of Cloud Computing*, International Journal of Engineering Science and Technology, 3(9), pp. 7149-7155.

66. Kuyoro S.O., Ibikunle F., Awodele O., *Cloud Computing Security Issues & Challenge*, IJCN, Vol. 3 Issue 5: 2011, pp. 247-255.

67. Mahesh S.Giri, Bhupesh Gaur and Deepak Tomar (2015). *A Survey on Data Integrity Techniques in Cloud Computing*, International Journal of Computer Applications, Volume 122 – No.2, pp. 27 -32.

68. Meiko Jensen, JorgSchwenk, Nils Gruschka, Luigi Lo Iacon, *On technical Security Issues in Cloud Computing*, Proc. of IEEE International Conference on Cloud Computing (CLOUD-II, 2009), pp. 109-116, India, 2009.

69. Patrick Van Eecke, 2017. *Cloud Computing Legal issues*, DLA Piper, Everything Matters, pp. 1 -10.

70. Robinson, N., Valeri, L., Cave, J., Starkey, T., Grauz, H., Creese, S., & Hopkins, P. (2010). *The cloud: Understanding the security, privacy and trust challenges*. Brussels: Directorate-General Information Society and Media, European Commission. doi:10.1017/CBO9780511564765.012.

71. S. Subashini and V. Kavitha, *A survey on security issues in service delivery models of cloud computing*, J. Netw. Comput. Appl., vol. 34, no. 1, pp. 1–11, 2011.

72. Subashini S., V. Kavitha, *A survey on security issues in service delivery models of cloud computing*, Journal of Network and Computer Applications, Vol. 34(1), pp 1–11, Academic Press Ltd., UK, 2011, ISSN: 1084-8045.

73. Sultan Aldossary and William Allen (2016). *Data Security, Privacy, Availability and Integrity in Cloud Computing: Issues and Current Solutions*, International Journal of Advanced Computer Science and Applications, Vol. 7, No. 4, pp.485-498.

74. Wejdan Bajaber, Manahil AlQulaity and Fahd S. Alotaibi (2017). *Different Techniques to Ensure High Availability in Cloud Computing*, International Journal of Advanced Research in Computer and Communication Engineering, Vol. 6, Issue 11, pp. 6-16.

75. Younis, Y., Merabti, M. & Kifayat, K. (2013). *Secure cloud computing for critical infrastructure: A survey*. Liverpool John Moores University, United Kingdom, Tech. Rep.

76. Zhang X., N. Wuwong, H. Li, and X. J. Zhang, *Information Security Risk Management Framework for the Cloud Computing Environments*, in proceedings of 10th IEEE International Conference on Computer and Information Technology, pp. 1328- 1334, 2010.

77. Margaret Rouse, *Message passing interface (MPI)*, 2013

78. PCQ Bureau, *Understanding MapReduce Programming Model in Hadoop*, December 8, 2015

79. Krishnakumar, *Introduction to Map-Reduce Programming model*, 2016

80. Siva, *MapReduce Programming Model*, 2014

81. Nguyen Quang Hung, *MapReduce*.

82. Christophe Bisciglia, Aaron Kimball, & Sierra Michels-Slettvet, *Distributed Computing Seminar, Lecture 2: MapReduce Theory and Implementation*, Summer 2007,

83. Smruti R. Sarangi, DryadLIN, Distributed Computation Department of Computer Science Indian Institute of Technology New Delhi, India

84. A. Srinivasan, *Cloud Computing*, 2014

85. S. Sharma, M. Mahrishi, *Implementation of Trust Model on Cloudsim in Cloud based on Service Parametric Model*.

86. Muyiwa Iyowu, *Cloud Computing Comparative Study - OpenStack vs OpenNebula*, 2016

87. A. Jiyani, M. Mahrishi, NAM: a nearest acquaintance modeling approach for VM allocation using R-Tree, International Journal of Computers and Applications, 2018

88. Ahmed Shawish and Maria Salama, *Cloud Computing: Paradigms and Technologies, Inter-cooperative Collective Intelligence: Techniques and Applications,* Studies in Computational Intelligence 495, 2014

89. Manchun Pandit, *Complete Guide of Hadoop Ecosystem and components,* 2018

90. Gery Menegaz, *What is Hadoop, and how does it relate to cloud?* 2014

91. Manchun Pandit, *What I Hadoop? How Hadoop is Connected with the Cloud?* 2018

92. MICKEY ALON, INSIGHTERA'S CEO AND CO-FOUNDER, *Apache Hadoop as A Service,* 2018

Printed in Great Britain
by Amazon